# Consumer Behavior

# Consumer Behavior

Edited by Erik Madsen

CLANRYE
INTERNATIONAL
www.clanryeinternational.com

Clanrye International,
750 Third Avenue, 9ᵗʰ Floor,
New York, NY 10017, USA

ISBN: 978-1-63240-683-5


**Cataloging-in-Publication Data**

Consumer behavior / edited by Erik Madsen.
p. cm.
Includes bibliographical references and index.
ISBN 978-1-63240-683-5
1. Consumer behavior. 2. Consumers' preferences. 3. Consumers--Attitudes. I. Madsen, Erik.
HF5415.32 .C66 2018
658.834 2--dc23

For information on all Clanrye International publications visit our website at www.clanryeinternational.com

LANRYE
NTERNATIONAL

# Contents

**Preface** ........................................................................................................................ **VII**

Chapter 1    **An Introduction to Consumer Behavior** .................................................... 1
     a.   Consumer ........................................................................................... 1
     b.   Consumer Behavior ........................................................................ 2
     c.   Nature of Consumer Behavior ...................................................... 39
     d.   Scope of Consumer Behavior ........................................................ 40

Chapter 2    **Decision Making Process: A Consumer-Centric Approach** .......... 43
     a.   Decision-making .............................................................................. 43
     b.   Consumer Decision Making .......................................................... 54
     c.   Levels of Decision Making ............................................................ 78
     d.   Buyer Decision Process .................................................................. 81
     e.   Consumer Decision Making Process ............................................ 87

Chapter 3    **Consumer Behavior: Methods and Models** ..................................... 97
     a.   Marketing Research ......................................................................... 97
     b.   Advertising Management ............................................................... 108
     c.   Models of Consumers ..................................................................... 157
     d.   Models of Consumer Behavior .................................................... 158
     e.   Model of Consumer Buying .......................................................... 161
     f.   Model of Industrial Buying ........................................................... 165

Chapter 4    **Consumer Groups: An Integrated Study** .......................................... 172
     a.   Consumer Groups ........................................................................... 172
     b.   Consumer Reference Groups ........................................................ 180
     c.   Reference Group Appeals .............................................................. 182

Chapter 5    **Impact of Culture on Consumer Behavior** ...................................... 185
     a.   Culture ............................................................................................... 185
     b.   Consumer Culture .......................................................................... 188
     c.   Consumer Culture Theory ............................................................. 198
     d.   Components of Culture .................................................................. 201
     e.   Measurement of Culture ................................................................ 202
     f.   Sub-culture ....................................................................................... 203

g.   Exposure to other Cultures.................................................................................................205

h.   Cross-cultural Consumer Analysis.....................................................................................206

i.   Strategies for Multinational Companies...........................................................................208

Chapter 6   **Opinion Leadership and its Role in Consumer Behavior**..............................................**215**

a.   Opinion Leadership.............................................................................................................215

b.   Opinion Leaders..................................................................................................................217

**Permissions**

**Index**

# Preface

Consumer behavior refers to the research and study of particular groups of buyers, focusing on their buying needs, buying pattern, their thoughts and opinions about the brand. It is vital because it enables the company to produce products that are relevant to the customer and therefore help in growing the company and developing it into a brand. Most of the topics introduced in this book cover new techniques and the applications of consumer behavior. This textbook attempts to assist those with a goal of delving into this field.

A short introduction to every chapter is written below to provide an overview of the content of the book:

**Chapter 1 -** Consumer behavior refers to the study of people in relation with the choices they make in terms of selection, usage, experiences and ideas to meet their needs. It is concerned with varying affects, attitudes and preferences, and the effect they have on buying behavior of the consumers. The study tries to understand consumption pattern. It focuses on what, why, when and where consumers buy products. This chapter is an overview of the subject matter incorporating all the major aspects of consumer behavior; **Chapter 2 -** Decision-making can be defined as selecting from available options, and is goal-oriented and a problem solving method. When consumer decision-making is discussed, it becomes primarily a problem solving process. It involves collecting information, analyzing them and then choosing the best alternative. The section strategically encompasses and incorporates the major components and key concepts of consumer decision making, providing a complete understanding; **Chapter 3 -** The behavior of a consumer differs in the choosing of a marketplace. The decision is affected by few reasons, which the subject studies. It can be classified into economic view, cognitive view, passive view, and emotional view. This is referred to as the consumer model. It is based on the various approaches a costumer, who holds different perspectives, makes at the market place. Many models have been developed to deal with consumer behavior. They are economic model, psychological model, psychoanalytic model and sociological model. This chapter discusses the methods of consumer behavior in a critical manner providing key analysis to the subject matter; **Chapter 4 -** Consumer groups are groups who possess a need to purchase a good or service in order to satisfy them. These groups are mainly classified on the basis of number and size, regularity of contact, and structure and hierarchy. Moreover, a consumer group feels the need to take reference or compare itself with another group. The group to which a consumer group compares itself to is called a reference group. The aspects elucidated in this section are of vital importance, and provide a better understanding of consumer groups and communications; **Chapter 5 -** Consumerism is an ideology that propagates the idea to buy goods and services in an ever-increasing manner. After the Industrial Revolution, this idea led to overproduction, which in turn gave birth to planned advertising. This section also deals with consumer socialization, which puts focus on how early year experiences pave way for future consumer behavior; **Chapter 6 -** Opinion leadership is the higher form of media that interprets and advocates the media content. This can greatly influence ideas and perceptions of individuals or groups who hold the opinion leader in high esteem. These leaders play the role of authoritative figure, trend setter and of a local opinion leader. Consumer behavior in consumer behavior is best understood in confluence with the major topics listed in the following chapter.

I extend my sincere thanks to the publisher for considering me worthy of this task. Finally, I thank my family for being a source of support and help.

**Editor**

# An Introduction to Consumer Behavior

Consumer behavior refers to the study of people in relation with the choices they make in terms of selection, usage, experiences and ideas to meet their needs. It is concerned with varying affects, attitudes and preferences, and the effect they have on buying behavior of the consumers. The study tries to understand consumption pattern. It focuses on what, why, when and where consumers buy products. This chapter is an overview of the subject matter incorporating all the major aspects of consumer behavior.

## Consumer

A consumer is a person or organization that uses economic services or commodities.

In economic systems *consumers* are utilities expressed in the decision to trade or not.

Consumers buying fruit in Nanjing, China

### Economics and Marketing

The *consumer* is the one who pays to consume goods and services produced. As such, *consumers* play a vital role in the economic system of a nation. Without consumer demand, producers would lack one of the key motivations to produce: to sell to consumers. The *consumer* also forms part of the chain of distribution.

Recently in marketing instead of marketers generating broad demographic profiles and Fisio-graphic profiles of market segments, marketers have started to engage in personalized marketing, permission marketing, and mass customization.

Largely due the rise of the Internet, consumers are shifting more and more towards becoming "prosumers", consumers that are also producers (often of information and media on the social web) or influence the products created (e.g. by customization, crowdfunding or publishing their preferences) or actively participate in the production process or use interactive products.

## Law and Politics

The law primarily uses the notion of the consumer in relation to consumer protection laws, and the definition of consumer is often restricted to living persons (i.e. not corporations or businesses) and excludes commercial users. A typical legal rationale for protecting the consumer is based on the notion of policing market failures and inefficiencies, such as inequalities of bargaining power between a consumer and a business. As of all potential voters are also consumers, consumer protection takes on a clear political significance.

Concern over the interests of consumers has also spawned activism, as well as incorporation of consumer education into school curricula. There are also various non-profit publications, such as *Which?*, *Consumer Reports* and *Choice Magazine*, dedicated to assist in consumer education and decision making.

In India, the Consumer Protection Act 1986 differentiates the consummation of a commodity or service for personal use or to earn a livelihood. Only consumers are protected per this act and any person, entity or organization purchasing a commodity for commercial reasons are exempted from any benefits of this act.

## Consumer Behavior

Consumer Behavior may be defined as "the interplay of forces that takes place during a consumption process, within a consumers' self and his environment.

- this interaction takes place between three elements viz. knowledge, affect and behavior;

- it continues through pre-purchase activity to the post purchase experience;

- it includes the stages of evaluating, acquiring, using and disposing of goods and services".

The "consumer" includes both personal consumers and business/industrial/organizational consumers.

Consumer behavior explains the reasons and logic that underlie purchasing decisions and consumption patterns; it explains the processes through which buyers make decisions. The study includes within its purview, the interplay between cognition, affect and behavior that goes on within a consumer during the consumption process: selecting, using and disposing off goods and services.

   i.  Cognition:

This includes within its ambit the "knowledge, information  processing and thinking" part; It includes the mental processesc involved in processing of information, thinking and interpretation of stimuli (people, objects, things, places and events). In our case, stimuli would be product or service offering; it could be a brand or even  anything to do with the 4Ps.

ii.  Affect:

This is the " feelings" part. It includes the favorable or unfavorable feelings and corresponding emotions towards a stimuli (eg. towards a product or service offering or a brand). These vary in direction, intensity and persistence.

iii.  Behavior:

This is the "visible" part. In our case, this could be the purchase activity: to buy or not a buy (again specific to a product or service offering, a brand or  even related to any of the 4 Ps).

The interaction is reciprocal between each of the three towards each other and with the environment.

Other Definitions:

"The behavior that consumers display in searching for, purchasing, using, evalauting and disposing of products and services that they expect will satisfy their needs."

- Schiffman and Kanuk

".....the decision process and physical activity engaged in when evaluating, acquiring, using or disposing of goods and services."

- Loudon and Bitta

" The study of consumers as they exchange something of value for a product or service that satisfies their needs"

- Wells and Prensky

"Those actions directly involved in obtaining, consuming and disposing of products and services including the decision processes that precede and follow these actions".

-Engel, Blackwell, Miniard

"the dynamic interaction of effect and cognition, behavior and the environment by which human beings conduct the exchange aspects of their lives"

-American Marketing Association

Consumer behaviour is the study of individuals, groups, or organizations and the processes they use to select, secure, use, and dispose of products, services, experiences, or ideas to satisfy their needs and wants. It is also concerned with the social and economic impacts that purchasing and consumption behaviour has on both the consumer and wider society. Consumer behaviour blends elements from psychology, sociology, social anthropology, marketing and economics, especially behavioural economics. It examines how emotions, attitudes and preferences affect buying behaviour. Characteristics of individual consumers such as demographics, personality lifestyles and behavioural variables such as usage rates, usage occasion, loyalty, brand advocacy, willingness to provide referrals, in an attempt to understand people's wants and consumption are all investigated in formal studies of consumer behaviour. The study of consumer behaviour also investigates the influences, on the consumer, from groups such as family, friends, sports, reference groups, and society in general.

The Galeries Royales Saint-Hubert shopping arcade in Belgium. Consumer behaviour,
in its broadest sense, is concerned with how consumers select and use goods and services.

The study of consumer behaviour is concerned with all aspects of purchasing behaviour - from pre-purchase activities through to post-purchase consumption and evaluation activities. It is also concerned with all persons involved, either directly or indirectly, in purchasing decisions and consumption activities including brand-influencers and opinion leaders. Research has shown that consumer behaviour is difficult to predict, even for experts in the field. However, new research methods such as ethnography and consumer neuroscience are shedding new light on how consumers make decisions.

Customer relationship management (CRM) databases have become an asset for the analysis of customer behaviour. The voluminous data produced by these databases enables detailed examination of behavioural factors that contribute to customer re-purchase intentions, consumer retention, loyalty and other behavioural intentions such as the willingness to provide positive referrals, become brand advocates or engage in customer citizenship activities. Databases also assist in market segmentation, especially behavioural segmentation such as developing loyalty segments, which can be used to develop tightly targeted, customized marketing strategies on a one-to-one basis.

## The Purchase Decision and its Context

Understanding purchasing and consumption behaviour is a key challenge for marketers. Consumer behaviour, in its broadest sense, is concerned with understanding both how purchase decisions are made and how products or services are consumed or experienced.

In a family unit, the adult female often makes brand choices on behalf
the entire household, while children can be important influencers

Some purchase decisions involve long, detailed processes that include extensive information search to select between competing alternatives. Other purchase decisions, such as impulse buys, are made almost instanteously with little or no investment of time or effort in information search.

Some purchase decisions are made by groups (such as families, households or businesses) while others are made by individuals. When a purchase decision is made by a small group, such as a household, different members of the group may become involved at different stages of the decision process and may perform different roles. For example, one person may search for information while another may physically go to the store, buy the product and transport it home. It is customary to think about the types of decision roles; such as:

- The Initiator - the person who proposes a brand (or product) for consideration;

- The Influencer- someone who recommends a given brand;

- The Decider- the person who makes the ultimate purchase decision;

- The Purchaser - the one who orders or physically buys it;

- The User - the person who uses or consumes the product.

For most purchase decisions, each of the decision roles must be performed, but not always by the same individual. For example, in the case of family making a decision about a dining-out venue, the mother may initiate the process by intimating that she is too tired to cook, the children are important influencers in the overall purchase decision, but both parents may act as joint deciders performing a gate-keeping role by vetoing unacceptable alternatives and encouraging more acceptable alternatives. The importance of children as influencers in a wide range of purchase contexts should never be underestimated and the phenomenon is known as pester power.

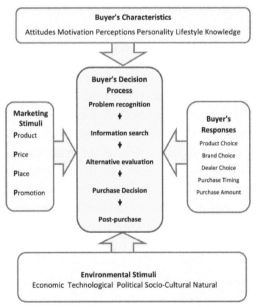

The purchasing decision model

To understand the mental processes used in purchasing decisions, some authors employ the concept of the *black box*; a figurative term used to describe the cognitive and affective processes used by a consumer during a purchase decision. The decision model situates the black box in a broader environment which shows the interaction of external and internal stimuli (e.g.consumer characteristics, situational factors, marketing influences and environmental factors) as well as consumer responses. The black box model is related to the black box theory of behaviourism, where the focus extends beyond processes occurring *inside* the consumer, and also includes the *relation* between the stimuli and the consumer's response.

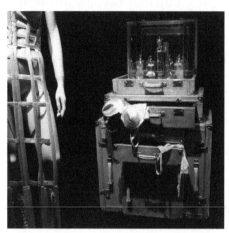

The purchase of up-market perfumes, often purchased as gifts, are high involvement
decisions because the gift symbolises the relationship between the giver and the intended recipient

The decision model assumes that purchase decisions do not occur in a vacuum. Rather they occur in real time and are affected by other stimuli, including external environmental stimuli and the consumer's momentary situation. The elements of the model include: interpersonal stimuli (between people) or intrapersonal stimuli (within people), environmental stimuli and marketing stimuli. Marketing stimuli include actions planned and carried out by companies, whereas environmental stimuli include actions or events occurring in the wider operating environment and include social factors, economic, political and cultural dimensions. In addition, the buyer's black box includes buyer characteristics and the decision process, which influence the buyer's responses.

The black box model considers the buyer's response as a result of a conscious, rational decision process, in which it is assumed that the buyer has recognized a problem, and seeks to solve it through a commercial purchase. In practice some purchase decisions, such as those made routinely or habitually, are not driven by a strong sense of problem-solving. Such decisions are termed *low-involvement* and are characterized by relatively low levels of information search/ evaluation activities. In contrast, *high involvement* decisions require a serious investment of time and effort in the search/ evaluation process. Low involvement products are typically those that carry low levels of economic or psycho-social risk. High involvement products are those that carry higher levels of risk and are often expensive, infrequent purchases. Regardless of whether the consumer faces a high or low involvement purchase, he or she needs to work through a number of distinct stages of a decision process.

## Overview of the Consumer's Purchase Decision Process

The consumer buying process is usually depicted as consisting of 5 distinct stages:

The purchase decision begins with the *problem recognition* stage which occurs when the consumer identifies a need, typically defined as the difference between the consumer's current state and their desired state. The strength of the need drives the entire decision process. *Information search* describes the phase where consumers scan both their internal memory and external sources for information about products or brands that will potentially satisfy their need. The aim of the information search is to identify a list of options that represent realistic purchase options. Throughout the entire process, the consumer engages in a series of mental *evaluations of alternatives*, searching for the best value. Towards the end of the evaluation stage, consumers form a purchase intention, which may or may not translate into an actual *product purchase*. Even when consumers decide to proceed with an actual purchase, the decision-process is not complete until the consumer consumes or experiences the product and engages in a final *post purchase evaluation*; a stage in which the purchaser's actual experience of the product is compared with the expectations formed during the information search and evaluation stages. The stages of the decision process normally occur in a fixed sequence. However it should be noted that information search and evaluation can occur throughout the entire decision process, including post-purchase.

## Problem Recognition

The first stage of the purchase decision process begins with *problem recognition* (also known as category need or need arousal). This is when the consumer identifies a need, typically defined as the difference between the consumer's current state and their desired or ideal state. A simpler way of thinking about problem recognition is that it is where the consumer decides that he or she is 'in the market' for a product or service to satisfy some need or want. The strength of the underlying need drives the entire decision process.

The purchase of a mobile phone may trigger the desire for accessories such as this phone mount for use in a car

Theorists identify three broad classes of problem-solving situation relevant for the purchase decision:

Extensive problem-solving → Purchases that warrant greater deliberation, more extensive information search and evaluation of alternatives

Typically expensive purchases, or purchases with high social visibility e.g. fashion, cars

Limited problem-solving → Known or familiar purchases, regular purchases, straight re-buys

Typically low-priced items

Routinized problem-solving → Repeat purchases, habitual purchases

Consumers become aware of a problem in a variety of ways including:

- *Out-of-Stock/ Natural Depletion*: When a consumer needs to replenish stocks of a consumable item e.g. ran out of milk or bread.

- *Regular purchase*: When a consumer purchases a product on a regular basis e.g. newspaper, magazine.

- *Dissatisfaction*: When a consumer is not satisfied with the current product or service.

- *New Needs or Wants*: Lifestyle changes may trigger the identification of new needs e.g. the arrival of a baby may prompt the purchase of a cot, stroller and car-seat for baby.

- *Related products*: The purchase of one product may trigger the need for accessories, spare parts or complementary goods and services e.g. the purchase of a printer leads to the need for ink cartridges; the purchase of a digital camera leads to the need for memory cards.

- *Marketer-induced problem recognition*: When marketing activity persuades consumers of a problem (usually a problem that the consumer did not realise they had).

- *New Products or Categories*: When consumers become aware of new, innovative products that offer a superior means of fulfilling a need. Disruptive technologies such as the advent of wireless free communications devices can trigger a need for plethora of products such as a new mouse or printer.

## Information Search and Evaluation of Alternatives

Touchpoints associated with stages of the purchase decision

During the information search and evaluation stages, the consumer works through processes designed to arrive at a number of brands (or products) that represent viable purchase alternatives. Typically consumers first carry out an *internal search*; that is a scan of memory for suitable brands. The evoked set is a term used to describe the set of brands that a consumer can elicit from memory and is typically a very small set of some 3- 5 alternatives. Consumers may choose to supplement the number of brands in the evoked set by carrying out an *external search* using sources such as the Internet, manufacturer/brand websites, shopping around, product reviews, referrals from peers and the like.

Consumer evaluation can be viewed as a distinct stage. Alternatively, evaluation may occur continuously throughout the entire decision process. The fact that a consumer is aware of a brand does not necessarily mean that it is being considered as a potential purchase. For instance, the consumer may be aware of certain brands, but not favorably disposed towards them (known as the *inept set*). Such brands will typically be excluded from further evaluation as purchase options. For other brands, the consumer may have indifferent feelings (the *inert set*). As the consumer approaches the actual purchase, he or she distills the mental list of brands into a set of alternatives that represent realistic purchase options, known as the *consideration set*. By definition, the consideration set refers to the "small set of brands which a consumer pays close attention to when making a purchase decision".

Traditionally, one of the main roles of advertising and promotion was to increase the likelihood that a brand name was included in the consumer's evoked set. Repeated exposure to brand names through intensive advertising was the primary method for increasing *top-of-mind brand awareness*. However, the advent of the Internet means that consumers can obtain brand/product information from a multiplicity of different platforms. In practice, this means that the consideration set has assumed greater importance. The implication for marketers is that relevant brand information should be disseminated as widely as possible and included on any forum where consumers are likely to search for product or brand information. Thus, marketers require a rich understanding of the typical consumer's touchpoints.

Consumers evaluate alternatives in terms of the functional and psycho-social benefits offered. Functional benefits are the tangible outcomes that can be experienced by the consumer such as taste or appearance. Psycho-social benefits are the more abstract outcomes such as the social currency that might accrue from wearing an expensive suit or driving a 'hot' car. Brand image is an important psycho-social attribute. Consumers have both positive and negative beliefs about a given brand. Consumer beliefs may differ depending on the consumer's prior experience and the effects of selective perception, distortion and retention.

The marketing organization needs a deep understanding of the benefits most valued by consumers and therefore which attributes are most important in terms of the consumer's purchase decision. It also needs to monitor other brands in the customer's consideration set to optimise planning for its own brand.

During the evaluation of alternatives, the consumer ranks or assesses the relative merits of different options available. No universal evaluation process is used by consumers across all-buying situations. Instead, consumers generate different evaluation criteria depending on each unique buying situation. Thus the relevant attributes vary according to each product category and across different types of consumers. For example, attributes important for evaluating a restaurant would include food quality, price, location, atmosphere, quality of service and menu selection. Consumers, depending on their geographic, demographic, psychographic and behavioural characteristics, will decide which attributes are important to them. After evaluating the different product attributes, the consumer ranks each attribute from highly important to least important. These priorities are directly related to the consumer's needs and wants. Thus, the consumer arrives at a weighted score for each product - representing the consumer's subjective assessment of individual attribute scores weighted in terms of their importance, to arrive at a total mental score or rank for each product under consideration.

## Purchase Decision

Once the alternatives have been evaluated, the consumer is ready to make a purchase decision. Sometimes purchase intention does not translate into an actual purchase. The extent to which purchase intentions result in actual sales is known as the *sales conversion* rate.

Organizations use a variety of techniques to improve conversion rates. The provision of easy credit or payment terms may encourage purchase. Sales promotions such as the opportunity to receive a premium or enter a competition may provide an incentive to buy now rather than later. Advertising messages with a strong *call-to-action* are yet another device used to convert customers. A call-to-action is any device designed to encourage immediate sale. Typically, a call-to-action includes specific wording in an advertisement or selling pitch that employs imperative verbs such as "Buy now" or "Don't wait". Other types of calls-to-action might provide consumers with strong reasons for purchasing immediately such an offer that is only available for a limited time (e.g. 'Offer must expire soon'; 'Limited stocks available') or a special deal usually accompanied by a time constraint (e.g. 'Order before midnight to receive a free gift with your order'; 'Two for the price of one for first 50 callers only'). The key to a powerful call-to-action is to provide consumers with compelling reasons to purchase promptly rather than defer purchase decisions.

Happy hour, where two drinks can be purchased for the price of one, is a strong call-to-action because it encourages consumers to buy now rather than defer purchasing to a later time

As consumers approach the actual purchase decision, they are more likely to rely on personal sources of information. For this reason, personal sales representatives must be well versed in giving sales pitches and in tactics used close the sale. Methods used might include: 'social evidence', where the salesperson refers to previous success and satisfaction from other customers buying the product. 'Scarcity attraction' is another technique, where the salesperson mentions that the offer is limited, as it forces the consumer to make a quicker decision, and therefore less time evaluating alternatives.

## Post-purchase Evaluation

Following purchase and after experiencing the product or service, the consumer enters the final stage, namely post-purchase evaluation. The consumer's purchase and post-purchase activities have the potential to provide important feedback to marketers. Foxall (2005) suggested that post-purchase evaluation provides key feedback because it influences future purchase patterns and consumption activities.

The post purchase stage is where the consumer examines and compares product features, such as price, functionality, and quality with their expectations. Post purchase evaluation can be viewed as the steps taken by consumers to correlate their expectations with perceived value, and thus influences the consumer's next purchase decision for that good or service. For example, if a consumer buys a new phone and his or her post-purchase evaluation is positive, he/she will be encouraged to purchase the same brand or from the same company in the future. This is also known as "post-purchase intention". On the contrary, if a consumer is dissatisfied with the new phone, he or she may take actions to resolve the dissatisfaction. Consumer actions, in this instance, could involve requesting a refund, making a complaint, deciding not to purchase the same brand or from the same company in the future or even spreading negative product reviews to friends or acquaintances, possibly via social media.

After acquisition, consumption or disposition, consumers may feel some uncertainty in regards to the decision made, generating in some cases regret. Post-decision dissonance (also known as cognitive dissonance ) is the term used to describe feelings of anxiety that occur in the post purchase stage; and refers to the consumer's uneasy feelings or concerns as to whether or not the correct decision was made at purchase. Some consumers, for instance, may regret that they did not purchase one of the other brands they were considering.This type of anxiety can affect consumers' subsequent behaviour

Consumers use a number of strategies to reduce post purchase dissonance. A typical strategy is to look to peers or significant others for validation of the purchase choice. Marketing communications can also be used to remind consumers that they made a wise choice by purchasing Brand X.

When consumers make unfavorable comparisons between the chosen option and the options forgone, they may feel *post-decision regret*. Consumers can also feel short-term regret when they avoid making a purchase decision, however this regret can dissipate over time. Through their experiences consumers can learn and also engage in a process that's called *hypothesis testing*. This refers to the formation of hypotheses about the products or a service through prior experience or word of mouth communications. There are four stages that consumers go through in the hypothesis testing: Hypothesis generation, exposure of evidence, encoding of evidence and integration of evidence.

## Internal Influences on Purchase Decision

Purchasing behaviour is also influenced by a range of internal influences such as psychological, demographic and personality factors. Demographic factors include income level, psychographics (lifestyle), age, occupation and socio-economic status. Personality factors include knowledge, attitudes, personal values, beliefs, emotions and feelings. Psychological factors include an individual's motivation, attitudes, personal values and beliefs. Other factors that may affect the purchase decision include the environment and the consumer's prior experience with the category or brand.

## Motivations and Emotions

The consumer's underlying motivation drives consumer action, including information search and the purchase decision. The consumer's attitude to a brand (or *brand preference*) is described as a link between the brand and a purchase motivation. These motivations may be negative - that is to avoid pain or unpleasantness, or positive - that is to achieve some type of sensory gratification.

One approach to understanding motivations, was developed by Abraham Maslow. The *hierarchy of needs* is based on five levels of needs, organized accordingly to the level of importance.

Maslow's five needs are:

- *Physiological* - basic levels of needs such as food, water and sleep

- *Safety*- the need for physical safety, shelter and security

- *Belonging*- the need for love, friendship and also a desire for group acceptance

- *Esteem*- The need for status, recognition and self-respect

- *Self-actualization* – The desire for self-fulfillment (e.g. personal growth, artistic expression)

Maslow's hierarchy suggests that people seek to satisfy basic needs such
as food and shelter before higher order needs become meaningful

Physiological needs and safety needs are the so-called lower order needs. Consumers typically use most of their resources (time, energy and finances) attempting to satisfy these lower order needs before the higher order needs of belonging, esteem and self-actualization become meaningful. Part of any marketing program requires an understanding of which motives drive given product choices. Marketing communications can illustrate how a product or brand fulfills these needs. Maslow's approach is a generalised model for understanding human motivations in a wide variety of contexts, but is not specific to purchasing decisions.

A decision to purchase an analgesic preparation is motivated
by the desire to avoid pain (negative motivation)

A decision to buy an ice-cream sundae is motivated by the desire
for sensory gratification (positive motivation)

Another approach proposes eight *purchase* motivations, five negative motives and three positive motives, which energise purchase decisions as illustrated in the table below. These motivations are believed to provide positive reinforcement or negative reinforcement.

| Rossiter and Percy's Purchase Motivations & Emotions | |
|---|---|
| **Motivation** | **Emotional Sequence** |
| **NEGATIVE** | |
| Problem removal | Annoyance → Relief |
| Problem avoidance | Fear → Relaxation |
| Incomplete satisfaction | Disappointment → Optimism |
| Mixed approach avoidance | Conflict → Peace-of-mind |

| Normal depletion | Mild annoyance → Convenience |
|---|---|
| **POSITIVE** | |
| Sensory gratification | Dull (or neutral) → Sensory anticipation |
| Intellectual simulation | Bored (or neutral) → Excited |
| Social approval/ conformity | Apprehensive (or ashamed) → Flattered/ proud |

In the marketing literature, the consumer's motivation to search for information and engage in the purchase decision process is sometimes known as *involvement*. Consumer involvement has been defined as "the personal relevance or importance of a message [or a decision]". Purchase decisions are classified as low involvement when consumers suffer only a small psycho-social loss in the event that the make a poor decision. On the other hand, a purchase decision is classified as high involvement when psycho-social risks are perceived to be relatively high. The consumer's level of involvement is dependent on a number of factors including, perceived risk of negative consequences in the event of a poor decision, the product category - especially the social visibility of the product and the consumer's prior experience with the category.

## Perception

Part of marketing strategy is to ascertain how consumers gain knowledge and use information from external sources. The perception process is where individuals receive, organize and interpret information in order to attribute some meaning. Perception involves three distinct processes: sensing information, selecting information and interpreting information. Sensation is also part of the perception process, and it is linked direct with responses from the senses creating some reaction towards the brand name, advertising and packaging. The process of perception is uniquely individual and may depend on a combination of internal and external factors such as experiences, expectations, needs and the momentary set.

When exposed to a stimulus, consumers may respond in entirely different ways due to individual perceptual processes. A number of processes potentially support or interfere with perception. *Selective exposure* occurs when consumers decide whether to be exposed to information inputs. *Selective attention* occurs when consumers focus on some messages to the exclusion of others. *Selective comprehension* is where the consumer interprets information in a manner that is consistent with their own beliefs. *Selective retention* occurs when consumers remember some information while rapidly forgetting other information. Collectively the processes of selective exposure, attention, comprehension and retention lead individual consumers to favour certain messages over others. The way that consumers combine information inputs to arrive at a purchase decision is known as *integration*.

Marketers are interested in consumer perceptions of brands, packaging, product formulations, labelling and pricing. Of especial interest is the *threshold of perception* (also known as the *just noticeable difference*) in a stimulus. For example, how much should a marketer lower a price before consumers recognise it as a bargain? In addition, marketers planning to enter global markets need to be aware of cultural differences in perception. For example, westerners associate the colour white with purity, cleanliness and hygiene, but in eastern countries white is often associated with mourning and death. Accordingly, white packaging would be an inappropriate colour choice for food labels on products to be marketed in Asia.

## Prior Experience

The consumer's prior experience with the category, product or brand can have a major bearing on purchase decision-making. Experienced consumers (also called experts) are more sophisticated consumers; they tend to be more skillful information searchers, canvass a broader range of information sources and use complex heuristics to evaluate purchase options. Novice consumers, on the other hand, are less efficient information searchers and tend to perceive higher levels of purchase risk on account of their unfamiliarity with the brand or category. When consumers have prior experience, they have less motivation to search for information, spend less effort on information search but can process new information more efficiently. One study, for example, found that as consumer experience increases, consumers consider a wider range of purchase alternatives (that is, they generate a larger consideration set, but only at the product category level).

## External Influences on Purchase Decision

Purchasing behaviour can also be affected by external influences, such as culture, sub-culture, social class, reference groups, family and situational determinants.

## Culture

Culture is the broadest and most abstract of the external factors. Culture refers to the complexity of learning meanings, values, norms, and customs shared by members of a society. Cultural norms are relatively stable over time, therefore, culture has a major impact on consumer behaviour. Marketers interested in global expansion are especially interested in understanding cross-cultural differences in purchasing and consumption. For instance, Ferrari, one of the world's top brands found that Chinese consumers are very different from their Western counterparts. Whereas consumers in the US, UK and Australia expect to wait 12 months for a custom-made Ferrari, prospective Chinese buyers want to drive the vehicle off the showroom floor. China is an 'instant-gratification market'. Buyers see their friends riding around in a luxury car and want to have the same as quickly as possible. To meet the growing demand for luxury goods, Ferrari and other luxury car makers have been forced to modify their production processes for Asian markets.

## Subcultures

People with shared interests, such as skaters and bladers, tend to form informal groups known as subcultures

Subcultures may be based on age, geographic, religious, racial, and ethnic differences. More often, however, a subculture occurs when people with shared interests form a loose-knit group with a distinctive identity (sometimes called *consumer tribes*). Members of subcultures are self-selected, and signal their membership status by adopting symbols, rituals or behaviours that are widely understood by other members of the tribe (e.g. a dress code, hairstyle or even a unique way of speaking). For example, within youth culture it is possible to identify a number of sub-groups with common interests such as skaters and bladers, surfers, ravers, punks, skinheads, Goths, homies and others.

Harley-Davidson enthusiasts are an example of a consumption subculture

A different type of subculture is a *consumption subculture* which is based on a shared commitment to a common brand or product. In other words, consumption subcultures cut across demographic, geographic and social boundaries. The most well-known example of a consumption subculture is that of Harley-Davidson owners. Ethnographic researchers who have studied Harley riders believe that there are only two types of motor cyclists, Harley owners and the rest. Harley-Davidson has leveraged the values of this subculture by establishing the Harley Owners Group (HOG).

Subcultures are important to marketers for several reasons. Firstly. given that subcultures can represent sizeable market segments which are profitable and influential, there are obvious advantages in developing and selling products and services that meet the needs of subculture members. Secondly, and perhaps less obviously, many new fads and fashions emerge spontaneously from within these tribal groups. Trend-spotters are accordingly interested in studying the lifestyles and activities of tribes in a effort to spot new trends before they go mainstream.

## Social Class

Social class refers to relatively homogenous divisions in a society, typically based on socio-economic variables such as educational attainment, income and occupation. Social class can be very difficult to define and measure, however marketers around the world tend to use a conventional classification which divides any given population into five socio-economic quintiles (e.g. In Australia the groups AB, C, D, E and FG, where AB is the top socio-economic quintile, but in much of Asia the quintiles are labelled I, II, III, IV and V where I is the top quintile). In Australia, for example, the AB socio-economic group account for just 24% of the population, but control 50% of discretionary spending. The top quintiles (i.e. AB socio-economic segments) are of particular interest to marketers of luxury goods and services such as travel, dining-out, entertainment, luxury cars, investment or wealth management services, up-market consumer electronics and designer labels (e.g. Louis Vuitton).

## Reference Groups

A reference group is defined as "a group whose presumed perspectives or values are being used by an individual as the basis for his or her judgment, opinions, and actions." Reference groups are important because they are used to guide an individual's attitudes, beliefs and values. Insights into how consumers acquire a given value system can obtained from an understanding of group influence and group socialisation processes.

A number of distinct types of reference groups can be identified:

*Aspirational groups* refer to a group to which an individual does not currently belong, but possibly aspires to become a member because the group possesses characteristics which are admired.

*Associative Reference Groups* refers to a group or groups to which an individual belongs, such as friends, family and work groups that can exert a positive influence on consumers.

*Disassociative Reference Groups* - a group which has a negative image; individuals may disapprove of the disassociative group's values, attitudes or behaviours and may seek to distance themselves from such groups.

*Opinion Leaders* can exert considerable social influence because of their product knowledge, expertise and credibility. In the marketing literature, opinion leaders are also known as influencers, mavens and even hubs. Opinion leaders are specific to a product category, so that an opinion leader for computers is not likely to be an opinion leader for fashion. Typically, opinion leaders have high levels of involvement with the product category, are heavy users of the category and tend to be early adopters of new technologies within the category. Journalists, celebrities and bloggers are good examples of an opinion leader due to their broad social networks and increased ability to influence people's decisions . Indeed, recent evidence suggests that bloggers may be emerging as a more important group of opinion leaders than celebrities.

In order to leverage the value of opinion leaders in marketing strategies, it is important to be able to identify the unique opinion leaders for each category or situation and this can be very challenging. Some techniques that can be used are through key informants, socio-metric techniques and self-questionnaires. More often, however, marketers use gut instinct to identify opinion leaders. For example, marketers of athletic shoes have been known to provide gym/ aerobic instructors with free shoes in the hope that class members will adopt the same brand as the instructor. Marketers of cosmetics and skincare preparations regularly provide fashion editors with free samples in the hope that their products will be mentioned in fashion magazines.

## Consumer Decision Styles

A number of theorist have argued that certain fundamental decision-making styles can be identified. A decision-making style is defined as a "mental orientation characterising a consumer's approach to making choices." Sproles and Kendall (1986) developed a consumer style inventory (CSI) consisting of eight factors, such as price-sensitivity, quality-consciousness, brand-consciousness, novelty-seeking, fashion-consciousness and habit. Based on these factors, the authors developed a typology of eight distinct decision-making styles:

Shoppers who shop just for the fun of it are known as recreational shoppers

- Quality conscious/Perfectionist: Quality-consciousness is characterised by a consumer's search for the very best quality in products; quality conscious consumers tend to shop systematically making more comparisons and shopping around.

- Brand-conscious: Brand-consciousness is characterised by a tendency to buy expensive, well-known brands or designer labels. Those who score high on brand-consciousness tend to believe that the higher prices are an indicator of quality and exhibit a preference for department stores or top-tier retail outlets.

- Recreation-conscious/ Hedonistic: Recreational shopping is characterised by the consumer's engagement in the purchase process. Those who score high on recreation-consciousness regard shopping itself as a form of enjoyment.

- Price-conscious: A consumer who exhibits price-and-value consciousness. Price-conscious shoppers carefully shop around seeking lower prices, sales or discounts and are motivated by obtaining the best value for money

- Novelty/fashion-conscious: characterised by a consumer's tendency to seek out new products or new experiences for the sake of excitement; who gain excitement from seeking new things; they like to keep up-to-date with fashions and trends, variety-seeking is associated with this dimension.

- Impulsive: Impulsive consumers are somewhat careless in making purchase decisions, buy on the spur of the moment and are not overly concerned with expenditure levels or obtaining value. Those who score high on impulsive dimensions tend not to be engaged with the object at either a cognitive or emotional level.

- Confused (by over-choice): characterised by a consumer's confusion caused by too many product choices, too many stores or an overload of product information; tend to experience information overload.

- Habitual / brand loyal: characterised by a consumer's tendency to follow a routine purchase pattern on each purchase occasion; consumers have favourite brands or stores and have formed habits in choosing, the purchase decision does not involve much evaluation or shopping around.

The Consumer Styles Inventory (CSI) has been extensively tested and retested in a wide variety of countries and purchasing contexts. Many empirical studies have observed cross-cultural variations in decisions styles, leading to numerous adaptations or modifications of the CSI scale for use in specific countries. Consumer decision styles are important for marketers because they describe behaviours that are relatively stable over time and for this reason, they are useful for market segmentation.

## Other Topics in Consumer Behaviour

The purchase of an up-market sports car carries both financial risk and social risk, because it is an expensive purchase and it makes a highly visible statement about the driver

In addition to understanding the purchasing decision, marketers are interested a number of different aspects of consumer behaviour that occur before, during and after making a purchase choice. Areas of particular interest include: risk perception and risk reduction activities; brand switching, channel switching, brand loyalty, customer citizenship behaviours and post purchase behavioural intentions and behaviours, including brand advocacy, referrals, word of mouth activity etc.

## Risk Perception and Risk Reduction Activities

The consumer's perceptions of risk are a major consideration in the pre-purchase stage of the purchasing decision. Perceived risk is defined as "the consumer's perceptions of the uncertainty and adverse consequences of engaging in an activity". Risk consists of two dimensions: *consequences* - the degree of importance or the severity of an outcome and *uncertainty* - the consumer's subjective assessment of the likelihood of occurrence. For example, many tourists are fearful of air travel because, although the probability of being involved in a airline accident is very low, the consequences are potentially dire.

The marketing literature identifies many different types of risk, of which five are the most frequently cited:

Facilitating trial of a product may help to alleviate risk perceptions

- Financial Risk: the potential financial loss in the event of a poor decision

- Performance Risk (also known as *functional risk*): The idea that a product or service will not perform as intended

- Physical Risk: the potential for physical harm if something goes wrong with a purchase

- Social Risk: the potential for loss of social status associated with a purchase

- Psychological Risk: the potential for a purchase to result in a loss of self-esteem

If a consumer perceives a purchase to be risky, he or she will engage in strategies to reduce the perceived risk until it is within their tolerance levels or, if they are unable to do so, withdraw from the purchase. Thus, the consumer's perceptions of risk drive information search activities.

Services marketers have argued that risk perception is higher for services because they lack the search attributes of products (i.e. tangible properties that can be inspected prior to consumption). In terms of risk perception, marketers and economists identify three broad classes of purchase; search goods, experience goods and credence goods with implications for consumer evaluation processes. Search goods, which include most tangible products, possess tangible characteristics that allow consumers to evaluate quality prior to purchase and consumption. Experience goods, such as restaurants and clubs, can only be evaluated with certainty after purchase or consumption. In the case of credence goods, such as many professional services, the consumer finds it difficult to fully appreciate the quality of the goods even after purchase and consumption has occurred. Difficulties evaluating quality after consumption may arise because the cost of obtaining information is prohibitive, or because the consumer lacks the requisite skills and knowledge to undertake such evaluations. These goods are called credence products because the consumer's quality evaluations depend entirely on the trust given to the product manufacturer or service provider.

Typical risk-reduction strategies used include:

*Prospective purchasers carefully inspect the merchandise before purchasing expensive gold jewellery*

- Advertising and Promotional Messages: Pay closer attention to product or brand related promotion including advertising messages

- Shopping Around: Comparing offers and prices, inspecting the merchandise

- Buy Known Brand: Using a known, reputable brand as an indicator of quality merchandise

- Buy from Reputable Store: Relying on a reputable retail outlet as an indicator of quality

- Product Reviews: Reading independent reviews in main media (e.g. newspapers, magazines), written by independent experts

- Online product reviews or consumer-generated testimonials: Reading about the experiences of other consumers (e.g. TripAdvisor, Amazon customer reviews)

- Sampling or Limited-scale Trial: Where practical, obtaining samples, free trial or a 'test-drive' prior to purchase

- Manufacturer Specifications: Reading information provided by manufacturers e.g. brochures or specs

- Referrals: Obtaining referrals from friends or relatives

- Sales Representatives: Talking to sales reps in retail outlets

- Product Guarantees: Looking for formal guarantees or warranties

## New Product Adoption and Diffusion of Innovations

Within consumer behaviour, a particular area of interest is the study of how innovative new products, services, ideas or technologies spread through groups. Insights about how innovations are diffused (i.e., spread) through populations can assist marketers to speed up the new product adoption process and fine-tune the marketing program at different stages of the diffusion process. In addition, diffusion models provide benchmarks against which new product introductions can be tracked.

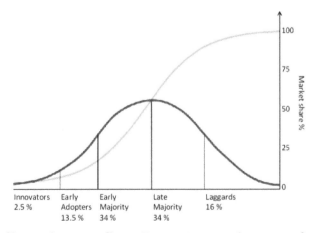

The diffusion of innovations according to Rogers. As successive groups of consumers adopt the innovation(shown in blue), its market share (yellow) will eventually reach saturation level

A sizeable body of literature has been devoted to the diffusion of innovation. Research studies tend to fall into two broad categories; general diffusion research - an approach that seeks to understand the general process of diffusion and applied diffusion research - studies that describe the diffusion of specific products at particular moments in time or within given social communities. Collectively these studies suggest a certain regularity in the adoption process; initially few members adopt the innovation but over time, successive, overlapping waves of people begin to adopt the innovation. This pattern contributes to a generalised S-shaped curve. However, the exact shape and timing of curves varies in different product markets such that some innovations are diffused relatively quickly, while others can take many years to achieve broad market acceptance.

The diffusion model developed by Everett Rogers is widely used in consumer marketing because it segments consumers into five groups, based on their rate of new product adoption. Rogers defines the diffusion of innovation as the process by which that innovation is "communicated through certain channels over time among the members of a social system." Thus the diffusion process has a number of elements, the innovation, the communication channels, time and the social system. An innovation is any new idea, object or process that is perceived as new by members of the social system. Communication channels are the means by which information about the innovation is transmitted to members of the social system and may include mass media, digital media and personal communications between members of the social system. Time refers to the rate at which the innovation is picked up by the members of the social system.

Table: Adopter Categories

| Adopter Group | Proportion of All Adopters | Psycho-social and Demographic Characteristics |
|---|---|---|
| Innovators | 2.5% | • adopt new products or concepts well ahead of the social community<br>• venturesome; like new ideas<br>• are willing to accept some uncertainty/ risk in purchase decision-making<br>• are active information seekers<br>• cosmopolitan; move in broad social circles<br>• have access to financial resources (which helps absorb potential losses when innovations fail)<br>• tend to be heavy users or category enthusiasts (e.g. tech-heads are the first to adopt new communications technologies)<br>• tend to be younger, well-educated and affluent |
| Early adopters | 13.5% | • second group to adopt new products or concepts<br>• not too far ahead of the community in terms of innovativeness<br>• have the respect of their social communities<br>• potential adopters look to early adopters as role models<br>• are important opinion leaders<br>• higher social status and well-educated |

| | | |
|---|---|---|
| Early majority | 34% | • third group to adopt new products or concepts<br>• adopt innovations only marginally ahead of the community average<br>• tend to be more deliberate in purchase decision-making<br>• average social status and education levels |
| Late majority | 34% | • adopt new products or concepts slightly later than average<br>• skeptical in purchase decision-making<br>• adoption is often a response to social community pressures |
| Laggards | 16% | • last group to adopt new products or concepts<br>• highly cautious; need to be confident that an innovation will not fail before purchasing<br>• are the most risk-averse of all adopter segments; dislike change<br>• traditionalists; resistant to change; look to the past<br>• somewhat isolated within their social community<br>• often adopt innovations when they are becoming obsolete<br>• tend to be older, less well educated and less affluent |

A number of factors contribute to the rate at which innovations are diffused through a social community.

Facilitating a 'test-drive' can encourage consumers to speed up adoption rates

- Relative advantage: the degree to which an innovation is perceived to be superior to alternatives

- Compatibility: the extent to which an innovation fits in with an individual's values, lifestyles and past experiences

- Complexity: the degree to which an innovation is perceived to be easy or difficult to understand and use

- Trialability: the extent to which an individual can experiment with the innovation, on a limited scale, prior to adoption

- Observability: the degree to which the results of the innovation are visible to other members of the social community

Innovations with some or all of these factors are more likely to be adopted quickly. Accordingly, marketing communications may stress the innovation's relative benefits over other solutions to the consumer's problem. Marketing messages may also focus on compatibility and observability. Marketers can also facilitate adoption by offering limited scale trial (e.g. samples, test drives, sale on approval), enabling consumers to develop and understanding of the innovation and how it is used prior to purchase.

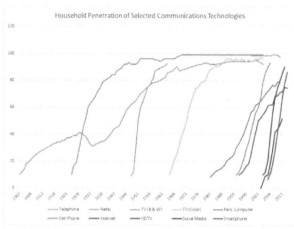

The rate of diffusion is speeding up

Studies have shown that the diffusion rate for many new technologies is speeding up. The figure, *Household Penetration of Selected Communications Technologies* (right), illustrates U.S. household penetration rates of selected communications technologies, measured as a percentage of all households. The slope of the curve becomes steeper with each successive innovation indicating a more rapid diffusion rate. For example, it took decades for the telephone to achieve 50 percent penetration rates beginning in around 1900, but it took less than five years for cellphones to achieve the same penetration rates. In order to explain the increasing pace of adoption, some have pointed to supply-side issues such as reduced barriers to entry and lower costs of innnovation, while others have argued that consumers drive adoption rates because they place a high value on the convenience of new innovations.

## Brand-switching

Brand-switching occurs when a consumer chooses to purchase a brand that is different to the regular or customary brand purchased. Consumers switch brands for a variety of reasons including that the store did not have the regular brand or the consumer's desire for variety or novelty in brand choice. In the fast moving consumer goods market (FMCG), the incidence of switching is relatively high. A great deal of marketing activity is targeted at brand-switchers. Rossiter and Bellman have proposed a classification of consumers based on brand-loyalty/ switching behaviour:

- *Brand Loyals*: Purchase preferred brand on almost every purchase occasion

- *Favourable Brand Switchers*: Exhibit moderate preference for the brand or brands that they buy and can be readily enticed to purchase competing brands

- *Other Brand Switchers*: Normally purchase a competing brand, possibly because they are unaware of our brand or due to a negative experience with our brand

- *New Category Users*: Those who are unaware of a category but have potential to become new users

Marketers are particularly interested in understanding the factors that lead to brand-switching. A global, large sample survey carried out by Nielsen shows that four in 10 shoppers (41%) said that getting a better price would encourage them to switch brands (or service provider/retailer); 26% said quality was an incentive to switch; 15% looked for a better service agreement and 8% said that improved features are a switching incentive. However, it should be noted that cross-cultural differences were observed among respondents. Price was the major switch incentive for more than half of North Americans (61%) and Europeans (54%) but price and quality held equal sway in Asia-Pacific and Middle East/Africa, with roughly one-third of respondents each in both regions reporting that both price and quality were the major incentives to switching.

The concept of *switching costs* (also known as switching barriers) is pertinent to the understanding of brand switching. Switching costs refer to the costs incurred by a consumer when he or she switches from one supplier to another (or from one brand to another). Although switching costs are often monetary, the concept can also refer to psychological costs such as time, effort and inconvenience incurred as a result of switching. When switching costs are relatively low, as in the case of many fast moving consumer goods (FMCG), the incidence of brand switching tends to be higher. An example of switching that includes both monetary and psychological costs is when Android or Apple users wish to switch to a different platform, they would need to sacrifice their data, including purchased music tracks, apps or media and may also need to learn new routines to become an efficient user.

## Channel-switching

The advent of category killers, such as Australia's Officeworks, has contributed to an increase in channel switching behaviour

Channel-switching (not to be confused with zapping or channel surfing on TV) is the action of consumers switching to a different purchasing environment (or distribution channel) to purchase goods, such as switching from brick-and-mortar stores to online catalogues, or the internet. A number of factors have led to an increase in channel switching behaviour; the growth of e-commerce, the globalization of markets, the advent of Category killers (such as Officeworks and Kids 'R Us) as well as changes in the legal/ statutory environment. For instance, in Australia and New Zealand, following a relaxation of laws prohibiting supermarkets from selling therapeutic goods, consumers are gradually switching away from pharmacies and towards supermarkets for the purchase of minor analgesics, cough and cold preparations and complementary medicines such as vitamins and herbal remedies.

For the consumer, channel switching offers a more diverse shopping experience. However, marketers need to be alert to channel switching because of its potential to erode market share. Evidence of channel switching can suggest that disruptive forces are at play, and that consumer behaviour is undergoing fundamental changes. A consumer may be prompted to switch channels when the product or service can be found cheaper, when superior models become available, when a wider range is offered, or simply because it is more convenient to shop through a different channel (e.g online or one-stop shopping). As a hedge against market share losses due to switching behaviour, some retailers engage in multi-channel retailing.

## Impulse Buying

Impulse purchases are unplanned purchases. Impulse buying can be defined as "a sudden and powerful urge to buy immediately" and occurs when a consumer purchases an item which they had no intention of purchasing prior to entering the store. Impulse buying can be influenced by external stimuli such as store characteristics and sale promotions, internal stimuli such as enjoyment and self-identity, situational and product related factors such as time and money available, and demographic and socio-cultural factors such as gender, age, and education. Stern introduced the four broad classifications of impulse buying including pure impulse buying, reminded impulse buying, suggestion impulse buying, and planned impulse buying:

Large family-sized cakes are more likely to be a planned purchase,
while the individual portions are much more likely to be an unplanned purchase

- *Pure impulse buying* - Occurs outside of the normal purchase behaviour where a consumer experiences a strong emotion of desire towards a product that he/she did not initially plan to buy. This is type of impulse buying is commonly influenced by low prices and even the approval to touch the product as this will create the imagine of actually owning the product.

- *Reminded impulse buying* - Occurs when a consumer remembers the need for a product by seeing it in a store. This is triggered through various techniques such as in-store advertising or sensory marketing. For example, a consumer may be reminded to buy ingredients for a barbecue when he/she drives past a butcher store.

- *Suggestion impulse buying* - Occurs when a consumer sees a product that they have no prior knowledge about, envisions a use for it, and decides that they need it. An example of suggestion impulse buying is when a consumer is encouraged to purchase an electric hand-mixer after having picked up a brochure from the baking department of a home-ware store. The brochure convinces the consumer of the hand-mixer's superiority over the wooden spoon she has been using. Marketing techniques that can also trigger suggestion impulse buying include long-term warranties or a free trial period.

- *Planned impulse buying* - Involves a partially planned intention of buying, however specific product or categories are not yet determined. In this case, the consumer's purchasing decision can be encouraged by retailing staff, or even their peers who can persuade the consumer to purchase a substitute or provide reassurance about an alternative brand choice.

Recent research carried out by Nielsen International suggests that about 72 percent of FMCG purchases are planned, but that 28 percent of supermarket purchases are unplanned or impulse purchases. The top unplanned purchases in the food category are candy (lollies), chocolate, cookies (biscuits), frozen desserts and snacks and the top unplanned purchases in the non-food category are cosmetics, air-fresheners, toothbrushes, hand-soaps and hand/body lotions. This explains why supermarkets place these types of products at the front of the store or near the checkout where the consumer spends more time and is more likely to notice them and therefore more likely to pop them into the shopping basket. Retailers use insights from this type of research to design stores in ways that maximise opportunities for impulse-buying.

## Affect: Emotions, Feelings and Mood

The consumer's affective state has implications for a number of different dimensions of consumer behaviour, including information search, evaluation of alternatives; product choice, service encounters, complaining and also in advertising responses. Westbrook (1987 , p. 259) defines affect as a "class of mental phenomena uniquely characterised by a consciously experienced, subjective feeling state, commonly accompanying emotions and moods" suggesting that these concepts are closely related. Research suggests that affect plays an important role in underlying attitudes, as well as shaping evaluation and decision-making.

Consumer researchers have noted the difficulties separating the concepts of affect, emotions, feelings and mood. The line between emotions and mood is difficult to draw and consumer researchers often use the concepts interchangeably. Yet other researchers note that a detailed understanding of the relationship between affect and consumer behaviour has been hampered by the lack of research in the area. Indeed, within the consumer behaviour literature, there is widespread agreement that the role of emotions is an area that is currently under-researched and is in need of greater attention, both theoretically and empirically.

## Affect and Information Search

Studies have found that people in a positive mood are more efficient at information search activities. That, is they are more efficient at processing information, are able to integrate information by identifying useful relationships and arrive at creative solutions to problems. Due to their efficiency processing information, those who are in a positive mood are generally quicker to make decisions and easier to please. Research consistently shows that people in a positive mood are more likely to evaluate information positively. As online environments become more important as a consumer search tool, it may be prudent for web designers to consider site-design issues such as ease of navigation, lest poor design contribute to customer frustration thereby engendering a bad mood and ultimately leading to unfavourable product/brand evaluations.

## Affect and Choice

The immediate hedonic pleasure of eating candy often outweighs
the longer term benefit of a healthier food choice

Affect may play an important role in impulse-buying decisions. Research suggests that consumers place higher weightings on immediate affective rewards and punishments, while delayed rewards receive less weighting. For instance, the immediate hedonic pleasure of eating a sweet treat often outweighs the longer term benefits of eating a healthy alternative such as fruit. This occurs because the immediate emotional gain is a strong driver, and one that consumers can readily visualise whereas the more distant goal lacks sufficient strength to drive choice.

## Affect and Customer Satisfaction

The relationship between affect and customer satisfaction is an area that has received considerable academic attention, especially in the services marketing literature. The proposition that there is a positive relationship between affect and satisfaction is well supported in the literature. In a meta-analysis of the empirical evidence, carried out in 2001, Szymanski et al, suggest that affect may be both an antecedent to and an outcome of satisfaction. Emotions elicited during consumption are proposed to leave affective traces in memory, traces that are available for consumers to access and integrate into their satisfaction assessments.

## Affect and Advertising

Emotion can play an important role in advertising. In advertising, it is common to identify advertising with two different approaches to persuasion: (a) *thinking ads*- those that require cognitive processing (also known as the *central route to persuasion*) and, (b) *feeling ads* - those that are processed at an emotional level (also known as the *peripheral route*). Advertisers can bypass cognitive, rational processing which can lead to counter-arguing by simply appealing to the emotions. Neuro-imaging studies suggest that when evaluating brands, consumers primarily use emotions (personal feelings and experiences) rather than information (brand attributes, features, and facts).

It is relatively widely accepted that emotional responses require fewer processing resources (i.e. are easier) and also result in more enduring associations with the brand being advertised. Feelings elicited by the advertising message can shape attitudes towards the brand and to the advertisement.

## Customer Loyalty

Customer loyalty, defined as "the relationship between an individual's relative attitude and repeat patronage" (Dick and Basu, 1994: p. 99). Thus, by definition, loyalty has both an attitudinal component and a behavioural component.

Dick and Basu proposed four types of loyalty based on relative attitude and patronage behaviour:

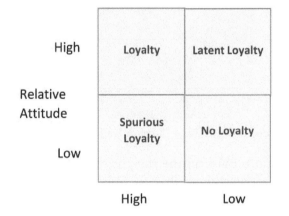

Dick and Basu's Loyalty Matrix

- *No Loyalty*: Characterised by low relative attitude and low repeat patronage behaviour. May occur when competing brands are seen as similar or in the case of new brands (or categories) where insufficient time has elapsed for loyalty to become established.

- *Spurious Loyalty*: Characterised by low relative attitude and high repeat patronage. Spurious loyalty occurs when the consumer undertakes repeat purchasing due to situational factors such as access, convenience or shelf placement. Spurious loyalty can also occur when there are no genuine alternatives or the consumer is 'locked-in' to purchasing a given brand due to some quasi-contractual arrangement or membership status which creates difficulties for switching. In other words, where switching costs are relatively high, high patronage behaviour may be observed despite the absence of a favourable attitude towards the brand. An example would be a consumer who always purchases petrol from the same outlet on the way to work because there are no other outlets in the vicinity.

- *Latent Loyalty*: Characterised by high relative attitude and low repeat patronage. Latent loyalty occurs when situational factors over-ride strong favourable attitudes. For example, a person may have a preferred restaurant but may not patronize it, due to the preferences of dining companions.

- *Loyalty*: (i.e. true loyalty) Characterised by favourable attitude and favourable patronage behaviour. For marketers, true loyalty is the ideal situation.

Frequent flyer schemes are among the most well known of the reward programs

Loyalty marketing programs are built on the insight that it costs 5-20 times more to acquire a new customer than to retain an existing customer. Marketers use a variety of loyalty programs to strengthen customer attitudes towards the brand (or service provider/ retailer) in order to retain customers, minimise customer defections and strengthen loyalty bonds with existing customers. Broadly there are two types of program: reward and recognition programs. In a Reward Program, the customer accumulates points for each purchase, and the points can subsequently be exchanged for goods or services. Recognition Programs operate on a quasi-membership basis where the consumer is issued with a card that upon presentation leads to various entitlements such as free upgrades, special privileges or access to products/services that are not normally available to non-members, and that acknowledge the loyal customer's "VIP" status. For example, a hotel might recognise loyal patrons by providing a complimentary fruit bowl and bottle of champagne in the room on arrival. Whereas reward programs are motivated by the consumer's desire for material possessions, recognition programs are motivated by the consumer's need for esteem, recognition and status. Many commercial loyalty programs are hybrid schemes, combining elements of both reward and recognition. In addition, not all reward programs are designed to encourage loyalty. Certain reward programs are designed to encourage other types of positive customer behaviour such as the provision of referrals or providing positive word-of-mouth (WOM) recommendations.

Loyalty marketing can involve the use of databases and sophisticated software to analyse and profile customer loyalty segments with a view to identifying the most desirable segments, setting goals for each segment and ultimately attempting to increase the size of the loyal customer base.

## Customer Citizenship Behaviour

Customer citizenship behaviour refers to actions that are not part of the customer's normal behaviour, that are of a voluntary or discretionary in nature and which are thoughtful, considerate and helpful. Citizenship behaviour often requires some type of sacrifice on the part of customers. Service marketers are particularly interested in citizenship behaviour because it harnesses the consumer's labour power, and therefore increases organisational efficiency. It also has the potential to improve service quality.

The service marketing literature identifies a number of distinct types of citizenship behaviour:

- *Voice*: When customers direct their complaint to the service provider in order to rectify and maintain the relationship

- *Display of Affiliation*: When customers communicate with others their relationship with the organization e.g. provide word-of-mouth referrals.

- *Policing*: The observation of other customers to ensure their appropriate behaviour

- *Flexibility*: Customer willingness to adapt to situations beyond their control.

- *Service Improvement*: Providing ideas and suggestions which may aid in the organization's improvement.

- *Positive Word-of-mouth Referral or Recommendation*: Favourable communication regarding brand, product, an organization or a service.

- *Benevolent Act of Service*: A willingness to help employees in performing service.

- *Suggestions for Service Improvement*: Suggestions that do not arise from specific service failures

## Research Methods Used in Consumer Behaviour

To gain insights into consumer behaviour, researchers uses the standard battery of market research methods such as surveys, depth interviews and focus groups. Increasingly, researchers are turning to newer methodologies and technologies in an effort to seek deeper understandings of why consumers behave in certain ways. These newer methods include *ethnographic research* (also known as participant observation) and *neuroscience* as well as experimental lab designs. In addition, researchers often turn to separate disciplines for insights with potential to inform the study of consumer behaviour. For instance, behavioural economics is adding fresh, new insights into certain aspects of consumer behaviour.

### Ethnographic Research

Ethnographic research or ethnography has its origins in anthropology. However, marketers use ethnographic research to study the consumer in terms of cultural trends, lifestyle factors, attitudes and the way that social context influences product selection, consumption and usage. Ethnographic research, also called *participant observation*, attempts to study consumer behaviour in natural settings rather than in artificial environment such as labs. Different types of ethnographic research are used in marketing including;

Product usage studies are used to improve packaging design

- Observed product usage: observing regular product usage at home or work, to gain insights into how products are opened, prepared, consumed, stored, disposed etc to gain insights into the usefulness of packaging, labelling and general usage

- Day-in-the-life studies: extended visits during product usage situations to gain insights into norms and consumer expectations

- Accompanied purchase or shop-alongs: researcher accompanies a shopper on a purchase expedition to gain insights into consumer responses to merchandising and other sales tactics

- Cultural studies: similar to traditional ethnography; extended stays with a group or tribe with a view to uncovering the fundamental rules and conventions that govern behaviour

- Guerilla ethnography: random observations in public settings to help establish research questions or to gain quick insights into specific behaviours

- Mystery shopping: observations in the retail context with a view to gaining insights into the customer's service experience

- Multiple methodologies: combining ethnographic research methods with conventional research techniques with a view to triangulating results

Trendspotters such as Faith Popcorn's BrainReserve make extensive use of ethnographic research to spot emergent trends.

## Consumer Neuroscience

*Consumer neuroscience* also known as *neuromarketing* refers to the commercial use of neuroscience when applied to the investigation of marketing problems and consumer research. Some researchers have argued that the term *consumer neuroscience* is preferred over neuromarketing or other alternatives.

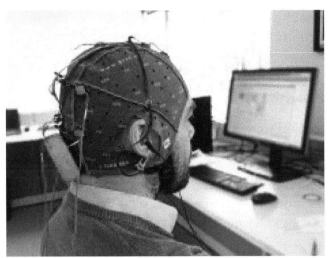

Neuromarketing uses sophisticated biometric sensors such as EEG to study consumer responses to specific stimuli

Consumer neuroscience employs sophisticated bio-metric sensors, such as electroencephalography (EEG), functional magnetic resonance imaging (fMRI) and eye-tracking, to study the ways that consumers respond to specific stimuli such as product displays, brands, packaging information or other marketing signals. Such tests reveal stimuli that trigger the brain's pleasure centre.

Consumer neuroscience has become a mainstream component of consumer research methods. International market research company, Nielsen Research, has recently added neuromarketing to its services by acquiring Innerscope, a company specialising in neuromarketing research thus enabling Nielsen to add neuromarketing research to the suite of services available to clients.

Consumer neuroscience research has led to some surprising findings:

*Framing value* : For example, one study reported on a magazine subscription where potential subscribers were offered two options:

(a) online subscription for $59 and;

(b) a combined online and print for $129 a year.

Most people chose the online only option. However, when a third option was introduced: print only for $129 (i.e. *the decoy*), the online and print option seemed like better value and a significant number of people switched to that option. In other words, the *decoy* price assists in framing value. Marketers use a variety of methods to *frame value*: e.g. quote monthly payment options rather than total price as the former seems more reasonable.

*Choice Fatigue*: Research by Sheena Iyengar experimented with the number of gourmet jams on display. When consumers were faced with a large number of alternatives (24 jams), 60% of consumers stopped and looked but only a few (3%) actually made a purchase. However, when consumers faced with fewer brands (6 jams), were more likely to make a purchase with 30% going on to buy something. Similar results have been observed in other categories. The findings suggest that while consumers appreciate being given some choice, the process of making a selection is painful and can lead to choice fatigue. An issue for marketers and retailers is to determine the 'sweet spot' where consumers are given sufficient choice to satisfy their desire for variety, but not become overwhelmed by it.

*Decision Paralysis*: One study examined the wording used to solicit philanthropic donations. Consumers were exposed to variants in the advertising copy execution:

(a) "Would you be willing to help by giving a donation?" and;

(b) "Would you be willing to help by giving a donation? Every penny will help."

Those given the second option were almost twice as likely to donate. The researchers concluded that people are more likely to take action when given parameters. By clarifying that "even a penny" could make a difference, the second line provides guidance and makes the request more achievable. For marketers, the implication is that when asking consumers to take an action, specifying a small step helps to break through the action paralysis. This finding also suggests that even small differences in advertising copy can lead to improved outcomes.

## Sustainable Consumer Behavior

Sustainable consumer behaviour is consumers' behaviors that improve social and environmental performance as well as meet their needs. It studies why and how consumers do or do not incorporate sustainability issues into their consumption behaviour. Also, it studies what products consumers do or do not buy, how they use them and what they do with them afterwards. One mechanism to spread information about sustainable consumer behaviour is word of mouth.

From a conventional marketing perspective, consumer behaviour has focused largely on the purchase stage of the total consumption process. This is because it is the actual point at which a contract is made between the buyer and seller, money is paid and the ownership of products transfers to the consumer. Yet from a social and environmental perspective, consumer behaviour needs to be understood as a whole since a product affects all stages of a consumption process.

## Total Consumption Process

### Know the difference between need and want

Need and want recognition occur when a consumer senses a difference between what he or she perceives to be the idea versus the actual state of affairs.

### Information Search

There are three key sources for searching information, in other words personal, commercial and public sources. Especially, the mass media, which is a public source, increasingly provide information about the environmental costs and benefits of consumption. Consumers become aware of them through these sources.

### Evaluation of Alternatives

In this stage, environmental concerns which are expressed as environmental costs, risks and benefits, will contribute to the evaluation of options in deciding what to buy. One way to evaluate more sustainable consumption is to consider the total customer cost which incurs in acquisition, use and post-use phases.

## Purchase

Consumers have to trade off the environmental benefits against other attributes such as higher price, better performance and better design. In addition they may need to change the manner of behaviour that they usually do.

## Use

In this stage, maintenance, repair, use frequency and type of use are of interest. Some key products such as homes, cars and domestic appliances, much of the sustainability impact accrue after the purchase phase during use or post-use. Again, this is why the total consumption process approach is needed.

## Post-use

In the final stage, consumers can keep, reuse (for example by selling, trading or giving a product to others) and dispose of a product. Some materials such as paper, glass, metal can be recycled or reused in production process. This phase has become significantly important due to the overloaded landfill.

## The Consumer Behaviour Influence

Buying and consuming an individual product, like a cup of coffee on the way to work or class, might seem such a trivial action that, although it refreshes us, it leaves no lasting impression or memory. However, that action will combine with those of other consumers to contribute to the economic success of the coffee retailer, the overall growth in the economy and the volume of waste with which local government must deal. It will influence the demand for, and the price of, coffee beans and milk, and in doing so will influence the lives and prosperity of thousands of farmers throughout the world, and shape their investment and planting decisions for next year. It will have knock-on impacts in terms of the demand for pesticides, fertilizer, packaging materials and energy. The economic impact of that coffee will contribute to the future share price of the retailers and the levels of income and investment they will enjoy. At a national level, it will contribute to national prosperity and in doing so will influence the future policies on taxation and interest rates.

We tend to think of consumption as an economic phenomenon that addresses our individual wants and drives the economy through our collective behaviour, but it is also social and cultural process through which we all express our identity and establish our place within society. It is also a physical process that literally consumes resources. What we eat, how we heat our homes and how we travel to work or for pleasure may seem like nobody`s businesses except our own. However, the collective consequences of those consumption decisions, and the ways in which our needs are met, are a principal driver behind climate change that will have consequences for people, countries and species across the globe.

Consumers' purchasing behaviour will determine the success or failure of new products and services that are marketed on the basis of their sustainability performance. Because of the role consumers in determining sustainability impacts during the use and disposal phases of the consumption process, their overall behaviour will also strongly influence the sustainability performance of all goods and services.

## Attitude, Knowledge and Behaviour Gap

There exist some inconsistencies in consumers' behaviours.

## Attitude and Behaviour Gap

Despite the significant increase in consumers' environmental awareness, many of them have not taken their concerns into consideration in their actual consumption choices and behaviours. This can be due to consumers' selfishness, which is they don't want to give up or change the way they live, or the associated costs and taxes.

## Knowledge and Behaviour Gap

There is a discrepancy between what behaviour consumers think is socially and environmentally sustainable and what behaviour actually is. For instance, many people in the U.S. limit their use of spray cans as they want to minimize their contribution to the impact on the ozone layer. Their behaviour is not environmentally significant because the substances that affect the ozone layer have already been banned in the U.S. long ago. This can be due to consumers' lack of knowledge about general environmental impacts of consumption.

## Three Theories Explanation

## Rational Explanations

This emphasizes the economics of sustainable consumption, and how consumers weigh up the functional benefits and relatively affordability of a product and service. Behavioural models based around economical rationality tend to assume a high degree of self-interest on the part of the consumer.

## Psychological Explanations

As a complement to rational explanations for consumer behaviour, there has been research into the psychology of sustainable consumption and more emotional and irrational explanations of our behaviour. Much of this focuses on consumers` attitudes and beliefs about sustainable issues. Three important sets of attitudes that influence consumers willingness to engage with sustainability issues are perceived personal relevance, social responsibility and trust.

## Sociological Explanations

Our behaviour as consumers is not simply a reflection of the rational dimensions of the costs and benefits of a particular consumption activity and what we know about it, nor is it fully explained by how we perceive the consumption activity as an individual. It is also explained by how we think our consumption activities will be perceived by others, and how that might be reflect and influence our place in society.

## Forms of Sustainable Consumption Behaviour

Progress toward more sustainable consumption is therefore not simply a question of what products and services are purchased, it is about the adoption of a lifestyle in which sustainability is reflected in all aspects of consumers` behaviour. The most advanced form of sustainable consumption behaviour is among those identified as voluntary simplifiers, whose lifestyle is based around five key values:

### Material Simplicity

Involving consuming fewer products and services, and tending to seek out products that are resource efficient, durable and with a reduced ecological impact.

### Human Scale

Following the principal of "small is beautiful" in tending toward working and living environments that are smaller, simpler and less centralized.

### Self-determination

Through a reduced reliance on large commercial businesses, or even large public-sector organization, to meet one`s need, or even to influence what those needs might be.

### Ecological Awareness

In terms of conservation of resources and reduction of waste in order to protect the environment.

### Personal Growth

Emphasizing the creation of satisfaction through experiences and development of personal abilities instead of commercially provided consumption experiences.

In recent years many of the key traits of voluntary simplification have been exhibited in a less extreme, but more widespread way, through the phenomenon of downshifting. Downshifting involves a change of lifestyle and consumption patterns that exchange a relatively highly paid/lower stress but more rewarding, and shifting to a lower level of material consumption but a higher level of quality of life and personal satisfaction.

### Sustainable Consumption Choices

From a sustainability perspective, we know that all types of consumption are not equally important in terms of their sustainability impacts. Greater progress may come from focusing on consumption behaviours linked to those products with the most significant impacts. The European Environmental Impact of Product Project provides a rigorous analysis of research into the environmental impact of products consumed by households. The project`s input-output-based methodology assesses 255 domestic product types against a wide range of environmental impacts. It concludes that 70-80% of total impacts relate to food and drink consumption; housing (including domestic energy use); and transport (including commuting, leisure and holiday travel). Ideally, all aspects of our consumption behaviours and production systems will become oriented toward sustainability, but initially significant progress would be achieved through:

## Sustainable Food and Drink Consumption Choices

Consumption level that are more conductive to health; a reduced consumption of meat products due to their contribution to climate change; choosing organically produced and locally sourced, seasoned produce; and greater composting of biodegradable food waste

## Sustainable Housing Consumption Choices

Including more emphasis on purchasing homes constructed using sustainable materials and choosing and creating homes with high levels of insulation and energy efficiency. This also involves energy usage within the home based on sustainable energy source, and the avoidance of energy waste while living in the home (e.g. through energy-efficient refrigerator and energy saving bulbs).

## Sustainable Travel Behaviour

Which may mean reducing the amount of travel undertaken (e.g. through home-working or teleconference service) or finding alternative transport means for journeys such as cycling for leisure rather than driving. In terms of tourism consumption behaviours, it means seeking tourism offerings that try to protect the global and local environment and also the cultures within tourism destinations.

## Toward Behaviour Change

Behaviour change in consumption is nowadays becoming a guiding principle for sustainable development policy. However, switching unsustainable consumer behaviours to sustainable demanours is far from straightforward. Individual behaviours are deeply rooted in social and institutional contexts. We are influenced by what others around us say and do, and by the institutional rules as we make choice on our own. In fact, we have been already locked into unsustainable behaviours regardless of having best intentions.

Making sustainable consumption choices are significantly related to the role of habit and routine behaviours. Habits can be thought of as procedural strategies to reduce the cognitive effort associated with making choices, particularly in situations that are relatively stable. They allow us to perform routine actions with a minimum of deliberation and often only limited awareness. Moreover, the evidence suggests that habit is a crucial component in a wide variety of environmentally-significant activities: travel behaviour, shopping patterns, household chores, waste disposal, leisure activities, and even personal hygiene. Habits are formed through repetition and reinforcement. Andersen (1982) identifies three stages in the formation of a new habit. The first stage, or declarative stage, involves information processing relating to a particular choice or action. At this stage the attitudinal and affective responses to this information are both important. The information challenges the existing choice, but at this stage does not actually change coffee-buying behaviour. In the second knowledge compilation stage, however, this information is converted into a new routine by exercising a different choice in practice. When the action itself is associated with a clear positive reinforcement, and repeated over time, a 'cognitive script' is developed which enables to repeat the same action in similar circumstances with very little cognitive effort. This final procedural stage locks into a new coffee-buying habit and virtually without thinking now the ethically traded coffee is tossed into the supermarket trolley week after week. At this stage, the behaviour is more or less automatized and bypasses rational deliberation almost completely.

In many cases, people appear to be locked into behaviours and behavioural patterns that seem to be resistant to change. In fact, they are changing continually and sometimes radically in a short period. The uptake of smart phones, widescreen plasma TVs, standby modes in electronic appliances patterns of holiday travel and travel behaviour: these are examples of technological and behavioural change occurring in only a decade. The sorts of changes are a kind of 'creeping evolution' of social and technological norms. Individuals alter their behaviours and sometimes individual behaviour initiates new social trends. At some higher or deeper level, in other words, individuals find themselves responding to societal and technological changes that are initiated elsewhere. Therefore, we should develop policies to encourage pro-environmental and pro-social consumer behaviours informed by some kind of understanding of the dimensions of and possibilities for behavioural change.

Sustainable consumer behaviour is a complex and evolving subject, and simply answers rarely provide substantive progress toward creating a more sustainable society. From a sustainable perspective, consumption needs to be understood more holistically as a total process, as part of a broader consumer lifestyle and as a process that is strongly influenced by the social context in which it takes place. Individual changes in purchasing behaviour can contribute to progress toward sustainability, but progress also depends on supports from deeper changes occurring within consumer lifestyle and throughout society.

## Nature of Consumer Behavior

i.   The subject deals with issues related to *cognition, affect and behavior* in consumption behaviors, against the backdrop of *individual* and *environmental* determinants. The *individual* determinants pertain to an individual's internal self and include psychological components like personal motivation and involvement, perception, learning and memory, attitudes, self-concept and personality, and, decision making. The *environmental* determinants pertain to external influences surrounding an individual and include sociological, anthropological and economic components like the family, social groups, reference groups, social class, culture, sub-culture, cross-culture, and national and regional influences.

ii.  The subject can be studied at *micro or macro levels* depending upon whether it is analyzed at the individual level or at the group level.

iii. The subject is interdisciplinary. It has borrowed heavily from *psychology* (the study of the individual: individual determinants in buying behavior), *sociology* (the study of groups: group dynamics in buying behavior), social psychology (the study of how an individual operates in group/groups and its effects on buying behavior), *anthropology* (the influence of society on the individual: cultural and cross-cultural issues in buying behavior), and *economics* (income and purchasing power).

iv.  Consumer behavior is *dynamic and interacting in nature*. The three components of cognition, affect and behavior of individuals alone or in groups keeps on changing; so does the environment. There is a continuous interplay or interaction between the three components themselves and with the environment. This impacts consumption pattern and behavior and it keeps on evolving and it is highly dynamic.

v.   Consumer behavior involves the process of *exchange* between the buyer and the seller, mutually beneficial for both.

vi.  As a field of study it is *descriptive* and also *analytical/ interpretive*. It is *descriptive* as it explains consumer decision making and behavior in the context of individual determinants and environmental influences. It is *analytical/ interpretive*, as against a backdrop of theories borrowed from psychology, sociology, social psychology, anthropology and economics, the study analyzes consumption behavior of individuals alone and in groups. It makes use of qualitative and quantitative tools and techniques for research and analysis, with the objective is to understand and predict consumption behavior.

vii. It is a *science as well as an art*. It uses both, *theories* borrowed from social sciences to understand consumption behavior, and *quantitative and qualitative tools and techniques* to predict consumer behavior.

## Scope of Consumer Behavior

The study of consumer behavior deals with understanding consumption patterns and behavior. It includes within its ambit the answers to the following:

- 'What' the consumers buy: goods and services

- 'Why' they buy it: need and want

- 'When' do they buy it: time: day, week, month, year, occasions etc.

- 'Where' they buy it: place

- 'How often they buy' it: time interval

- 'How often they use' it: frequency of use

The scope of consumer behavior includes not only the actual buyer but also the various roles played by him/ different individuals.

Basic Components

i)   *Decision making* (Cognitive and Affect): This includes the stages of decision making: Need recognition, Information search, Evaluation of alternatives, Purchase activity, Post purchase behavior.

ii)  *Actual purchase (Behavior):* This includes the visible physical activity of buying of goods and/ or service.  It is the result of the interplay of many individual and environmental determinants which are invisible.

iii) *Individual determinants and environmental influences*: The environmental factors affect the decision process indirectly, through way of affecting individual determinants.

*iv) Buying roles*: Actual Buyer vis a vis other users. There are five buying roles, viz., Initiator, Influencer, Decider, User, Buyer. The *initiator* is the person who identifies that there exists a need or want; the *influencer* is the one who influences the purchase decision, the actual purchase activity and/or the use of the product or service; the *decider* is the one who decides whether to buy, what to buy, when to buy, from where to buy, and how to buy; the *buyer* is theone who makes the actual purchase; and, the *user* is the person (s) who use the product or service. These five roles may be played by one person or by different persons. A person may assume one or more of these roles. This would depend on the product or service in question. *Examples: Let us take two examples.*

Example 1:

A child goes to a kindergarten school. She comes back home and asks her parents to buy her a set of color pencils and crayons. Now the roles played are:

1. Initiator: the child in nursery school

2. Influencer: a fellow classmate

3. Decider: the father or the mother

4. Buyer: the father or the mother

5. User: the child

Example 2:

The lady of a house who is a housewife and spends her day at home doing household chores watches TV in her free time. That is her only source of entertainment. The TV at home is giving problem.  She desires a new TV set, and says that she wants an LCD plasma TV. Now the roles played are:

1. Initiator: the housewife (mother)

2. Influencer: a friend / neighbour

3. Decider: the husband or the son

4. Buyer: the husband or the son

5. User: the family

*Consumer behavior focuses specifically on* the Buyer and often User.But also analyzes impact of other roles.

*v) Buyers and Sellers*: They are the key elements in consumer behavior. They have needs and wants and go through a complex buying process, so as to be able to satisfy the need through purchase of the good or service offering. They enter into an exchange process with the seller, which leaves both the parties (buyer and seller) better off than before. In fact the exchange process is value enhancing in nature, leading to satisfaction of both the parties.

# References

- "An Institutional Analysis of Consumer Law". Vanderbilt Journal of Transnational Law. Archived from the original on March 2, 2007. Retrieved 2007-01-29

- Cross, Robert G. (1997). Revenue management: hard-core tactics for market domination. Broadway Books. pp. 66–71. ISBN 978-0-553-06734-7

- J. Scott Armstrong (1991). "Prediction of Consumer Behavior by Experts and Novices" (PDF). Journal of Consumer Research. Journal of Consumer Research Inc. 18: 251–256. doi:10.1086/209257

- "The relationships among service quality, perceived value, customer satisfaction, and post-purchase intention in mobile value-added services". Computers in Human Behavior. 25: 887–896. 2009. doi:10.1016/j.chb.2009.03.003

- Lynn R. Kahle; Angeline G. Close (2011). Consumer Behavior Knowledge for Effective Sports and Event Marketing. New York: Routledge. ISBN 978-0-415-87358-1

- Mitchell, V-W, "Consumer Perceived Risk: Conceptualisations and Models", European Journal of Marketing , Vol. 33 no. 1/2, pp.163 – 195

- Elizabeth A. Minton; Lynn R. Khale (2014). Belief Systems, Religion, and Behavioral Economics. New York: Business Expert Press LLC. ISBN 978-1-60649-704-3

- Khosla, Swati (2010). "Consumer psychology: The essence of Marketing". International Journal of Educational Administration. 2 (2): 220–220. Retrieved 2012-05-16

- Dholakia1, R.R., Zhao, M. and Dholakia, N., "Multichannel retailing: A case study of early experiences.," Journal of Interactive Marketing, vol. 19, March, pp 63–74, 2009, DOI: 10.1002/dir.20035

- Lynn R. Kahle; Pierre Valette-Florence (2012). Marketplace Lifestyles in an Age of Social Media. New York: M.E. Sharpe, Inc. ISBN 978-0-7656-2561-8

- Winchester, J. R. and Bogomolova, S., "Positive and negative brand beliefs and brand defection/uptake", European Journal of Marketing, Vol. 42, No. 5/6, 2008, pp.553 – 570

- Weber, Elke U.; Baron, Jonathan (2001-01-01). Conflict and Tradeoffs in Decision Making. Cambridge University Press. ISBN 9780521772389

- Bhakat, Ravi Shankar; Muruganantham, G. "A Review of Impulse Buying Behavior". International Journal of Marketing Studies. 5 (3). doi:10.5539/ijms.v5n3p149

- Flynn, L. R., Goldsmith, R. E. and Eastman, J. K., "Opinion leaders and opinion seekers: Two new measurement scales," Journal of Academy of Marketing Science, vol. 24, no. 2, pp 137-147

- Stern, Hawkins (1962-01-01). "The Significance of Impulse Buying Today". Journal of Marketing. 26 (2): 59–62. JSTOR 1248439. doi:10.2307/1248439

- Chaffey, D. (2006). Internet marketing (3rd ed.. ed.). Harlow: Financial Times Prentice Hall. p. 109. ISBN 1405871814

- Durvasula, S., Lysonski, S. and Andrews, J.C. (1993), "Cross-cultural generalizability of a scale for profiling consumers' decision-making styles", The Journal of Consumer Affairs, Vol. 27 No. 1, pp. 55-65

- Jain, R. and Sharma, A., "A Review on Sproles & Kendall's Consumer Style Inventory (CSI) for Analyzing Decision Making Styles of Consumers," Indian Journal of Marketing, Vol. 43, no. 3, 2013

- Bauer, H. H., Sauer, N. E., and Becker, C., "Investigating the relationship between product involvement and consumer decision-making styles," Journal of Consumer Behaviour. Vol. 5, 2006 342–354

# Decision Making Process: A Consumer-Centric Approach

Decision-making can be defined as selecting from available options, and is goal-oriented and a problem solving method. When consumer decision-making is discussed, it becomes primarily a problem solving process. It involves collecting information, analyzing them and then choosing the best alternative. The section strategically encompasses and incorporates the major components and key concepts of consumer decision making, providing a complete understanding.

## Decision-making

Sample flowchart representing the decision process

In psychology, decision-making is regarded as the cognitive process resulting in the selection of a belief or a course of action among several alternative possibilities. Every decision-making process produces a final choice; it may or may not prompt action. Decision-making is the process of identifying and choosing alternatives based on the values and preferences of the decision-maker.

## Overview

Decision-making can be regarded as a problem-solving activity terminated by a solution deemed to be satisfactory. It is therefore a process which can be more or less rational or irrational and can be based on explicit or tacit knowledge.

Human performance with regard to decisions has been the subject of active research from several perspectives:

- Psychological: examining individual decisions in the context of a set of needs, preferences and values the individual has or seeks.

- Cognitive: the decision-making process regarded as a continuous process integrated in the interaction with the environment.

- Normative: the analysis of individual decisions concerned with the logic of decision-making, or communicative rationality, and the invariant choice it leads to.

A major part of decision-making involves the analysis of a finite set of alternatives described in terms of evaluative criteria. Then the task might be to rank these alternatives in terms of how attractive they are to the decision-maker(s) when all the criteria are considered simultaneously. Another task might be to find the best alternative or to determine the relative total priority of each alternative (for instance, if alternatives represent projects competing for funds) when all the criteria are considered simultaneously. Solving such problems is the focus of multiple-criteria decision analysis (MCDA). This area of decision-making, although very old, has attracted the interest of many researchers and practitioners and is still highly debated as there are many MCDA methods which may yield very different results when they are applied on exactly the same data. This leads to the formulation of a decision-making paradox.

Logical decision-making is an important part of all science-based professions, where specialists apply their knowledge in a given area to make informed decisions. For example, medical decision-making often involves a diagnosis and the selection of appropriate treatment. But naturalistic decision-making research shows that in situations with higher time pressure, higher stakes, or increased ambiguities, experts may use intuitive decision-making rather than structured approaches. They may follow a recognition primed decision that fits their experience and arrive at a course of action without weighing alternatives.

The decision-maker's environment can play a part in the decision-making process. For example, environmental complexity is a factor that influences cognitive function. A complex environment is an environment with a large number of different possible states which come and go over time. Studies done at the University of Colorado have shown that more complex environments correlate with higher cognitive function, which means that a decision can be influenced by the location. One experiment measured complexity in a room by the number of small objects and appliances present; a simple room had less of those things. Cognitive function was greatly affected by the higher measure of environmental complexity making it easier to think about the situation and make a better decision.

## Problem Analysis

It is important to differentiate between problem analysis and decision-making. Traditionally, it is argued that problem analysis must be done first, so that the information gathered in that process may be used towards decision-making.

Characteristics of problem analysis

- Analyze performance, what should the results be against what they actually are

- Problems are merely deviations from performance standards

- Problems must be precisely identified and described

- Problems are caused by a change from a distinctive feature

- Something can always be used to distinguish between what has and hasn't been affected by a cause

- Causes of problems can be deduced from relevant changes found in analyzing the problem

- Most likely cause of a problem is the one that exactly explains all the facts, while having the fewest assumptions (Occam's razor).

Characteristics of decision-making

- Objectives must first be established

- Objectives must be classified and placed in order of importance

- Alternative actions must be developed

- The alternatives must be evaluated against all the objectives

- The alternative that is able to achieve all the objectives is the tentative decision

- The tentative decision is evaluated for more possible consequences

- The decisive actions are taken, and additional actions are taken to prevent any adverse consequences from becoming problems and starting both systems (problem analysis and decision-making) all over again

- There are steps that are generally followed that result in a decision model that can be used to determine an optimal production plan

- In a situation featuring conflict, role-playing may be helpful for predicting decisions to be made by involved parties

## Analysis Paralysis

Analysis paralysis is the state of over-analyzing (or over-thinking) a situation so that a decision or action is never taken, in effect paralyzing the outcome.

## Information Overload

Information overload is "a gap between the volume of information and the tools we have to assimilate" it. Excessive information affects problem processing and tasking, which affects decision-making. Crystal C. Hall and colleagues described an "illusion of knowledge", which means that as individuals encounter too much knowledge it can interfere with their ability to make rational decisions.

## Post-decision Analysis

Evaluation and analysis of past decisions is complementary to decision-making.

## Decision-making Techniques

Decision-making techniques can be separated into two broad categories: group decision-making techniques and individual decision-making techniques. Individual decision-making techniques can also often be applied by a group.

## Group

- Consensus decision-making tries to avoid "winners" and "losers". Consensus requires that a majority approve a given course of action, but that the minority agree to go along with the course of action. In other words, if the minority opposes the course of action, consensus requires that the course of action be modified to remove objectionable features.

- Voting-based methods:

    o Majority requires support from more than 50% of the members of the group. Thus, the bar for action is lower than with consensus.

    o Plurality, where the largest block in a group decides, even if it falls short of a majority.

    o Range voting lets each member score one or more of the available options. The option with the highest average is chosen. This method has experimentally been shown to produce the lowest Bayesian regret among common voting methods, even when voters are strategic.

- Delphi method is structured communication technique for groups, originally developed for collaborative forecasting but has also been used for policy making.

- Dotmocracy is a facilitation method that relies on the use of special forms called Dotmocracy Sheets to allow large groups to collectively brainstorm and recognize agreement on an unlimited number of ideas they have authored.

- Participative decision-making occurs when an authority opens up the decision-making process to a group of people for a collaborative effort.

- Decision engineering uses a visual map of the decision-making process based on system dynamics and can be automated through a decision modeling tool, integrating big data, machine learning, and expert knowledge as appropriate.

## Individual

- Decisional balance sheet: listing the advantages and disadvantages (benefits and costs, pros and cons) of each option, as suggested by Plato's *Protagoras* and by Benjamin Franklin.

- Simple prioritization: choosing the alternative with the highest probability-weighted utility. This may involve considering the opportunity cost of different alternatives.

- Satisficing: examining alternatives only until the first acceptable one is found. The opposite is maximizing or optimizing, in which many or all alternatives are examined in order to find the best option.

- Acquiesce to a person in authority or an "expert"; "just following orders".

- Anti-authoritarianism: taking the most opposite action compared to the advice of mistrusted authorities.

- Flipism e.g. flipping a coin, cutting a deck of playing cards, and other random or coincidence methods – or prayer, tarot cards, astrology, augurs, revelation, or other forms of divination, superstition or pseudoscience.

- Automated decision support: setting up criteria for automated decisions.

- Decision support systems: using decision-making software when faced with highly complex decisions or when considering many stakeholders, categories, or other factors that affect decisions.

## Steps

### GOFER

In the 1980s, psychologist Leon Mann and colleagues developed a decision-making process called GOFER, which they taught to adolescents, as summarized in the book *Teaching Decision Making To Adolescents*. The process was based on extensive earlier research conducted with psychologist Irving Janis. GOFER is an acronym for five decision-making steps:

1. Goals: Survey values and objectives.

2. Options: Consider a wide range of alternative actions.

3. Facts: Search for information.

4. Effects: Weigh the positive and negative consequences of the options.

5. Review: Plan how to implement the options.

### Decide

In 2008, Kristina Guo published the DECIDE model of decision-making, which has six parts:

1. Define the problem

2. Establish or Enumerate all the criteria (constraints)

3. Consider or Collect all the alternatives

4. Identify the best alternative

5. Develop and implement a plan of action

6. Evaluate and monitor the solution and examine feedback when necessary

## Other

In 2007, Pam Brown of Singleton Hospital in Swansea, Wales, divided the decision-making process into seven steps:

1. Outline your goal and outcome.

2. Gather data.

3. Develop alternatives (i.e., brainstorming).

4. List pros and cons of each alternative.

5. Make the decision.

6. Immediately take action to implement it.

7. Learn from and reflect on the decision.

In 2009, professor John Pijanowski described how the Arkansas Program, an ethics curriculum at the University of Arkansas, used eight stages of moral decision-making based on the work of James Rest:

1. Establishing community: Create and nurture the relationships, norms, and procedures that will influence how problems are understood and communicated. This stage takes place prior to and during a moral dilemma.

2. Perception: Recognize that a problem exists.

3. Interpretation: Identify competing explanations for the problem, and evaluate the drivers behind those interpretations.

4. Judgment: Sift through various possible actions or responses and determine which is more justifiable.

5. Motivation: Examine the competing commitments which may distract from a more moral course of action and then prioritize and commit to moral values over other personal, institutional or social values.

6. Action: Follow through with action that supports the more justified decision.

7. Reflection in action.

8. Reflection on action.

## Group Stages

According to B. Aubrey Fisher, there are four stages or phases that should be involved in all group decision-making:

- Orientation. Members meet for the first time and start to get to know each other.

- Conflict. Once group members become familiar with each other, disputes, little fights and arguments occur. Group members eventually work it out.

- Emergence. The group begins to clear up vague opinions by talking about them.

- Reinforcement. Members finally make a decision and provide justification for it.

It is said that establishing critical norms in a group improves the quality of decisions, while the majority of opinions (called consensus norms) do not.

## Rational and Irrational

In economics, it is thought that if humans are rational and free to make their own decisions, then they would behave according to rational choice theory. Rational choice theory says that a person consistently makes choices that lead to the best situation for himself or herself, taking into account all available considerations including costs and benefits; the rationality of these considerations is from the point of view of the person himself, so a decision is not irrational just because someone else finds it questionable.

In reality, however, there are some factors that affect decision-making abilities and cause people to make irrational decisions – for example, to make contradictory choices when faced with the same problem framed in two different ways.

## Cognitive and Personal Biases

Biases usually affect decision-making processes. Here is a list of commonly debated biases in judgment and decision-making:

- Selective search for evidence (also known as confirmation bias): People tend to be willing to gather facts that support certain conclusions but disregard other facts that support different conclusions. Individuals who are highly defensive in this manner show significantly greater left prefrontal cortex activity as measured by EEG than do less defensive individuals.

- Premature termination of search for evidence: People tend to accept the first alternative that looks like it might work.

- Cognitive inertia is unwillingness to change existing thought patterns in the face of new circumstances.

- Selective perception: People actively screen out information that they do not think is important. In one demonstration of this effect, discounting of arguments with which one disagrees (by judging them as untrue or irrelevant) was decreased by selective activation of right prefrontal cortex.

- Wishful thinking is a tendency to want to see things in a certain – usually positive – light, which can distort perception and thinking.

- Choice-supportive bias occurs when people distort their memories of chosen and rejected options to make the chosen options seem more attractive.

- Recency: People tend to place more attention on more recent information and either ignore or forget more distant information. The opposite effect in the first set of data or other information is termed *primacy effect*.

- Repetition bias is a willingness to believe what one has been told most often and by the greatest number of different sources.

- Anchoring and adjustment: Decisions are unduly influenced by initial information that shapes our view of subsequent information.

- Groupthink is peer pressure to conform to the opinions held by the group.

- Source credibility bias is a tendency to reject a person's statement on the basis of a bias against the person, organization, or group to which the person belongs. People preferentially accept statement by others that they like.

- Incremental decision-making and escalating commitment: People look at a decision as a small step in a process, and this tends to perpetuate a series of similar decisions. This can be contrasted with *zero-based decision-making*.

- Attribution asymmetry: People tend to attribute their own success to internal factors, including abilities and talents, but explain their failures in terms of external factors such as bad luck. The reverse bias is shown when people explain others' success or failure.

- Role fulfillment is a tendency to conform to others' decision-making expectations.

- Underestimating uncertainty and the illusion of control: People tend to underestimate future uncertainty because of a tendency to believe they have more control over events than they really do.

- Framing bias: This is best avoided by increasing numeracy and presenting data in several formats (for example, using both absolute and relative scales).

  o Sunk-cost fallacy is a specific type of framing effect that affects decision-making. It involves an individual making a decision about a current situation based on what they have previously invested in the situation. An example of this would be an individual that is refraining from dropping a class that they are most likely to fail, due to the fact that they feel as though they have done so much work in the course thus far.

- Prospect theory involves the idea that when faced with a decision-making event, an individual is more likely to take on a risk when evaluating potential losses, and are more likely to avoid risks when evaluating potential gains. This can influence one's decision-making depending if the situation entails a threat, or opportunity.

- Optimism bias is a tendency to overestimate the likelihood of positive events occurring in the future and underestimate the likelihood of negative life events. Such biased expectations are generated and maintained in the face of counter evidence through a tendency to discount undesirable information. An optimism bias can alter risk perception and decision-making in many domains, ranging from finance to health.

- Reference class forecasting was developed to eliminate or reduce cognitive biases in decision-making.

## Cognitive Styles

## Optimizing vs. Satisficing

Herbert A. Simon coined the phrase "bounded rationality" to express the idea that human decision-making is limited by available information, available time and the mind's information-processing ability. Further psychological research has identified individual differences between two cognitive styles: *maximizers* try to make an optimal decision, whereas *satisficers* simply try to find a solution that is "good enough". Maximizers tend to take longer making decisions due to the need to maximize performance across all variables and make tradeoffs carefully; they also tend to more often regret their decisions (perhaps because they are more able than satisficers to recognise that a decision turned out to be sub-optimal).

## Intuitive vs. Rational

The psychologist Daniel Kahneman, adopting terms originally proposed by the psychologists Keith Stanovich and Richard West, has theorized that a person's decision-making is the result of an interplay between two kinds of cognitive processes: an automatic intuitive system (called "System 1") and an effortful rational system (called "System 2"). System 1 is a bottom-up, fast, and implicit system of decision-making, while system 2 is a top-down, slow, and explicit system of decision-making. System 1 includes simple heuristics in judgment and decision-making such as the affect heuristic, the availability heuristic, the familiarity heuristic, and the representativeness heuristic.

## Combinatorial vs. Positional

Styles and methods of decision-making were elaborated by Aron Katsenelinboigen, the founder of predispositioning theory. In his analysis on styles and methods, Katsenelinboigen referred to the game of chess, saying that "chess does disclose various methods of operation, notably the creation of predisposition-methods which may be applicable to other, more complex systems."

Katsenelinboigen states that apart from the methods (reactive and selective) and sub-methods (randomization, predispositioning, programming), there are two major styles: positional and combinational. Both styles are utilized in the game of chess. According to Katsenelinboigen, the two styles reflect two basic approaches to uncertainty: deterministic (combinational style) and indeterministic (positional style). Katsenelinboigen's definition of the two styles are the following.

The combinational style is characterized by:

- a very narrow, clearly defined, primarily material goal; and
- a program that links the initial position with the final outcome.

In defining the combinational style in chess, Katsenelinboigen wrote: "The combinational style features a clearly formulated limited objective, namely the capture of material (the main constituent element of a chess position). The objective is implemented via a well-defined, and in some cases, unique sequence of moves aimed at reaching the set goal. As a rule, this sequence leaves no options for the opponent. Finding a combinational objective allows the player to focus all his energies on efficient execution, that is, the player's analysis may be limited to the pieces directly partaking in the combination. This approach is the crux of the combination and the combinational style of play.

The positional style is distinguished by:

- a positional goal; and

- a formation of semi-complete linkages between the initial step and final outcome.

"Unlike the combinational player, the positional player is occupied, first and foremost, with the elaboration of the position that will allow him to develop in the unknown future. In playing the positional style, the player must evaluate relational and material parameters as independent variables. … The positional style gives the player the opportunity to develop a position until it becomes pregnant with a combination. However, the combination is not the final goal of the positional player – it helps him to achieve the desirable, keeping in mind a predisposition for the future development. The pyrrhic victory is the best example of one's inability to think positionally."

The positional style serves to:

- create a predisposition to the future development of the position;

- induce the environment in a certain way;

- absorb an unexpected outcome in one's favor; and

- avoid the negative aspects of unexpected outcomes.

## Influence of Myers-briggs Type

According to Isabel Briggs Myers, a person's decision-making process depends to a significant degree on their cognitive style. Myers developed a set of four bi-polar dimensions, called the Myers-Briggs Type Indicator (MBTI). The terminal points on these dimensions are: *thinking* and *feeling*; *extroversion* and *introversion*; *judgment* and *perception*; and *sensing* and *intuition*. She claimed that a person's decision-making style correlates well with how they score on these four dimensions. For example, someone who scored near the thinking, extroversion, sensing, and judgment ends of the dimensions would tend to have a logical, analytical, objective, critical, and empirical decision-making style. However, some psychologists say that the MBTI lacks reliability and validity and is poorly constructed.

Other studies suggest that these national or cross-cultural differences in decision-making exist across entire societies. For example, Maris Martinsons has found that American, Japanese and Chinese business leaders each exhibit a distinctive national style of decision-making.

## Neuroscience

Decision-making is a region of intense study in the fields of systems neuroscience, and cognitive neuroscience. Several brain structures, including the anterior cingulate cortex (ACC), orbitofrontal cortex and the overlapping ventromedial prefrontal cortex are believed to be involved in decision-making processes. A neuroimaging study found distinctive patterns of neural activation in these regions depending on whether decisions were made on the basis of perceived personal volition or following directions from someone else. Patients with damage to the ventromedial prefrontal cortex have difficulty making advantageous decisions.

A common laboratory paradigm for studying neural decision-making is the two-alternative forced choice task (2AFC), in which a subject has to choose between two alternatives within a certain time. A study of a two-alternative forced choice task involving rhesus monkeys found that neurons in the parietal cortex not only represent the formation of a decision but also signal the degree of certainty (or "confidence") associated with the decision. Another recent study found that lesions to the ACC in the macaque resulted in impaired decision-making in the long run of reinforcement guided tasks suggesting that the ACC may be involved in evaluating past reinforcement information and guiding future action. A 2012 study found that rats and humans can optimally accumulate incoming sensory evidence, to make statistically optimal decisions.

Emotion appears able to aid the decision-making process. Decision-making often occurs in the face of uncertainty about whether one's choices will lead to benefit or harm. The somatic-marker hypothesis is a neurobiological theory of how decisions are made in the face of uncertain outcome. This theory holds that such decisions are aided by emotions, in the form of bodily states, that are elicited during the deliberation of future consequences and that mark different options for behavior as being advantageous or disadvantageous. This process involves an interplay between neural systems that elicit emotional/bodily states and neural systems that map these emotional/bodily states. A recent lesion mapping study of 152 patients with focal brain lesions conducted by Aron K. Barbey and colleagues provided evidence to help discover the neural mechanisms of emotional intelligence.

Although it is unclear whether the studies generalize to all processing, subconscious processes have been implicated in the initiation of conscious volitional movements.

## In Adolescents vs. Adults

During their adolescent years, teens are known for their high-risk behaviors and rash decisions. Recent research has shown that there are differences in cognitive processes between adolescents and adults during decision-making. Researchers have concluded that differences in decision-making are not due to a lack of logic or reasoning, but more due to the immaturity of psychosocial capacities that influence decision-making. Examples of their undeveloped capacities which influence decision-making would be impulse control, emotion regulation, delayed gratification and resistance to peer pressure. In the past, researchers have thought that adolescent behavior was simply due to incompetency regarding decision-making. Currently, researchers have concluded that adults and adolescents are both competent decision-makers, not just adults. However, adolescents' competent decision-making skills decrease when psychosocial capacities become present.

Recent research has shown that risk-taking behaviors in adolescents may be the product of interactions between the socioemotional brain network and its cognitive-control network. The socioemotional part of the brain processes social and emotional stimuli and has been shown to be important in reward processing. The cognitive-control network assists in planning and self-regulation. Both of these sections of the brain change over the course of puberty. However, the socioemotional network changes quickly and abruptly, while the cognitive-control network changes more gradually. Because of this difference in change, the cognitive-control network, which usually regulates the socioemotional network, struggles to control the socioemotional network when psychosocial capacities are present.

When adolescents are exposed to social and emotional stimuli, their socioemotional network is activated as well as areas of the brain involved in reward processing. Because teens often gain a sense of reward from risk-taking behaviors, their repetition becomes ever more probable due to the reward experienced. In this, the process mirrors addiction. Teens can become addicted to risky behavior because they are in a high state of arousal and are rewarded for it not only by their own internal functions but also by their peers around them.

Adults are generally better able to control their risk-taking because their cognitive-control system has matured enough to the point where it can control the socioemotional network, even in the context of high arousal or when psychosocial capacities are present. Also, adults are less likely to find themselves in situations that push them to do risky things. For example, teens are more likely to be around peers who peer pressure them into doing things, while adults are not as exposed to this sort of social setting.

A recent study suggests that adolescents have difficulties adequately adjusting beliefs in response to bad news (such as reading that smoking poses a greater risk to health than they thought), but do not differ from adults in their ability to alter beliefs in response to good news. This creates biased beliefs, which may lead to greater risk taking.

## Consumer Decision Making

A consumer purchase is actually *a response to a problem*. Consumer Decision Making pertains to making *decisions regarding product and service offerings*. It may be defined as a process of gathering and processing information, evaluating it and selecting the best possible option so as to solve a problem or make a buying choice.

Consumer Decision Making pertains to the following decisions:

a) What to buy: Products and Services (and the Brands?)

b) How much to buy: Quantity

c) Where to buy: Place

d) When to buy: Time

e) How to buy: Payment terms.

*All purchase decisions are not similar. The effort put into each decision making is different.*

## Market Segmentation

Market segmentation is the process of dividing a broad consumer or business market, normally consisting of existing and potential customers, into sub-groups of consumers (known as *segments*) based on some type of shared characteristics. In dividing or segmenting markets, researchers typically look for shared characteristics such as common needs, common interests, similar lifestyles or even similar demographic profiles. The overall aim of segmentation is to identify *high yield segments* – that is, those segments that are likely to be the most profitable or that have growth potential – so that these can be selected for special attention (i.e. become target markets).

Many different ways to segment a market have been identified. Business-to-business (B2B) sellers might segment the market into different types of businesses or countries. While business to consumer (B2C) sellers might segment the market into demographic segments, lifestyle segments, behavioral segments or any other meaningful segment.

**S-T-P Approach**

| Segmentation | Targeting | Positioning |
|---|---|---|
| • Select base for segmentation | • Evaluate segments' attractiveness | • Develop position for each segment |
| • Profile segments' characteristics | • Select one or more segments as targets | • Develop marketing program for each segment |

The STP approach highlights the three areas of decision-making

Market segmentation assumes that different market segments require different marketing programs – that is, different offers, prices, promotion, distribution or some combination of marketing variables. Market segmentation is not only designed to identify the most profitable segments, but also to develop profiles of key segments in order to better understand their needs and purchase motivations. Insights from segmentation analysis are subsequently used to support marketing strategy development and planning. Many marketers use the S-T-P approach; Segmentation→ Targeting → Positioning to provide the framework for marketing planning objectives. That is, a market is segmented, one or more segments are selected for targeting, and products or services are positioned in a way that resonates with the selected target market or markets.

## Market Segmentation: Brief Historical Overview

The Model T Ford *Henry Ford famously said "Any customer can have a car painted any color that he wants so long as it is black"*

The business historian, Richard S. Tedlow, identifies four stages in the evolution of market segmentation:

- Fragmentation (pre 1880s): The economy was characterised by small regional suppliers who sold goods on a local or regional basis

- Unification or Mass Marketing (1880s–1920s): As transportation systems improved, the economy became unified. Standardised, branded goods were distributed at a national level. Manufacturers tended to insist on strict standardisation in order to achieve scale economies with a view to penetrating markets in the early stages of a product's life cycle. e.g. the Model T Ford

- Segmentation (1920s–1980s): As market size increased, manufacturers were able to produce different models pitched at different quality points to meet the needs of various demographic and psychographic market segments. This is the era of market differentiation based on demographic, socio-economic and lifestyle factors.

- Hyper-segmentation (1980s+): a shift towards the definition of ever more narrow market segments. Technological advancements, especially in the area of digital communications, allow marketers to communicate with individual consumers or very small groups. This is sometimes known as *one-to-one* marketing.

Wendell R. Smith is generally credited with being the first to introduce the concept of market segmentation into the marketing literature with the publication of his article, "Product Differentiation and Market Segmentation as Alternative Marketing Strategies." Smith's article makes it clear that he had observed "many examples of segmentation" emerging and to a certain extent saw this as a natural force in the market that would "not be denied." As Schwarzkopf points out, Smith was codifying implicit knowledge that had been used in advertising and brand management since the 1920s.

Contemporary market segmentation emerged in the twentieth century as marketers responded to two pressing issues. Demographic and purchasing data were available for groups but rarely for individuals and secondly, advertising and distribution channels were available for groups, but rarely for single consumers. Between 1902 and 1910, George B Waldron, working at Mahin's Advertising Agency in the United States used tax registers, city directories and census data to show advertisers the proportion of educated vs illiterate consumers and the earning capacity of different occupations etc. in a very early example of simple market segmentation. In 1924 Paul Cherington developed the 'ABCD' household typology; the first socio-demographic segmentation tool. With access to group level data only, brand marketers approached the task from a tactical viewpoint. Thus, segmentation was essentially a brand-driven process.

Until relatively recently, most segmentation approaches have retained this tactical perspective in that they address immediate short-term decisions; such as describing the current "market served" and are concerned with informing marketing mix decisions. However, with the advent of digital communications and mass data storage, it has been possible for marketers to conceive of segmenting at the level of the individual consumer. Extensive data is now available to support segmentation at very narrow groups or even for the single customer, allowing marketers to devise a customised offer with an individual price which can be disseminated via real-time communications.

## Criticisms of Market Segmentation

The limitations of conventional segmentation have been well documented in the literature. Perennial criticisms include:

- that it is no better than mass marketing at building brands

- that in competitive markets, segments rarely exhibit major differences in the way they use brands

- that it fails to identify sufficiently narrow clusters

- geographic/demographic segmentation is overly descriptive and lacks sufficient insights into the motivations necessary to drive communications strategy

- difficulties with market dynamics, notably the instability of segments over time and structural change which leads to segment creep and membership migration as individuals move from one segment to another

Market segmentation has many critics. But in spite of its limitations, market segmentation remains one of the enduring concepts in marketing and continues to be widely used in practice. One American study, for example, suggested that almost 60 percent of senior executives had used market segmentation in the past two years.

## Market Segmentation Strategy

A key consideration for marketers is whether to segment or not to segment. Depending on company philosophy, resources, product type or market characteristics, a businesses may develop an undifferentiated approach or *differentiated approach*. In an undifferentiated approach (also known as *mass marketing*), the marketer ignores segmentation and develops a product that meets the needs of the largest number of buyers. In a differentiated approach the firm targets one or more market segments, and develops separate offers for each segment.

Even simple products like salt are highly differentiated in practice.

In consumer marketing, it is difficult to find examples of undifferentiated approaches. Even goods such as salt and sugar, which were once treated as commodities, are now highly differentiated. Consumers can purchase a variety of salt products; cooking salt, table salt, sea-salt, rock salt, kosher salt, mineral salt, herbal or vegetable salts, iodized salt, salt substitutes and if that is not enough choice, at the brand level, gourmet cooks are likely to make a major distinction between Maldon salt and other competing brands.The following table outlines the main strategic approaches.

Table: Main Strategic Approaches to Segmentation

| Number of seg-ments | Segmentation strategy | Comments |
|---|---|---|
| Zero | Undifferentiated strategy | Mass marketing: no segmentation |
| One | Focus strategy | Niche marketing: focus efforts on a small, tightly defined target market |
| Two or more | Differentiated strategy | Multiple niches: focus efforts on 2 or more, tightly defined targets |
| Thousands | Hypersegmentation | One-to-one marketing: customise the offer for each individual customer |

A number of factors are likely to affect a company's segmentation strategy:

- Company resources: When resources are restricted, a concentrated strategy may be more effective.

- Product variability: For highly uniform products (such as sugar or steel) an undifferentiated marketing may be more appropriate. For products that can be differentiated, (such as cars) then either a differentiated or concentrated approach is indicated.

- Product life cycle: For new products, one version may be used at the launch stage, but this may be expanded to a more segmented approach over time. As more competitors enter the market, it may be necessary to differentiate.

- Market characteristics: When all buyers have similar tastes, or are unwilling to pay a premium for different quality, then undifferentiated marketing is indicated.

- Competitive activity: When competitors apply differentiated or concentrated market segmentation, using undifferentiated marketing may prove to be fatal. A company should consider whether it can use a different market segmentation approach.

## Market Segmentation Process: S-T-P

The process of segmenting the market is deceptively simple. Seven basic steps describe the entire process including segmentation, targeting and positioning. In practice, however, the task can be very laborious since it involves poring over loads of data, and requires a great deal of skill in analysis, interpretation and some judgement. Although a great deal of analysis needs to be undertaken, and many decisions need to be made, marketers tend to use the so-called S-T-P process, that is Segmentation→ Targeting → Positioning, as a broad framework for simplifying the process  and outlined here:

Segmentation

1. Identify market (also known as the universe) to be segmented.

2. Identify, select and apply base or bases to be used in the segmentation

3. Develop segment profiles

Targeting

4. Evaluate each segment's attractiveness

5. Select segment or segments to be targeted

Positioning

6. Identify optimal positioning for each segment

7. Develop the marketing program for each segment

## Identifying the Market to be Segmented

The market for a given product or service known as the *market potential* or the *total addressable market (TAM)*. Given that this is the market to be segmented, the market analyst should begin by identifying the size of the potential market. For existing products and services, estimating the size and value of the market potential is relatively straight forward. However, estimating the market potential can be very challenging when a product or service is totally new to the market and no historical data on which to base forecasts exists.

A basic approach is to first assess the size of the broad population, then estimate the percentage likely to use the product or service and finally to estimate the revenue potential. For example, when the ride-sharing company, Uber, first entered the market, the owners assumed that Uber would be a substitute for taxis and hire cars. Accordingly, they calculated Uber's TAM based on the size of the existing taxi and car service business, which they estimated at $100 billion. They then made a conservative estimate that the company could reach 10 percent share of market and used this to estimate the expected revenue.

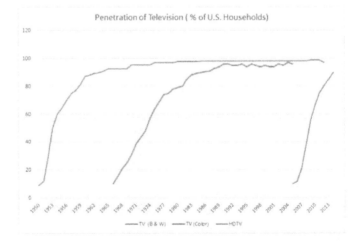

Penetration of Television ( % of U.S. Households)

To estimate market size, a marketer might evaluate adoption and growth rates of comparable technologies.

Another approach is to use historical analogy. For example, the manufacturer of HDTV might assume that the number of consumers willing to adopt high definition TV will be similar to the adoption rate for Color TV. To support this type of analysis, data for household penetration of TV, Radio, PCs and other communications technologies is readily available from government statistics departments. Finding useful analogies can be challenging because every market is unique. However, analogous product adoption and growth rates can provide the analyst with benchmark estimates, and can be used to cross validate other methods that might be used to forecast sales or market size.

A more robust technique for estimating the market potential is known as the Bass diffusion model, the equation for which follows:

$$N(t) - N(t-1) = [p + qN(t-1)/m] \times [m - N(t-1)]$$

Where:

- $N(t)$= the number of adopters in the current time period, ($t$)

- $N(t-1)$= the number of adopters in the previous time period, ($t$-$1$)

- $p$ = the coefficient of innovation

- $q$ = the coefficient of imitation (the social contagion influence)

- $m$ = an estimate of the number of eventual adopters

The major challenge with the Bass model is estimating the parameters for $p$ and $q$. However, the Bass model has been so widely used in empirical studies that the values of $p$ and $q$ for more than 50 consumer and industrial categories have been determined and are widely published in tables. The average value for p is 0.037 and for q is 0.327.

## Bases for Segmenting Consumer Markets

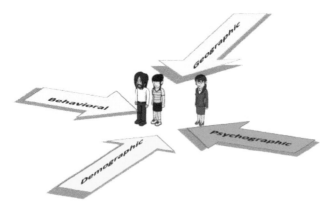

Major bases used for segmenting a market

A major step in the segmentation process is the selection of a suitable base. In this step, marketers are looking for a means of achieving internal homogeneity (similarity within the segments), and external heterogeneity (differences between segments). In other words, they are searching for a process that minimises differences between members of a segment and maximises differences between each segment. In addition, the segmentation approach must yield segments that are meaningful for the specific marketing problem or situation. For example, a person's hair colour may be a relevant base for a shampoo manufacturer, but it would not be relevant for a seller of financial services. Selecting the right base requires a good deal of thought and a basic understanding of the market to be segmented.

In reality, marketers can segment the market using any base or variable provided that it is identifiable, measurable, actionable and stable. For example, some fashion houses have segmented the market using women's dress size as a variable. However, the most common bases for segmenting consumer markets include: geographics, demographics, psychographics and behavior. Marketers normally select a single base for the segmentation analysis, although, some bases can be combined into a single segmentation with care. For example, geographics and demographics are often combined, but other bases are rarely combined. Given that psychographics includes demographic variables such as age, gender and income as well as attitudinal and behavioral variables, it makes little logical sense to combine psychographics with demographics or other bases. Any attempt to use combined bases needs careful consideration and a logical foundation.

| Segmentation base | Brief explanation of base (and example) | Typical segments |
| --- | --- | --- |
| **Demographic** | Quantifiable population characteristics. (e.g. age, gender, income, education, socio-economic status, family size or situation). | e.g. Young, Upwardly-mobile, Prosperous, Professionals (YUPPY); Double Income No Kids (DINKS); Greying, Leisured And Moneyed (GLAMS); Empty- nester, Full-nester |
| **Geographic** | Physical location or region (e.g. country, state, region, city, suburb, postcode). | e.g. New Yorkers; Remote, outback Australians; Urbanites, Inner-city dwellers |
| **Geo-demographic** or geoclusters | Combination of geographic & demographic variables. | e.g. Rural farmers, Urban professionals, 'sea-changers', 'tree-changers' |
| **Psychographics** | Lifestyle, social or personality characteristics. (typically includes basic demographic descriptors) | e.g. Socially Aware; Traditionalists, Conservatives, Active 'club-going' young professionals |
| **Behavioural** | Purchasing, consumption or usage behaviour. (e.g. Needs-based, benefit-sought, usage occasion, purchase frequency, customer loyalty, buyer readiness). | e.g. Tech-savvy (aka tech-heads); Heavy users, Enthusiasts; Early adopters, Opinion Leaders, Luxury-seekers, Price-conscious, Quality-conscious, Time-poor |

## Geographic Segmentation

Geographic segmentation divides markets according to geographic criteria. In practice, markets can be segmented as broadly as continents and as narrowly as neighborhoods or postal codes. Typical geographic variables include:

- Country e.g. USA, UK, China, Japan, South Korea, Malaysia, Singapore, Australia, New Zealand

- Region e.g. North, North-west, Mid-west, South, Central

- Population density: e.g. central business district (CBD), urban, suburban, rural, regional

- City or town size: e.g. under 1,000; 1,000–5,000; 5,000–10,000 ... 1,000,000–3,000,000 and over 3,000,000

- Climatic zone: e.g. Mediterranean, Temperate, Sub-Tropical, Tropical, Polar,

The geo-cluster approach (also called *geodemographic segmentation*) combines demographic data with geographic data to create richer, more detailed profiles. Geo-cluster approaches are a consumer classification system designed market segmentation and consumer profiling purposes. They classify residential regions or postcodes on the basis of census and lifestyle characteristics obtained from a wide range of sources. This allows the segmentation of a population into smaller groups defined by individual characteristics such as demographic, socio-economic or other shared socio-demographic characteristics.

Geographic segmentation may be considered the first step in international marketing, where marketers must decide whether to adapt their existing products and marketing programs for the unique needs of distinct geographic markets. Tourism Marketing Boards often segment international visitors based on their country of origin. By way of example, Tourism Australia undertakes marketing in 16 core geographic markets; of which China, UK, US, NZ and Japan have been identified as priority segments because they have the greatest potential for growth and are extremely profitable segments with higher than average expenditure per visit. Tourism Australia carries out extensive research on each of these segments and develops rich profiles of high priority segments to better understand their needs and how they make travel decisions. Insights from this analysis are used in travel product development, allocation of promotional budgets, advertising strategy and in broader urban planning decisions. For example, in light of the numbers of Japanese visitors, the city of Melbourne has erected Japanese signage in tourist precincts.

Caci's Acorn is one of the many proprietary products that allows for
geo-demographic segmentation of a consumer market

A number of proprietary geo-demographic packages are available for commercial use. Examples include Acorn in the United Kingdom, Nielsen's Claritas Prizm in the USA, Experian's Mosaic

Segmentation (active in North America, South America, UK, Europe, South Africa and parts of Asia-Pacific ) or Helix Personas (Australia, New Zealand and Indonesia). It should be noted that all these commercial packages combine geographics with behavioural, demographic and attitudinal data and yield a very large number of segments. For instance, the NZ Helix Personas segments New Zealand's relatively small population into 51 discrete personality profiles across seven geographic communities ( too numerous to itemise on this page). These commercial databases typically allow prospective clients access to limited scale demonstrations, and readers interested in learning more about how geo-demographic segmentation can benefit marketers and planners, are advised to experiment with the online demonstration software via these companies' websites.

Geographic segmentation is widely used in direct marketing campaigns to identify areas which are potential candidates for personal selling, letter-box distribution or direct mail. Geo-cluster segmentation is widely used by Governments and public sector departments such as urban planning, health authorities, police, criminal justice departments, telecommunications and public utility organisations such as water boards.

## Demographic Segmentation

Segmentation according to demography is based on consumer- demographic variables such as age, income, family size, socio-economic status, etc. Demographic segmentation assumes that consumers with similar demographic profiles will exhibit similar purchasing patterns, motivations, interests and lifestyles and that these characteristics will translate into similar product/brand preferences. In practice, demographic segmentation can potentially employ any variable that is used by the nation's census collectors. Typical demographic variables and their descriptors are as follows:

- Age: e.g. Under 5, 5–8 years, 9–12 years, 13–17 years, 18–24, 25–29, 30–39, 40–49, 50–59, 60+

- Gender: Male, Female

- Occupation: Professional, self-employed, semi-professional, clerical/ admin, sales, trades, mining, primary producer, student, home duties, unemployed, retired

- Social class (or socio-economic status): A, B, C, D, E, or I, II, III, IV or V (normally divided into quintiles)

- Marital Status: Single, married, divorced, widowed

- Family Life-stage: Young single; Young married with no children; Young family with children under 5 years; Older married with children; Older married with no children living at home, Older living alone

- Family size/ number of dependants: 0, 1–2, 3–4, 5+

- Income: Under $10,000; 10,000–20,000; 20,001–30,000; 30,001–40,000, 40,001–50,000 etc.

- Educational attainment: Primary school; Some secondary, Completed secondary, Some university, Degree; Post graduate or higher degree

- Home ownership: Renting, Own home with mortgage, Home owned outright

- Ethnicity: Asian, African, Aboriginal, Polynesian, Melanesian, Latin-American, African-American, American Indian etc.

- Religion: Catholic, Protestant, Muslim, Jewish, Buddhist, Hindu, Other

Scouts develop products for people of all ages

The Scouting movement offers an excellent example of demographic segmentation in practice. Scouts develops different products based on relevant age groups. In Australia, the segments are *Joeys* for boys and girls aged 6–7 years; *Cubs* for children ages 8– 10 years; *Scouts* for those aged 11–14 years; *Venturers* ages 15–17 years and *Rovers* aged 18–25 years. The Scouting movement provides members of each cohort with different uniforms and develops different activity programs for each segment. Scouts even cater to the needs of the over 25s offering them roles as scout leaders or volunteers. Scouts' segmentation is an example of a simple demographic segmentation analysis which utilises just a single variable, namely age.

In practice, most demographic segmentation utilises a combination of demographic variables. For instance, a segmentation approach developed for New Zealand by Nielsen Research combines multiple demographic variables including age, life-stage and socio-economic status. The proprietary segmentation product, known as geoTribes, segments the NZ market into 15 tribes, namely: *Rockafellas* – Affluent mature families; *Achievers* – Ambitious younger and middle aged families; *Fortunats* – Financially secure retirees and pre-retirees; *Crusaders* – Career-oriented singles and couples; *Preppies* – Mature children of affluent parents; *Independents* – Young singles and couples; *Suburban Splendour* – Middle class mature families; *Twixters* – Mature children living at home; *Debstars* – Financially extended younger families; *Boomers* – White collar post family pre-retirees; *True Blues* – Blue collar mature families and pre-retiree singles or couples; *Struggleville* – Struggling young and middle aged families; *Grey Power* – Better off retirees; *Survivors* – Retirees living on minimal incomes and *Slender Meanz* – People living in underprivileged circumstances.

The use of multiple segmentation variables normally requires analysis of databases using sophisticated statistical techniques such as cluster analysis or principal components analysis. It should be noted that these types of analysis require very large sample sizes. However, data-collection is expensive for individual firms. For this reason, many companies purchase data from commercial market research firms, many of whom develop proprietary software to interrogate the data. Proprietary packages, such as that mentioned in the preceding geoTribes by Nielsen example, offer clients access to an extensive database along with a program that allows users to interrogate the data via a 'user-friendly' interface. In other words, users do not need a detailed understanding of the 'back-end' statistical procedures used to analyse the data and derive the market segments. However, users still need to be skilled in the interpretation of findings for use in marketing decision-making.

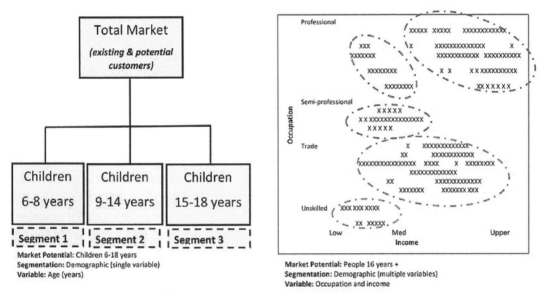

Visualisation of two approaches to demographic segmentation using one and two variables

The labels applied to some of the more popular demographic segments began to enter the popular lexicon in the 1980s. The following popular terms can be found in any good dictionary of popular language:

DINKS: Double (or dual) Income, No Kids. describes one member of a couple with above average household income and no dependent children, tend to exhibit discretionary expenditure on luxury goods and entertainment and dining out

GLAMs: Greying, Leisured and Moneyed. Retired older persons, asset rich and high income. Tend to exhibit higher spending on recreation, travel and entertainment

GUPPY: (aka GUPPIE) Gay, Upwardly Mobile, Prosperous, Professional; blend of gay and YUPPY (can also refer to the London-based equivalent of YUPPY)

MUPPY: (aka MUPPIE) Mid-aged, Upwardly Mobile, Prosperous, Professional

PREPPY: (American) Well educated, well-off, upper class young persons; a graduate of an expensive school. Often distinguished by a style of dress.

SITKOM: Single Income, Two Kids, Oppressive Mortgage. Tend to have very little discretionary income, struggle to make ends meet

TWEEN: (contraction of in-between). Young person who is approaching puberty, aged approximately 9–12 years; too old to be considered a child, but too young to be a teenager.

WASP: (American) White, Anglo-Saxon Protestant. Tend to be high-status and influential white Americans of English Protestant ancestry.

YUPPY: (aka YUPPIE) Young, Urban/ Upwardly-mobile, Prosperous, Professional. Tend to be well-educated, career-minded, ambitious, affluent and free spenders.

## Psychographic Segmentation

Psychographic segmentation, which is sometimes called lifestyle segmentation, is measured by studying the activities, interests, and opinions (AIOs) of customers. It considers how people spend their leisure, and which external influences they are most responsive to and influenced by. Psychographics is a very widely used basis for segmentation, because it enables marketers to identify tightly defined market segments and better understand consumer motivations for product or brand choice.

One of the most well-known psychographic segmentation analyses is the so-called Values And Lifestyles Segments (VALS), a proprietary psychometric method that measures attitudes, behaviours and demographics that align with brand preferences and new product adoption. The approach was originally developed by SBI International in the 1970s, and the typologies or segments have undergone several revisions over the years. As it currently stands, the VALs segments that describe the adult American population are: *Achievers* (26%), *Strivers* (24%), *Experiencers* (21%), Innovators, Thinkers, Believers, Makers and Survivors. The VALs segments are country specific and the developer offers VALs segmentation typologies for use in China, Japan, the Dominican Republic, Nigeria, UK and Venezuela.

Outside the USA, other countries have developed their own brand of proprietary psychographics segmentation. In Australia and New Zealand, Roy Morgan Research has developed the Values Segments which describes ten segments based on mindset, demographics and behaviors. The Values Segments are: *Visible Achievers* (20%); *Traditional Family Life* (19%); *Socially Aware* (14%); *Look-At-Me* (11%); *Conventional Family Life* (10%); *Something Better* (9%); *Young Optimists* (7%); *Fairer Deal* (5%); *Real Conservatives* (3%) and *Basic Needs* (2%). Market research company, Nielsen offers PALS (Personal Aspirational Lifestyle Segments), a values-based segmentation that ranks future lifestyle priorities, such as the importance of career, family, wanting to have fun, or the desire for a balanced lifestyle. PALS divides the Australian market into six groups, namely *Success Driven* (25%); *Balance Seekers* (23%); *Health Conscious* (22%), *Harmony Seekers* (11%), *Individualists* (11%) and *Fun Seekers* (8%).

In Britain, the psychographic segmentation typology, known as Values Modes has been in use for more than 30 years. In addition, a British lifestyles typology developed by McCann-Erickson is also in use. These segments include: *Avant-Guardians* (interested in change); *Pontificators* (traditionalists); *Chameleons* (follow the crowd) and *Sleepwalkers* (contented underachievers).

While many of these proprietary psychographic segmentation analyses are well-known, the majority of studies based on psychographics are custom designed. That is, the segments are developed for individual products at a specific time. One common thread among psychographic segmentation studies is that they use quirky names to describe the segments.

## Behavioral Segmentation

Behavioral segmentation divides consumers into groups according to their observed behaviors. Many marketers believe that behavioral variables are superior to demographics and geographics for building market segments. Typical behavioral variables and their descriptors include:

- Purchase/Usage Occasion: e.g. regular occasion, special occasion, festive occasion, gift-giving

- Benefit-Sought: e.g. economy, quality, service level, convenience, access

- User Status: e.g. First-time user, Regular user, Non-user

- Usage Rate/ Purchase Frequency: e.g. Light user, heavy user, moderate user

- Loyalty Status: e.g. Loyal, switcher, non-loyal, lapsed

- Buyer Readiness: e.g. Unaware, aware, intention to buy

- Attitude to Product or Service: e.g. Enthusiast, Indifferent, Hostile; Price Conscious, Quality Conscious

- Adopter Status: e.g. Early adopter, late adopter, laggard

Note that these descriptors are merely commonly used examples. Marketers customize the variable and descriptors for both local conditions and for specific applications. For example, in the health industry, planners often segment broad markets according to 'health consciousness' and identify low, moderate and highly health conscious segments. This is an applied example of behavioral segmentation, using attitude to product or service as a key descriptor or variable which has been customised for the specific application.

## Purchase/ Usage Occasion

Purchase or usage occasion segmentation focuses on analyzing occasions when consumers might purchase or consume a product. This approach customer-level and occasion-level segmentation models and provides an understanding of the individual customers' needs, behavior and value under different occasions of usage and time. Unlike traditional segmentation models, this approach assigns more than one segment to each unique customer, depending on the current circumstances they are under.

Cadbury segment consumers of their chocolate range according to usage occasion

For example, Cadbury has segmented the market into five segments based on usage and behavior:

- Immediate Eat (34%): Driven by the need to snack, indulge or an energy boost. Products that meet these needs include brands such as Kit-Kat, Mars Bars

- Home Stock (25%): Driven by the need to have something in the pantry to share with family in front of TV or for home snacking. Products that meet these needs are blocks or multi-packs

- Kids (17%): Driven by need for after school snacks, parties, treats. Products that meet these needs include Smarties and Milky Bars.

- Gift-giving (15%): Products purchased as gifts, needs include a token of appreciation, a romantic gesture or a special occasion. Products that meet these needs include boxed chocolates such as Cabury's Roses or Quality Street

- Seasonal (3.4%): Driven by need to give a present or create a festive atmosphere. The products are mainly purchased on feast days such as Christmas, Easter, Advent. Products that meet these needs include Easter eggs and Christmas tree decorations.

## Benefit-sought

Benefit sought (sometimes called *needs-based segmentation*) divides markets into distinct needs, perceived value, benefits sought or advantage that accrues from the purchase of a product or service. Marketers using benefit-sought segmentation might develop products with different quality levels, performance, customer service, special features or any other meaningful benefit and pitch different products at each of the segments identified. Benefit segmentation is one of the more commonly used approaches to segmentation and is widely used in many consumer markets including motor vehicles, fashion and clothing, furniture, consumer electronics and holiday-makers.

Loker and Purdue, for example, used benefit segmentation to segment the pleasure holiday travel market. The segments identified in this study were the naturalists, pure excitement seekers, escapists,

## Attitudinal Segments

Attitudinal segmentation provides insight into the mindset of customers, especially the attitudes and beliefs that drive consumer decision-making and behavior. An example of attitudinal segmentation comes from the UK's Department of Environment which segmented the British population into six segments, based on attitudes that drive behavior relating to environmental protection:

- Greens: Driven by the belief that protecting environment is critical; try to conserve whenever they can

- Conscious with a conscience: Aspire to be *green*; primarily concerned with wastage; lack awareness of other behaviors associated with broader environmental issues such as climate change

- Currently constrained: Aspire to be *green* but feel they cannot afford to purchase organic products; pragmatic realists

- Basic contributors: Sceptical about the need for behavior change; aspire to conform to social norms; lack awareness of social and environmental issues

- Long-term resistance: Have serious life priorities that take precedence before behavioral change is a consideration; their every day behaviors often have low impact on the environment but for other reasons than conservation

- Disinterested: View *greenies* as an eccentric minority; exhibit no interest in changing their behavior; may be aware of climate change but have not internalised it to the extent that it enters their decision-making process.

## Other Types of Consumer Segmentation

In addition to geographics, demographics, pyschographics and behavioral bases, marketers occasionally turn to other means of segmenting the market, or to develop segment profiles.

## Generational Segments

A generation is defined as "a cohort of people born within a similar span of time (15 years at the upper end) who share a comparable age and life stage and who were shaped by a particular span of time (events, trends and developments)." Generational segmentation refers to the process of dividing and analysing a population into cohorts based on their birth date. Generational segmentation assumes that people's values and attitudes are shaped by the key events that occurred during their lives and that these attitudes translate into product and brand preferences.

Demographers, studying population change, disagree about precise dates for each generation. Dating is normally achieved by identifying population peaks or troughs, which can occur at different times in each country. For example, in Australia the post-war population boom peaked in 1960, while the peak occurred somewhat later in the USA and Europe, with most estimates converging on 1964. Accordingly, Australian Boomers are normally defined as those born between 1945–1960; while American and European Boomers are normally defined as those born between 1945–64. Thus, the generational segments and their dates discussed here must be taken as approximations only.

The primary generational segments identified by marketers are:

- Builders: born 1920 to 1945

- Baby boomers: born about 1945–1965

- Generation X: born about 1966–1976

- Generation Y: also known as Millenials; born about 1977–1994

- Generation Z: also known as Centennials; born 1995–2015

| Unique characteristics of selected generations | | |
|---|---|---|
| **Millenials** | **Generation X** | **Baby Boomers** |
| Technology use (24%) | Technology use (12%) | Work ethic (17%) |
| Music/ popular culture (11%) | Work ethic (11%) | Respectful (14%) |
| Liberal/ tolerant (7%) | Conservative/ traditional (7%) | Values/ morals (8%) |
| Smarter (6%) | Smarter (6%) | Smarter (5%) |
| Clothes (5%) | Respectful (5%) | n.a. |

## Cultural Segmentation

Cultural segmentation is used to classify markets according to cultural origin. Culture is a major dimension of consumer behavior and can be used to enhance customer insight and as a component of predictive models. Cultural segmentation enables appropriate communications to be crafted to particular cultural communities. Cultural segmentation can be applied to existing customer data to measure market penetration in key cultural segments by product, brand, channel as well as traditional measures of recency, frequency and monetary value. These benchmarks form an important evidence-base to guide strategic direction and tactical campaign activity, allowing engagement trends to be monitored over time.

Cultural segmentation can also be mapped according to state, region, suburb and neighborhood. This provides a geographical market view of population proportions and may be of benefit in selecting appropriately located premises, determining territory boundaries and local marketing activities.

Census data is a valuable source of cultural data but cannot meaningfully be applied to individuals. Name analysis (onomastics) is the most reliable and efficient means of describing the cultural origin of individuals. The accuracy of using name analysis as a surrogate for cultural background in Australia is 80–85%, after allowing for female name changes due to marriage, social or political reasons or colonial influence. The extent of name data coverage means a user will code a minimum of 99 percent of individuals with their most likely ancestral origin.

## Selecting Target Markets

In targeting, a group of consumers is selected to become the focus of the marketing program

Another major decision in developing the segmentation strategy is the selection of market segments that will become the focus of special attention (known as *target markets*). The marketer faces a number of important decisions:

- What criteria should be used to evaluate markets?

- How many markets to enter (one, two or more)?

- Which market segments are the most valuable?

When a marketer enters more than one market, the segments are often labelled the *primary target market, secondary target market*. The primary market is the target market selected as the main focus of marketing activities. The secondary target market is likely to be a segment that is not as large as the primary market, but has growth potential. Alternatively, the secondary target group might consist of a small number of purchasers that account for a relatively high proportion of sales volume perhaps due to purchase value or purchase frequency.

In terms of evaluating markets, three core considerations are essential:

- Segment size and growth

- Segment structural attractiveness

- Company objectives and resources.

## Criteria for Evaluating Segment Attractiveness

There are no formulas for evaluating the attractiveness of market segments and a good deal of judgement must be exercised. Nevertheless, a number of considerations can be used to assist in evaluating market segments for overall attractiveness. The following lists a series of questions that can be asked.

## Segment Size and Growth

- How large is the market?

- Is the market segment substantial enough to be profitable? (Segment size can be measured in number of customers, but superior measures are likely to include sales value or volume)

- Is the market segment growing or contracting?

- What are the indications that growth will be sustained in the long term? Is any observed growth sustainable?

- Is the segment stable over time? (Segment must have sufficient time to reach desired performance level)

## Segment Structural Attractiveness

- To what extent are competitors targeting this market segment?

- Do buyers have bargaining power in the market?

- Are substitute products available?

- Can we carve out a viable position to differentiate from any competitors?

- How responsive are members of the market segment to the marketing program?

- Is this market segment reachable and accessible? (i.e., with respect to distribution and promotion)

## Company Objectives and Resources

- Is this market segment aligned with our company's operating philosophy?

- Do we have the resources necessary to enter this market segment?

- Do we have prior experience with this market segment or similar market segments?

- Do we have the skills and/or know-how to enter this market segment successfully?

## Developing the Marketing Program and Positioning Strategy

The marketing program is designed with the needs of the target market in mind

When the segments have been determined and separate offers developed for each of the core segments, the marketer's next task is to design a marketing program (also known as the marketing mix) that will resonate with the target market or markets. Developing the marketing program requires a deep knowledge of key market segment's purchasing habits, their preferred retail outlet, their media habits and their price sensitivity. The marketing program for each brand or product should be based on the understanding of the target market (or target markets) revealed in the market profile.

For example, Black and Decker, manufacturer of three brands of power tools and household appliances, has a marketing mix where each brand is pitched at different quality points and targets different segments of the market. This table is designed to illustrate how the marketing program must be fine-tuned for each market segment.

| Table: Black & Decker market segmentation | | | | | |
|---|---|---|---|---|---|
| **Segment** | **Product/ Brand** | **Product strategy** | **Price strategy** | **Promotion strategy** | **Place strategy** |
| Home-owners/ D-I-Y | Black & Decker | Quality adequate for occasional use | Lower priced | TV advertising during holidays | Mass distribution (lower-tier stores) |
| Weekend warriors | Firestorm | Quality adequate for regular use | Higher priced | Ads in D-I-Y magazines, shows | Selective distribution (top tier hardware stores) |
| Professional users | De Walt | Quality adequate for daily use | Highest price | Personal selling (sales reps call on job sites) | Selective distribution (top tier hardware stores) |

Positioning is the final step in the S-T-P planning approach; Segmentation→ Targeting → Positioning; a core framework for developing marketing plans and setting objectives. Positioning refers to decisions about how to present the offer in a way that resonates with the target market. During the research and analysis that forms the central part of segmentation and targeting, the marketer will have gained insights into what motivates consumers to purchase a product or brand. These insights will form part of the positioning strategy.

According to advertising guru, David Ogilvy, "Positioning is the act of designing the company's offering and image to occupy a distinctive place in the minds of the target market. The goal is to locate the brand in the minds of consumers to maximize the potential benefit to the firm. A good brand positioning helps guide marketing strategy by clarifying the brand's essence, what goals it helps the consumer achieve, and how it does so in a unique way."

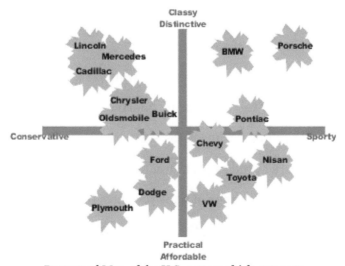

Perceptual Map of the U.S. motor vehicle category

The technique known as perceptual mapping is often used to understand consumers' mental representations of brands within a given category. Traditionally two variables (often, but not necessarily, price and quality) are used to construct the map. A sample of people in the target market are asked to explain where they would place various brands in terms of the selected variables. Results are averaged across all respondents, and results are plotted on a graph, as illustrated in the figure. The final map indicates how the *average* member of the population views the brand that make up a category and how each of the brands relates to other brands within the same category. While perceptual maps with two dimensions are common, multi-dimensional maps are also used.

**The burgers are better at HUNGRY JACK'S**

Hungry Jack's uses the same slogan in all its advertising, packaging and livery

There are a number of different approaches to positioning:

Dove positions itself as a beauty soap with one quarter moisturizer

1.  Against a competitor: e.g. Hungry Jack's tastes better

2.  Within a category: e.g. Within the prestige car category, Volvo is the safe alternative

3.  According to product benefit: e.g. Toothpaste with whitening

4.  According to product attribute: e.g. Dove is one quarter moisturizer

5.  For usage occasion: Cadbury Roses Chocolates – for gift giving or saying 'Thank-you'

6.  Along price lines e.g. a luxury brand or premium brand

7.  For a user: Johnson and Johnson range of baby products (No Tears Shampoo)

8.  Cultural symbols e.g. Australia's Easter Bilby (as a culturally appropriate alternative to the Easter Bunny).

## Bases for Segmenting Business Markets

Businesses can be segmented using type of industry, company size, geographic location, sales turnover or any other meaningful variable

Segmenting business markets is more straightforward than segmenting consumer markets. Businesses may be segmented according to industry, business size, business location, turnover, number of employees, company technology, purchasing approach or any other relevant variables.

Firmographics (also known as *emporographics* or *feature based segmentation*) is the business community's answer to demographic segmentation. It is commonly used in business-to-business markets (it's estimated that 81% of B2B marketers use this technique). Under this approach the target market is segmented based on features such as company size (either in terms of revenue or number of employees), industry sector or location (country and/or region).

In sales territory management, using more than one criterion to characterize the organization's accounts,such as segmenting sales accounts by government, business, customer, etc. and account size or duration, in effort to increase time efficiency and sales volume.

## Use in Customer Retention

The basic approach to retention-based segmentation is that a company tags each of its active customers on four axes:

Risk of customer cancellation of company service

> One of the most common indicators of high-risk customers is a drop off in usage of the company's service. For example, in the credit card industry this could be signaled through a customer's decline in spending on his or her card.

Risk of customer switching to a competitor

> Many times customers move purchase preferences to a competitor brand. This may happen for many reasons those of which can be more difficult to measure. It is many times beneficial for the former company to gain meaningful insights, through data analysis, as to why this change of preference has occurred. Such insights can lead to effective strategies for winning back the customer or on how not to lose the target customer in the first place.

Customer retention worthiness

> This determination boils down to whether the post-retention profit generated from the

customer is predicted to be greater than the cost incurred to retain the customer, and includes evaluation of customer lifecycles.

Tactics to use for retention of customer

This analysis of customer lifecycles is usually included in the growth plan of a business to determine which tactics to implement to retain or let go of customers. Tactics commonly used range from providing special customer discounts to sending customers communications that reinforce the value proposition of the given service.

## Segmentation: Algorithms and Approaches

The choice of an appropriate statistical method for the segmentation, depends on a number of factors including, the broad approach (a-priori or post-hoc), the availability of data, time constraints, the marketer's skill level and resources.

## A-priori Segmentation

According to the Market Research Association (MRA),a priori research occurs when "a theoretical framework is developed before the research is conducted". In other words, the marketer has an idea about whether to segment the market geographically, demographically, psychographically or behaviorally before undertaking any research. For example, a marketer might want to learn more about the motivations and demographics of light and moderate users in an effort to understand what tactics could be used to increase usage rates. In this case, the target variable is known – the marketer has already segmented using a behavioral variable – user status. The next step would be to collect and analyse attitudinal data for light and moderate users. Typical analysis includes simple cross-tabulations, frequency distributions and occasionally logistic regression or CHAID analysis.

The main disadvantage of a-priori segmentation is that it does not explore other opportunities to identify market segments that could be more meaningful.

## Post-hoc Segmentation

In contrast, post-hoc segmentation makes no assumptions about the optimal theoretical framework. Instead, the analyst's role is to determine the segments that are the most meaningful for a given marketing problem or situation. In this approach, the empirical data drives the segmentation selection. Analysts typically employ some type of clustering analysis or structural equation modeling to identify segments within the data. The figure alongside illustrates how segments might be formed using clustering, however note that this diagram only uses two variables, while in practice clustering employs a large number of variables. Post-hoc segmentation relies on access to rich data sets, usually with a very large number of cases.

## Statistical Techniques Used in Segmentation

Marketers often engage commercial research firms or consultancies to carry out segmentation analysis, especially if they lack the statistical skills to undertake the analysis. Some segmentation, especially post-hoc analysis, relies on sophisticated statistical analysis.

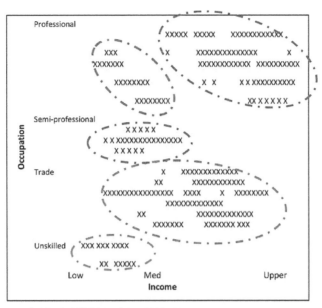

**Market Potential (Universe):** People 16 years +
**Segmentation:** Demographic (multiple variables)
**Variables:** Occupation and income

Visualisation of market segments formed using clustering methods

Common statistical approaches and techniques used in segmentation analysis include:

- Clustering algorithms – overlapping, non-overlapping and fuzzy methods; e.g. K-means or other Cluster analysis

- Conjoint analysis

- Ensemble approaches – such as random forests

- Chi-square automatic interaction detection – a type of decision-tree

- Factor analysis or principal components analysis

- Logistic regression

- Multidimensional scaling and canonical analysis

- Mixture models - e.g., EM estimation algorithm, finite-mixture models for simple Latent Class Analysis

- Model based segmentation using simultaneous and structural equation modeling e.g. LIS-REL

- Other algorithms such as artificial neural networks.

## Data Sources Used for Segmentation

Marketers use a variety of data sources for segmentation studies and market profiling. Typical sources of information include:

## Internal Sources

- Customer transaction records e.g. sale value per transaction, purchase frequency
- Patron membership records e.g. active members, lapsed members, length of membership
- Customer relationship management (CRM) databases
- In-house surveys
- Customer self-completed questionnaires or feedback forms

## External Sources

- Proprietary surveys or tracking studies (e.g. Nielsen's Scandata, single source surveys)
- Proprietary databases/ software (e.g. Cameo (UK), Experian, Helix Personas, Claritas' PRIZM, SBI's VALs and RMR's Values segments)
- Omnibus surveys
- Government agencies and departments (e.g. Department of Trade or Industry)
- Government statistician (e.g. Census data, retail surveys, household consumption surveys, employment and income data)
- Professional/ Industry associations/ Employer associations
- Census data
- Observed purchase behavior (e.g. data collected from online agencies such as Google )
- Data-mining techniques
- Commissioned research

## Levels of Decision Making

While decision making is defined as the selection of an alternative to solve a problem, the time and effort required to complete the process varies across buying situations. We may define three kinds problem solving spread over a continuum; these are referred to as the levels of consumer decision making; (i) Extensive problem solving (EPS) (ii) Limited problem solving (LPS) (iii) Routinized problem solving (RPS) or routinized response behavior. These are explained as follows:

*a) Extensive problem solving (EPS):* In EPS, the consumer is unfamiliar with the product/service category; he is not informed of the product or service offering, and thus, the situation requires extensive information search and evaluation.

The consumer is *not aware*:

- about the various decision criteria used to evaluate the product or service offering.

- of the various brands that are available and from which to evaluate.

The result is that the *purchase process involves significant effort on part of the consumer.* He has to gather knowledge about (i) the decision criteria;

(ii) the brands available; and (iii) make a choice amongst the brands.

The types of products and / situations where we generally have EPS:

1. These goods are ones of high involvement; they are expensive; they are infrequently bought; there is considerable amount of risk involved.

2. These are generally first time purchases

Examples: Jewellery, electronic goods, Real estate and property etc.

*b) Limited problem solving (LPS):* The consumer is familiar of the product or service offering; but he is unaware of the various brands. The case is one where the buyer is familiar wit the product category but unfamiliar with the brands.

The consumer:

- *is aware* of some brands and also of the various criteria used to evaluate the product or service offering.

- *is unaware* of the new brands that have been introduced.

- *has not evaluated* the brands amongst the awareness set and has not established preferences amongst the group of brands.

The result is that the *purchase process is more of a recurring purchase and it involves only a moderate effort on part of the consumer.* He has to gather knowledge to add/modify the existing knowledge that he has in his memory. Thereafter he has to make a decision.

The types of products and / situations where we generally have LPS:

1. These goods are ones of low involvement; they are generally moderately priced; they are frequently bought; there is lesser amount of risk involved.

2. These are generally recurring purchases.

Exceptions:

*They may also be cases where an expensive product is being repurchased.*

Examples: A laptop replacing a desktop, a second TV for the home.

*Routinized problem solving (RPS) or routinized response behavior:* The consumer is well informed and experienced with the product or service offering. The consumer *is aware* of both the decision criteria as well as the various brands available. Here, the goods are ones of low involvement; they are inexpensive; they are frequently bought; there is no risk involved. These are routine purchases and are a direct repetition, where the consumer may be brand loyal. The result is that the *purchase process involves no effort on part of the consumer*. It is simple and the process is completed quickly; purchases are routine and made out of habit.

The types of products and / situations where we generally have RPS:

1. These goods are ones of low involvement; they are inexpensive; they are frequently bought; there is no risk involved.

2. These are routine purchases and the consumer is brand loyal.

Examples: Staples, Cold drinks, Stationery etc.

Table: Comparisons between EPS, LPS and RPS

|                                          | EPS       | LPS          | RPS                     |
|------------------------------------------|-----------|--------------|-------------------------|
| **1. Complexity of decision making**     | High      | Medium       | Low                     |
| **2. Time taken to make     decisions**  | High      | Low to High  | Low                     |
| **3. Information gathering**             | Yes       | Yes          | No                      |
| **4. Information sources**               | Many      | Few          | Few or none             |
| **5. Awareness and knowledge of:**       | No        | Yes          | Yes                     |
| **a) Decision criteria**                 | No        | Somewhat     | Yes                     |
| **b) Alternative brands available**      |           |              |                         |
| **6. Evaluative criteria**               | Complex   | Moderate     | Simple (if at all)      |
| **7 Brands considered**                  | Many      | Few          | One (Repeat purchase)   |
| **8. Cognitive dissonance**              | High      | Rare         | None                    |

Table: Comparisons between EPS, LPS and RPS

|                                  | EPS                                       | LPS                                       | RPS                                             |
|----------------------------------|-------------------------------------------|-------------------------------------------|-------------------------------------------------|
| **1. Consumer Involvement**      | High                                      | Medium                                    | Low                                             |
| **2. Problem recognition**       | Actual state type to Desired State        | Actual state type to Desired State        | Actual state type                               |
| **3. Information search**        | Extensive<br><br>Internal and external sources | Limited<br><br>Mostly internal sources | Minimum Restricted to internal sources only.    |
| **4. Evaluation of alternatives**| Complex                                   | Moderate                                  | Simple (if at all)                              |

| 5. Purchase | Gradual after a cognitive process | Not so gradual | Immediate |
|---|---|---|---|
| 6. Post purchase processes | Cognitive dissonance is high. Brand loyalty if satisfied | Cognitive dissonance would be rare | Brand loyalty.Repeat purchase. |
| 7. Types of goods | Specialty goods | Mixed | Convenience |

## Buyer Decision Process

The buying decision process is the decision-making process used by consumers regarding market transactions before, during, and after the purchase of a good or service. It can be seen as a particular form of a cost–benefit analysis in the presence of multiple alternatives.

Common examples include shopping and deciding what to eat. Decision-making is a psychological construct. This means that although a decision can not be "seen", we can infer from observable behaviour that a decision has been made. Therefore, we conclude that a psychological "decision-making" event has occurred. It is a construction that imputes commitment to action. That is, based on observable actions, we assume that people have made a commitment to effect the action.

Nobel laureate Herbert A. Simon sees economic decision-making as a vain attempt to be rational. He claims (in 1947 and 1957) that if a complete analysis is to be done, a decision will be immensely complex. He also says that peoples' information processing ability is limited. The assumption of a perfectly rational economic actor is unrealistic. Consumers are influenced by emotional and non-rational considerations making attempts to be rational only partially successful.

### Stages

The stages of the buyer decision process were first introduced by Engel, Blackwell and Kollat in (1968).

- Problem/Need Recognition - Recognize what the problem or need is and identify the product or type of product which is required. Page text.

- Information Search - The consumer researches the product which would satisfy the recognized need.

- Evaluation of Alternatives - The consumer evaluates the searched alternatives. Generally, the information search reveals multiple products for the consumer to evaluate and understand which product would be appropriate.

- Purchase Decision - After the consumer has evaluated all the options and would be having the intention to buy any product, there could be now only two things which might just change the decision of the consumer of buying the product that is what the other peers of the consumer think of the product and any unforeseen circumstances. Unforeseen circumstances for example in this case could be financial losses which led to not buying of the product.

- Post Purchase Behaviour - After the purchase the consumer may experience post purchase dissonance feeling that buying another product would have been better. addressing post purchase dissonance spreads good word for the product and increases the chance of frequent repurchase.

These five stages are a framework to evaluate customers' buying decision process. However, it is not necessary that customers get through every stage, nor is it necessary that they proceed in any particular order. For example, if a customer feels the urge to buy chocolate, he or she might go straight to the purchase decision stage, skipping information search and evaluation.

## Problem/Need-recognition

Problem/Need-recognition is the first and most important step in the buying decision. Without the recognition of the need, a purchase cannot take place. The need can be triggered by internal stimuli (e.g. hunger, thirst) or external stimuli (e.g. advertising). Maslow held that needs are arranged in a hierarchy. According to Maslow's hierarchy, only when a person has fulfilled the needs at a certain stage, can he or she move to the next stage. The problem must be the products or services available. It's how the problem must be recognized.

## Information Search

The information search stage is the next step that the customers may take after they have recognized the problem or need in order to find out what they feel is the best solution. This is the buyer's effort at searching the internal and external business environments to identify and observe sources of information related to the focal buying decision.The field of information has come a long way in the last forty years, and has enabled easier and faster information discovery. Consumers can rely on print, visual, and/or voice media for getting information.

## Evaluation of Alternatives

At this stage, consumers evaluate different products/brands on the basis of varying product attributes, and whether these can deliver the benefits that the customers are seeking. This stage is heavily influenced by one's attitude, as "attitude puts one in a frame of mind: liking or disliking an object, moving towards or away from it". Another factor that influences the evaluation process is the degree of involvement. For example, if the customer involvement is high, then he/she will evaluate a number of brands; whereas if it is low, only one brand will be evaluated.

| Customer involvement | High | Medium | Low |
|---|---|---|---|
| Characteristics | High | Medium | Low |
| Number of brands examined | Many | Several | One |
| Number of sellers considered | Many | Several | Few |
| Number of product attributes evaluated | Many | Moderate | One |
| Number of external information sources used | Many | Few | None |
| Time spent searching | Considerable | Little | Minimal |

## Purchase Decision

This is the fourth stage, where the purchase takes place. According to Kotler, Keller, Koshy and Jha (2009), the final purchase decision can be disrupted by two factors: negative feedback from other customers and the level of motivation to comply or accept the feedback. For example, after going through the above three stages, a customer chooses to buy a Nikon D80 DSLR camera. However, because his good friend, who is also a photographer, gives him negative feedback, he will then be bound to change his preference. Secondly, the decision may be disrupted due to unanticipated situations such as a sudden job loss or the closing of a retail store.

## Post-purchase Behavior

These stages are critical to retain customers. In short, customers compare products with their expectations and are either satisfied or dissatisfied. This can then greatly affect the decision process for a similar purchase from the same company in the future, mainly at the information search stage and evaluation of alternatives stage. If customers are satisfied, this results in brand loyalty, and the information search and evaluation of alternative stages are often fast-tracked or skipped completely. As a result, brand loyalty is the ultimate aim of many companies.

On the basis of either being satisfied or dissatisfied, a customer will spread either positive or negative feedback about the product. At this stage, companies should carefully create positive post-purchase communication to engage the customers.

Also, cognitive dissonance (consumer confusion in marketing terms) is common at this stage; customers often go through the feelings of post-purchase psychological tension or anxiety. Questions include: "Have I made the right decision?", "Is it a good choice?", etc.

## Models of Buyer Decision-making

Making a few last minute decisions before purchasing a gold necklace from a Navy Exchange vendor

There are generally three ways of analysing consumer buying decisions:

- Economic models - largely quantitative and are based on the assumptions of rationality and near perfect knowledge. The consumer is seen to maximize their utility. Game theory can also be used in some circumstances.

- Psychological models - psychological and cognitive processes such as motivation and need recognition. They are qualitative rather than quantitative and build on sociological factors like cultural influences and family influences.

- Consumer behaviour models - practical models used by marketers. They typically blend both economic and psychological models.

In an early study of the buyer decision process literature, Frank Nicosia (Nicosia, F. 1966; pp 9–21) identified three types of buyer decision-making models. They are the univariate model (He called it the "simple scheme".) in which only one behavioural determinant was allowed in a stimulus-response type of relationship; the multi-variate model (He called it a "reduced form scheme".) in which numerous independent variables were assumed to determine buyer behaviour; and finally the "system of equations" model (He called it a "structural scheme" or "process scheme".) in which numerous functional relations (either univariate or multi-variate) interact in a complex system of equations. He concluded that only this third type of model is capable of expressing the complexity of buyer decision processes. Nicosia builds a comprehensive model involving five modules. The encoding module includes determinants like "attributes of the brand", "environmental factors", "consumer's attributes", "attributes of the organization", and "attributes of the message". Other modules in the system include, consumer decoding, search and evaluation, decision, and consumption.

Some neuromarketing research papers examined how approach motivation as indexed by electro-encephalographic (EEG) asymmetry over the prefrontal cortex predicts purchase decision when brand and price are varied. In a within-subjects design, the participants were presented purchase decision trials with 14 different grocery products (seven private label and seven national brand products) whose prices were increased and decreased while their EEG activity was recorded. The results showed that relatively greater left frontal activation (i.e., higher approach motivation) during the predecision period predicted an affirmative purchase decision. The relationship of frontal EEG asymmetry with purchase decision was stronger for national brand products compared with private label products and when the price of a product was below a normal price (i.e., implicit reference price) compared with when it was above a normal price. Higher perceived need for a product and higher perceived product quality were associated with greater relative left frontal activation.

For any high-involvement product category, the decision-making time is normally long and buyers generally evaluate the information available very cautiously. They also utilize an active information search process. The risk associated with such decision is very high.

## Cognitive and Personal Biases in Decision-making

It is generally agreed that biases can creep into our decision-making processes, calling into question the correctness of a decision. Below is a list of some of the more common cognitive biases.

- Selective search for evidence - We tend to be willing to gather facts that support certain conclusions but disregard other facts that support different conclusions.

- Selective perception - We actively screen out information that we do not think is salient.

- Premature termination of search for evidence - We tend to accept the first alternative that looks like it might work.

- Conservatism and inertia - Unwillingness to change thought patterns that we have used in the past in the face of new circumstances.

- Experiential limitations - Unwillingness or inability to look beyond the scope of our past experiences; rejection of the unfamiliar.

- Wishful thinking or optimism - We tend to want to see things in a positive light and this can distort our perception and thinking.

- Recency - We tend to place more attention on more recent information and either ignore or forget more distant information.

- Repetition bias - A willingness to believe what we have been told most often and by the greatest number of different of sources.

- Anchoring - Decisions are unduly influenced by initial information that shapes our view of subsequent information.

- Group think - Peer pressure to conform to the opinions held by the group.

- Source credibility bias - We reject something if we have a bias against the person, organization, or group to which the person belongs: We are inclined to accept a statement by someone we like.

- Incremental decision-making and escalating commitment - We look at a decision as a small step in a process and this tends to perpetuate a series of similar decisions. This can be contrasted with zero-based decision-making.

- Inconsistency - The unwillingness to apply the same decision criteria in similar situations..

- Attribution asymmetry - We tend to attribute our success to our abilities and talents, but we attribute our failures to bad luck and external factors. We attribute other's success to good luck, and their failures to their mistakes.

- Role fulfillment - We conform to the decision-making expectations that others have of someone in our position.

- Underestimating uncertainty and the illusion of control - We tend to underestimate future uncertainty because we tend to believe we have more control over events than we really do.

- Faulty generalizations - In order to simplify an extremely complex world, we tend to group things and people. These simplifying generalizations can bias decision-making processes.

- Ascription of causality - We tend to ascribe causation even when the evidence only suggests correlation. Just because birds fly to the equatorial regions when the trees lose their leaves, does not mean that the birds migrate *because* the trees lose their leaves.

## Neuroscience

Neuroscience is a useful tool and a source of theory development and testing in buyer decision-making research. Neuroimaging devices are used in Neuromarketing to investigate consumer behaviour.

## Buying Roles

Consumer decision making is a complex process. It is an interplay of reactions amongst a consumer and his cognition, affect and behavior on the one hand, as well as the environmental forces on the other hand.

The actual transaction/ exchange is preceded by considerable amount of thought processes and influences. This could be explained in terms of the five *"Buying Roles"* viz., Initiator, Influencer, Decider, Buyer and, User. The marketer needs to understand these roles so as to be able to frame suitable strategies to target them.

a) Initiator: The person who identifies a need and first suggests the idea of buying a particular product or service.

b) Influencer: The person(s) who influences the buyer in making his final choice of the product.

c) Decider: The person who decides on the final choice: what is to be bought, when, from where and how.

d) Buyer: The person who enters into the final transaction and exchange process or is involved in the physical activity of making a purchase.

e) User: The person(s) who actually consumes the product or service offering.

The various buying roles can be illustrated through examples:

Example1:

A kindergarten girl needs to buy color crayons to use in class.

i) Initiator: The girl

ii) Influencer: Her teacher or her classmates

iii) Decider: Either of the parents

iv) Buyer: Either of the parents or a sibling.

v) User: The girl herself.

Example 2:

The mother of the house is a housewife; she loves watching TV when her husband and children go for work. She has been complaining that the present TV set at home has been giving problem. She also says that the model is now an old one and that that the family should own a new model.

i) Initiator: The lady

ii) Influencer: Her neighbors and friends.

iii) Decider: Joint: Her husband, she herself and the children.

iv) Buyer: Husband or son or daughter or she herself.

v) User: The family.

Example 3:

A boy enters college and needs a laptop for doing assignments.

i) Initiator: The boy himself

ii) Influencer: His friends and classmates.

iii) Decider: The boy himself.

iv) Buyer: The boy himself.

v) User: The boy himself.

Note:

- *These five roles may be performed by one person or many persons.*

- *A person may perform more than one role.*

- *The role(s) that one assumes for a particular product purchase and in a particular purchase situation may differ to another product purchase and in another purchase situation.*

*It is even more noteworthy that:*

*As far as Buyer Behavior is concerned, the buyers role is the most important; it is he who enters into a transaction and final exchange.*

- *actual and final decision is always made at the time of transaction by the buyer.*

- *the decider may make a choice, but the exchange is entered into by the buyer*

## Consumer Decision Making Process

Marketers are interested in consumers' purchase behaviors, i.e., the decision making process. The consumers' decision making is a choice amongst various alternatives that address problematic issues like:

- what to buy;

- where to buy;

- when to buy;

- how to buy;

- how much to buy.

Consumer decision making involves a continuous flow of interactions among environmental factors, cognitive and affective processes and behavioral actions. *A consumers decision's are based on knowledge, affect and behavior related to the marketing mix.*

Stages in Consumer Decision Making Process: There are five stages in the consumer decision making process. These are:

1.  Need recognition/Problem recognition

2.  Pre-purchase information search

3.  Evaluation of alternatives

4.  Purchase decision

5. Post-purchase outcome and reactions

Each of these stages are explained as follows:

1. *Need recognition/Problem recognition*: This is a stage of perceiving a deficiency/need. A need could be triggered off by an *internal stimulus* or an *external stimulus*. For example, a person is thirsty and feels like having a cola drink. The stimulus is *internal*. On the other hand, while walking across the street, he sees a hoarding which shows a person having a frosted, chilled cola, and he too desires to have the same, the need is said to have been stimulated by an external stimuli.

A need or problem recognition could be *Simple* or *Complex*.

a) *Simple*: Simple problem recognition is similar to Structured Problems; They occur frequently as a routine and can be dealt with automatically without much effort.

b) *Complex*: A Complex problem recognition is similar to Unstructured Problems; They occur infrequently as unique and non-routine and need considerable effort to be solved.

A need or problem recognition could result when:

*a) the Actual State changes (AS type):*

- the product is failing, or the consumer is running short of it;

- there is a *problem* that exists.

- consumers who react in such situations are called AS Types.

Example: A product stops functioning and the customer needs a replacement; eg. A refrigerator; Samsung One door: Standard;

*b) the Desired State changing (DS type):*

- there is an *imbalance between the actual state and the desired state*

- another product seems better and superior to the one that is being currently used;

-consumers who react in such situations are called DS Types.

Example: The product is functioning properly; but the consumer wants to buy an upgraded model; eg., The refrigerator is functioning properly; However, the customer wants to buy another one which has more features and is more modern; Samsung Two doors: Deluxe: Frost free;

*Which of the particular styles operates' depends on the product or service in question as well as the situation.*

Whether a problem is an AS or DS Type also gets affected by an *individual and his personality*. Some consumers are AS Types, who realize that there is a problem after it has arisen, and so they go in for a purchase; They are *reactive* by nature; Eg. The consumer reacts after the refrigerator breaks down. Other consumers are the DS Types, who want to upgrade to better/newer products; They are *proactive*; Eg. Want to purchase a newer model of the refrigerator.

*A need is recognized in any of the following situations:*

- When a current product brand X is not performing well.

- When the current product brand X is nearing depletion.

- When another brand Y seems superior to the one currently owned, X.

Pre-purchase information search:

After a need is recognized, the consumer goes for an information search, so as to be able to make the right purchase decision. He gathers information about the:

(i) product category and the variations

(ii) various alternatives

(iii) various brands.

The amount of information a consumer will gather depends on the following:

i)  the consumer: demographics (age, gender, education), psychographics (learning, attitudes, involvement, personality type)

ii)  product category: differentiation and alternative brands available, risk, price, social visibility and acceptance of the product.

iii) situation: time available at hand, first time purchase, quantity of information required, availability of information.

- Types of Search Activity:

The information search activity may be of various types, viz, specific, ongoing and incidental.

(i)  Specific: This type of search activity is specific to the problem and/ immediate purchase; it is spurred as the need arises, and the consumer actively seeks information. Example: student enters college and needs to buy a laptop so that he can work on his assignments.

(ii) Ongoing: Here the search activity is a gradual process that could span over time. Example: the same student, has been thinking of purchasing the laptop since the past five years, and over these past 5-6 years, he has been gathering information specific to the laptop as a product category and also about the various brands available.

(iii) Incidental: This is a byproduct of another search activity or experiences. Consumers absorb information from their day to day routine activities and experiences. Example: the student goes to a mall; he has gone there to help his mother buy a microwave oven; there in the store, he attends a demonstration of a new laptop that is being launched.

## Information Sources

The information sources are of two types:

i) *Internal sources*: This includes the consumer and his self. He recalls information that is stored in his memory (comprising information gathered and stored, as well as his experiences, direct and indirect). *Internal sources seem sufficient when*:

- it is a routine purchase

- the product is of low involvement

ii) *External sources*: Here the consumer seeks information from the external environment. External sources of information include:

- Interpersonal communication (family, friends, work peers, opinion leaders etc.)

- Marketing communication or commercial information (advertisements, salespeople, company websites, magazines etc.)

- Other public sources (editorials, trade magazines and reports, consumer awareness programmes on TV, Internet etc.)

*External sources are resorted to in cases where:*

- past knowledge and experience is insufficient.

- the product is of high involvement and the risk of making a wrong decision is high.

*Evaluation of alternatives*: Once the consumer has gathered information and identified the alternatives, he compares the different alternatives available on certain criteria. This involves: i) Generation of choice alternatives; ii) Identification of evaluative criteria: Attributes and Benefits; iii) Application of Decision Rules.

i) *Generation of choice alternatives:*While generation of alternatives, a consumer moves from an evoked set towards the choice set.

- *Evoked set/Consideration set:* This is the set of alternatives that he actively considers while making a purchase decision; these exist either in his memory or feature prominently in the environment. The consumer perceives them to be acceptable.

- *Inept set:* These are those alternatives from the evoked set that the consumer excludes from further consideration, as he perceives them to be inferior and unacceptable.

- *Inert set*: These are those alternatives from the evoked set that the consumer excludes from further consideration, as he is indifferent towards them and perceives them as ones without much advantages or benefits.

- *Choice set:* This comprises the final set of one or two brands from which he finally decides.

ii) *Identification of Evaluative Criteria: Attributes and Benefits:* These are objective and subjective parameters of the brand that the consumer regards as important, and uses as standards to discriminate among the various alternatives. The consumer evaluates the different alternatives on one or few or many of these features and then makes a final choice.They are features that a consumer considers in choosing among alternatives; these could be functional/utilitarian in nature (benefits, attributes, features), or subjective/emotional/hedonic (emotions, prestige etc.). The major evaluative criteria are:

1. *Economic:* Price, Value *(Product Attributes, Brand image, Evaluation of Quality, Price, & Features).*

2. *Behavioral:* Need/motivation, Personality, self-concept and self-image, Lifestyle etc.

3. *Social influences:* Group influences, environmental issues etc.

iii) *Application of Decision Rules to make a final choice amongst alternatives:* The consumer uses certain decision rules. The decision rules help a consumer simplify the decision process; the various evaluative criteria are structured and integrated so as to simplify the evaluation process. There can be two kinds of Decision Rules, viz., Compensatory rules and Non-compensatory rules.

1. *Compensatory rules*: Under compensatory rules, the various evaluative criteria are listed as attributes. These attributes are scored and rated for the various alternative brands. A lower rating on an attribute may be offset by a higher rating on another; i.e. a higher rating on one attribute would compensate for a lower rating on another. Based on the final scores, the brands are ranked; the one with the highest score, being regarded as the best. The consumer would then select the brand that scores the highest among the various alternatives that have been evaluated. Compensatory rules could assume two forms: *simple* and *weighted.*

- *Simple summated*: The attributes are rated for each brand and the scores are totaled.

- *Weighted*: The attributes are first given weights relatively based on the level of importance; thereafter, the attributes are rated and finally scored after multiplication with the weights. The weighted scores are then totaled.

2. Non-Compensatory rules: Here, a negative evaluation of any one attribute eliminates the brand from consideration. A lower rating on an attribute cannot be offset by a higher rating on another; i.e. a higher rating on one attribute would not compensate for a lower rating on another. The consumer would then select the brand that scores the highest among the various alternatives that have been evaluated. Non-compensatory rules could assume three forms: conjunctive, disjunctive and lexicographic.

*Conjunctive rule*: A minimally acceptable cut off point is established for each attribute. The brands are evaluated, and, the brand that falls below the minimally acceptable limit on any of the attributes is eliminated/rejected.

*Disjunctive rule:* a minimally acceptable cut off point is established for each attribute. The brands are evaluated, and, the brand that falls above the cut off point on any of the attributes is selected.

*Lexicographic rule:* The various attributes are ranked in terms of perceived importance. First, the brands are evaluated on the attribute that is considered the most important. If a brand ranks considerably high than the others on this attribute, it is selected. In case the scores are competitive, the process may be repeated with the attribute considered next in importance.

*Sometimes the application of one rule may not be enough; And another may also be applied to reach a final decision.*

Table: Decision rules with Examples

| DECISION RULE | EXAMPLE |
|---|---|
| **Compensatory rule:** | The consumer chooses that laptop which he judges as the best when he balances the good and bad ratings with each other. |
| **Non Compensatory rules:**<br><br>**Conjuntive rule** | The consumer chooses that laptop that has no bad features. |
| **Disjunctive rule** | The consumer chooses that laptop that has at least one good feature. |
| **Lexicographic rule** | The consumer chooses that laptop that is the best on the most important of all features. |

d) Purchase decision: After the consumer has evaluated the various alternatives, he selects a particular brand. Consumer purchases may be trials/first purchases or repeat purchases.

*Trials/First purchase*: Trials could be elicited through market testing, or through promotional tactics such as free samples, coupons, etc.

*Repeat purchases*: If the consumer is satisfied, he would buy the brand again. Repeat purchases lead to brand loyalty.

The consumer may further have to make decisions on:

a) where to buy from? (Place: Real/brick and mortar or virtual/online);

b) whom to buy from? (Which store: Depends on reputation of seller, past experience, etc.)

c) when to buy? (Time: Emergency or Routine; During season, off season, sale, rebate etc.)

It is noteworthy that a *purchase intention* (desire to buy the most preferred brand) *may not always result in a purchase decision* in favor of the brand; it could get moderated by (i) Attitudes of others; and (2) Unexpected situational factors.

e) Post-purchase outcome and reactions: The post purchase outcome and reactions contains two stages; Stage I comprises *Post purchase Cognitive Dissonance, and S*tage II comprises *Product usage and reaction.*

*Stage I: Post purchase Cognitive Dissonance:*This is a feeling of tension and anxiety that a consumer experiences after the purchase of a product. The consumer begins to have a feeling of uncertainty with respect the performance of the product and begins to doubt his purchase decision "whether the decision was the right one?". He begins to ask himself the following questions:

a) Have I made the right choice?

b) Have I purchased the right brand?

c) Have I got value for money?

*The Fox and the Sour Grapes is a perfect example of Cognitive Dissonance.*

Cognitive dissonance generally occurs in cases where:

 (i)   the decision making and purchase relates to a high involvement product;

 (ii)  the purchase activity is irrevocable;

 (iii) the consumer cannot return the product;

 (iv)  the various alternatives have desirable features and are all comparable;

 (v)   the alternatives are also unique in some way or the other.

Consumers try to reduce this dissonance by:

(i)  gaining more product information;

(ii) discussing with other satisfied customers who have bought the same product/brand;

(iii)  going back to the dealer and asking for reassurances.

Other methods that consumers employ to reduce cognitive dissonance are by:

- rationalizing that the choice that they have made is the right one.

- refer to data (printed/audio visual) that supports and recommends the chosen product/brand.

- make others buy the same product/brand to reassure their choice.

Marketers also employ strategies to reduce this dissonance by providing guarantees and warranties, membership to company consumer forums and communication and follow up with the customers.

*Stage II: Product usage and reaction:*After the purchase, the consumer uses the product and re evaluates the chosen alternative in light of its performance viz. a viz. the expectations. This phase is significant as it (i) acts as an experience and gets stored in the memory; (ii) affects future purchase decisions; (iii) acts as a feedback. There could be three situations that can arise:

- *Performance meets expectations*:  This leads to a neutral feeling; Customer may think of more suitable alternatives next time.

- *Performance exceeds expectations*: The customer is satisfied and this leads to a positive feeling. He would tend to repeat purchase and it would lead to brand loyalty. He would also spread positive word of mouth.

- *Performance falls short of expectations*: Here, the customer is dissatisfied and this leads to a negative feeling. The customer would search for other alternatives, express grievances, spread negative word of mouth and may even resort to legal action.

It is important to note that the five staged decision making process is not so simple; it is complex.The decision making process is an interplay of reactions amongst a consumer and his cognition, affect and behavior on the one hand, as well as the environmental forces on the other hand. Further, the procedure may not always follow a linear order, and the decision making may not always proceed through all the five stages; it would vary across (i) the nature of the product (high and low involvement); (ii) the purchase situation (emergency or planned or routine); (iii) the personal characteristics of the consumer; and (iv) the type of problem solving (EPS, LPS and RPS).

## Implications for a Marketer

An understanding of the consumer decision making process, can help a marketer formulate appropriate marketing strategies. He can also model his marketing mix accordingly. The implications of understanding the dynamics of consumer behavior are discussed as follows:

1. *Need/Problem recognition*:

- A marketer can create an imbalance between the actual and desired state; it would trigger of the purchase decision process.

- He can launch newer models; marketing communication has a big role to play.

- He can focus on both functional (utilitarian) and emotional (hedonic) benefits that the product purchase could offer.

- He can activate a need through communication (advertisements, sales promotion, point-of-purchase stimuli, opinion leaders and reference groups).

2. *Pre-purchase information search*:

- Marketing communication has an important role at this stage.

- The marketer can identify the sources of information that the people generally access and use these to present information about his product and service offering.

- The marketer can also identify the functional or hedonic utility and use appeals accordingly.

- This would help create the right kind of cognitive and emotional touch point so as to elicit a favorable behavior (purchase).

- The marketer should be able to provide the right kind of information at the right place and at the right time.

- The marketer must make sure that his product and service offering forms a part of the evoked / consideration set.

a) For high involvement products: the marketer should ensure that information is available.

b) For low involvement products: he should use emotional appeals, POP stimuli etc.

3. *Evaluation of alternatives*:

-The marketer should be careful that his product is:

i)   positioned and promoted well;

ii) is readily available and displayed well;

iii) the product features prominently in the evoked/consideration set; and,

iv) he highlights those attributes and benefits that are regarded as most important to the consumers, and which they are most likely to evaluate while selecting an alternative.

- The marketer should inform and educate the customer about the various criteria to use for evaluation of alternatives.

- While doing so an intelligent marketer should focus on those attributes, where his product is better and/superior.

4. *Purchase decision*:

- The marketer should be careful to stock the product at the right place at the right time so that the consumer who has made a decision in favour of the brand can have access to the product; Else the consumer may have to change his decision at the last moment.

- As far as trial and first time purchases are concerned, the marketer should encourage trials through market testing, or through promotional tactics such as free samples, coupons, etc.

- For repeat purchases:

i) the marketer should make sure that he has satisfied the customer at the first time.

ii) that his offering is a part of the evoked/consideration set.

He should aim towards creation of brand loyalty.

5) *Post-purchase outcome and reactions*:

- The marketer can play an important role in reducing the dissonance that the consumer faces and reassuring him that the choice he made was the right one.

i) The marketer can communicate with the customer about the various attributes/features and benefits that the product has to offer in comparison with other alternatives.

ii) He can follow up with the customer and address queries and concerns if any (eg. follow up calls).

iii) Marketers' assurances with respect to warranties, guarantees and exchange can also pacify the cognitive dissonance state.

iv) Company websites with FAQs (frequently asked questions); satisfied customers' comments and blogs; and customer care information (eg. toll free numbers etc) can also prove to be helpful.

## References

- Pijanowski, John (February 2009). "The role of learning theory in building effective college ethics curricula". Journal of College and Character. 10 (3): 1–13. doi:10.2202/1940-1639.1088

- Kahneman, Daniel; Tversky, Amos, eds. (2000). Choices, values, and frames. New York; Cambridge, UK: Russell Sage Foundation; Cambridge University Press. p. 211. ISBN 0521621720. OCLC 42934579

- Kotler, Philip. "dl.ueb.edu.vn/bitstream/1247/2250/1/Marketing_Management_-_Millenium_Edition.pdf" (PDF). Pearson Customer Publishing. Archived from the original (PDF) on 1 February 2013. Retrieved 28 December 2012

- Reid, Robert D.; Bojanic, David C. (2009). Hospitality Marketing Management (5 ed.). John Wiley and Sons. p. 139. ISBN 978-0-470-08858-6. Retrieved 2013-06-08

- Bunn, Michele D. (January 1993). "Taxonomy of Buying Decision Approaches". Journal of Marketing. American Marketing Association. 57 (1): 38–56. doi:10.2307/1252056. JSTOR 1252056

- Kahneman, Daniel (2011). Thinking, fast and slow. New York: Farrar, Straus, and Giroux. ISBN 9780374275631. OCLC 706020998

- Niklas Ravaja, Outi Somervuori and Mikko Salminen (2012) Predicting purchase decision The role of hemispheric asymmetry over the frontal cortex, Journal of Neuroscience, Psychology, and Economics

- Ulea, Vera (2002). A concept of dramatic genre and the comedy of a new type: chess, literature, and film. Carbondale: Southern Illinois University Press. pp. 17–18. ISBN 0809324520. OCLC 51301095

- Hunt, Shelby; Arnett, Dennis (16 June 2004). "Market Segmentation Strategy, Competitive Advantage, and Public Policy". 12 (1). Australasian Marketing Journal: 1–25. Retrieved 18 March 2016

- Damasio, Antonio R. (1994). Descartes' error: emotion, reason, and the human brain. New York: Putnam. ISBN 0399138943. OCLC 30780083

- Paul Saffo quoted in: Foley, John (30 October 1995). "Managing information: infoglut". InformationWeek. Archived from the original on 2001-02-22. Retrieved 2015-07-26

- 'What is geographic segmentation' Kotler, Philip, and Kevin Lane Keller. Marketing Management. Prentice Hall, 2006. ISBN 978-0-13-145757-7

- Hoek, J., Gendall, P. and Esslemont, D., Market segmentation: A search for the Holy Grail?, Journal of Marketing Practice Applied Marketing Science, Vol. 2, no. 1, pp. 25–34, 1996

- Bardakci, A. and Whitelock, L., "Mass-customisation in Marketing: The Consumer Perspective," Journal of Consumer Marketing' vol. 20, no.5, 2003, pp. 463–479

- Forsyth, Donelson R. (2014) [1983]. Group dynamics (6th ed.). Belmont, CA: Wadsworth Cengage Learning. ISBN 9781133956532. OCLC 826872491

- Smit, E. G. and Niejens, P. C., 2000. "Segmentation Based on Affinity for Advertising," Journal of Advertising Research, vol. 40, no. 4, 2000, pp. 35–43

- Plous, Scott (1993). The psychology of judgment and decision making. Philadelphia: Temple University Press. ISBN 0877229139. OCLC 26548229

- Albaum, G. and Hawkins, D. I., "Geographic Mobility and Demographic and Socioeconomic Market Segmentation," Journal of the Academy of Marketing Science, vol. 11, no. 2. 1983, pp. 97–114

- Schacter, Daniel L.; Gilbert, Daniel Todd; Wegner, Daniel M. (2011) [2009]. Psychology (2nd ed.). New York: Worth Publishers. ISBN 9781429237192. OCLC 755079969

- Doos, L. Uttley, J. and Onyia, I., "Mosaic segmentation, COPD and CHF multimorbidity and hospital admission costs: a clinical linkage study," Journal of Public Health, Vo. 36, bno. 2, 2014, pp. 317–324

- Sharot, Tali (2011). The optimism bias: a tour of the irrationally positive brain (1st ed.). New York: Pantheon Books. ISBN 9780307378484. OCLC 667609433

- Ahmad, R., "Benefit Segmentation: A potentially useful technique of segmenting and targeting older consumers," International Journal of Market Research, Vol. 45, No. 3, 2003 <Online: (via WARC)

# Consumer Behavior: Methods and Models

The behavior of a consumer differs in the choosing of a marketplace. The decision is affected by few reasons, which the subject studies. It can be classified into economic view, cognitive view, passive view, and emotional view. This is referred to as the consumer model. It is based on the various approaches a costumer, who holds different perspectives, makes at the market place. Many models have been developed to deal with consumer behavior. They are economic model, psychological model, psychoanalytic model and sociological model. This chapter discusses the methods of consumer behavior in a critical manner providing key analysis to the subject matter.

## Marketing Research

Marketing research is "the process or set of processes that links the producers, customers, and end users to the marketer through information — information used to identify and define marketing opportunities and problems; generate, refine, and evaluate marketing actions; monitor marketing performance; and improve understanding of marketing as a process. Marketing research specifies the information required to address these issues, designs the method for collecting information, manages and implements the data collection process, analyzes the results, and communicates the findings and their implications."

It is the systematic gathering, recording, and analysis of qualitative and quantitative data about issues relating to marketing products and services. The goal of marketing research is to identify and assess how changing elements of the marketing mix impacts customer behavior. The term is commonly interchanged with market research; however, expert practitioners may wish to draw a distinction, in that *market* research is concerned specifically with markets, while *marketing* research is concerned specifically about marketing processes.

Marketing research is often partitioned into two sets of categorical pairs, either by target market:

- Consumer marketing research, and
- Business-to-business (B2B) marketing research

Or, alternatively, by methodological approach:

- Qualitative marketing research, and
- Quantitative marketing research

Consumer marketing research is a form of applied sociology that concentrates on understanding the preferences, attitudes, and behaviors of consumers in a market-based economy, and it aims to understand the effects and comparative success of marketing campaigns. The field of consumer marketing research as a statistical science was pioneered by Arthur Nielsen with the founding of the ACNielsen Company in 1923.

Thus, marketing research may also be described as the systematic and objective identification, collection, analysis, and dissemination of information for the purpose of assisting management in decision making related to the identification and solution of problems and opportunities in marketing.

## Role

The task of marketing research (MR) is to provide management with relevant, accurate, reliable, valid, and current market information. Competitive marketing environment and the ever-increasing costs attributed to poor decision making require that marketing research provide sound information. Sound decisions are not based on gut feeling, intuition, or even pure judgment.

Managers make numerous strategic and tactical decisions in the process of identifying and satisfying customer needs. They make decisions about potential opportunities, target market selection, market segmentation, planning and implementing marketing programs, marketing performance, and control. These decisions are complicated by interactions between the controllable marketing variables of product, pricing, promotion, and distribution. Further complications are added by uncontrollable environmental factors such as general economic conditions, technology, public policies and laws, political environment, competition, and social and cultural changes. Another factor in this mix is the complexity of consumers. Marketing research helps the marketing manager link the marketing variables with the environment and the consumers. It helps remove some of the uncertainty by providing relevant information about the marketing variables, environment, and consumers. In the absence of relevant information, consumers' response to marketing programs cannot be predicted reliably or accurately. Ongoing marketing research programs provide information on controllable and non-controllable factors and consumers; this information enhances the effectiveness of decisions made by marketing managers.

Traditionally, marketing researchers were responsible for providing the relevant information and marketing decisions were made by the managers. However, the roles are changing and marketing researchers are becoming more involved in decision making, whereas marketing managers are becoming more involved with research. The role of marketing research in managerial decision making is explained further using the framework of the "DECIDE" model.

## History

Marketing research has evolved in the decades since Arthur Nielsen established it as a viable industry, one that would grow hand-in-hand with the B2B and B2C economies. Markets naturally evolve, and since the birth of ACNielsen, when research was mainly conducted by in-person focus groups and pen-and-paper surveys, the rise of the Internet and the proliferation of corporate websites have changed the means by which research is executed.

Web analytics were born out of the need to track the behaviour of site visitors and, as the popularity of e-commerce and web advertising grew, businesses demanded details on the information created by new practices in web data collection, such as click-through and exit rates. As the Internet boomed,websites became larger and more complex and the possibility of two-way communication between businesses and their consumers became a reality. Provided with the capacity to interact with online customers, Researchers were able to collect large amounts of data that were previously unavailable, further propelling the Marketing Research Industry.

In the new millennium, as the Internet continued to develop and websites became more interactive, data collection and analysis became more commonplace for those Marketing Research Firms whose clients had a web presence. With the explosive growth of the online marketplace came new competition for companies; no longer were businesses merely competing with the shop down the road — competition was now represented by a global force. Retail outlets were appearing online and the previous need for bricks-and-mortar stores was diminishing at a greater pace than online competition was growing.With so many online channels for consumers to make purchases, companies needed newer and more compelling methods, in combination with messages that resonated more effectively, to capture the attention of the average consumer.

Having access to web data did not automatically provide companies with the rationale behind the behaviour of users visiting their sites,which provoked the marketing research industry to develop new and better ways of tracking, collecting and interpreting information. This led to the development of various tools like online focus groups and pop-up or website intercept surveys. These types of services allowed companies to dig deeper into the motivations of consumers, augmenting their insights and utilizing this data to drive market share.

As information around the world became more accessible, increased competition led companies to demand more of Market Researchers. It was no longer sufficient to follow trends in web behaviour or track sales data; companies now needed access to consumer behaviour throughout the entire purchase process.This meant the Marketing Research Industry, again, needed to adapt to the rapidly changing needs of the marketplace, and to the demands of companies looking fora competitive edge.

Today, Marketing Research has adapted to innovations in technology and the corresponding ease with which information is available. B2B and B2C companies are working hard to stay competitive and they now demand both quantitative ("What") and qualitative ("Why?") marketing research in order to better understand their target audience and the motivations behind customer behaviours.

This demand is driving Marketing Researchers to develop new platforms for interactive, two-way communication between their firms and consumers. Mobile devices such as SmartPhones are the best example of an emerging platform that enables businesses to connect with their customers throughout the entire buying process. Innovative research firms, such as *OnResearch* with their *OnMobile* app, are now providing businesses with the means to reach consumers from the point of initial investigation through to the decision and, ultimately, the purchase.

As personal mobile devices become more capable and widespread, the Marketing Research Industry will look to further capitalize on this trend. Mobile devices present the perfect channel for Research Firms to retrieve immediate impressions from buyers and to provide their clients with a holistic view of the consumers within their target markets, and beyond. Now, more than ever,innovation is the key to success for Marketing Researchers. Marketing Research Clients are beginning to demand highly personalized and specifically-focused products from the MR firms; big data is great for identifying general market segments, but is less capable of identifying key factors of niche markets, which now defines the competitive edge companies are looking for in this mobile-digital age.

## Characteristics

First, marketing *research is systematic.* Thus systematic planning is required at all the stages of the marketing research process. The procedures followed at each stage are methodologically sound, well documented, and, as much as possible, planned in advance. Marketing research uses the scientific method in that data are collected and analyzed to test prior notions or hypotheses. Experts in marketing research have shown that studies featuring multiple and often competing hypotheses yield more meaningful results than those featuring only one dominant hypothesis.

Marketing research is *objective.* It attempts to provide accurate information that reflects a true state of affairs. It should be conducted impartially. While research is always influenced by the researcher's research philosophy, it should be free from the personal or political biases of the researcher or the management. Research which is motivated by personal or political gain involves a breach of professional standards. Such research is deliberately biased so as to result in predetermined findings. The objective nature of marketing research underscores the importance of ethical considerations. Also, researchers should always be objective with regard to the selection of information to be featured in reference texts because such literature should offer a comprehensive view on marketing. Research has shown, however, that many marketing textbooks do not feature important principles in marketing research.

## Related Business Research

Other forms of business research include:

- Market research is broader in scope and examines all aspects of a business environment. It asks questions about competitors, market structure, government regulations, economic trends, technological advances, and numerous other factors that make up the business environment. Sometimes the term refers more particularly to the financial analysis of companies, industries, or sectors. In this case, financial analysts usually carry out the research and provide the results to investment advisors and potential investors.

- Product research — This looks at what products can be produced with available technology, and what new product innovations near-future technology can develop.

- Advertising research - is a specialized form of marketing research conducted to improve the efficacy of advertising. Copy testing, also known as "pre-testing," is a form of customized research that predicts in-market performance of an ad before it airs, by analyzing audience levels of attention, brand linkage, motivation, entertainment, and communication, as well as breaking down the ad's flow of attention and flow of emotion. Pre-testing is also used on ads still in rough (ripomatic or animatic) form. (Young, p. 213)

## Classification

Organizations engage in marketing research for two reasons: (1) to identify and (2) solve marketing problems. This distinction serves as a basis for classifying marketing research into problem identification research and problem solving research.

Problem identification research is undertaken to help identify problems which are, perhaps, not apparent on the surface and yet exist or are likely to arise in the future like company image, market characteristics, sales analysis, short-range forecasting, long range forecasting, and business trends research. Research of this type provides information about the marketing environment and helps diagnose a problem. For example, The findings of problem solving research are used in making decisions which will solve specific marketing problems.

The Stanford Research Institute, on the other hand, conducts an annual survey of consumers that is used to classify persons into homogeneous groups for segmentation purposes. The National Purchase Diary panel (NPD) maintains the largest diary panel in the United States.

Standardized services are research studies conducted for different client firms but in a standard way. For example, procedures for measuring advertising effectiveness have been standardized so that the results can be compared across studies and evaluative norms can be established. The Starch Readership Survey is the most widely used service for evaluating print advertisements; another well-known service is the Gallup and Robinson Magazine Impact Studies. These services are also sold on a syndicated basis.

- Customized services offer a wide variety of marketing research services customized to suit a client's specific needs. Each marketing research project is treated uniquely.

- Limited-service suppliers specialize in one or a few phases of the marketing research project. Services offered by such suppliers are classified as field services, coding and data entry, data analysis, analytical services, and branded products. Field services collect data through the internet, traditional mail, in-person, or telephone interviewing, and firms that specialize in interviewing are called field service organizations. These organizations may range from small proprietary organizations which operate locally to large multinational organizations with WATS line interviewing facilities. Some organizations maintain extensive interviewing facilities across the country for interviewing shoppers in malls.

- Coding and data entry services include editing completed questionnaires, developing a coding scheme, and transcribing the data on to diskettes or magnetic tapes for input into the computer. NRC Data Systems provides such services.

- Analytical services include designing and pretesting questionnaires, determining the best means of collecting data, designing sampling plans, and other aspects of the research design. Some complex marketing research projects require knowledge of sophisticated procedures, including specialized experimental designs, and analytical techniques such as conjoint analysis and multidimensional scaling. This kind of expertise can be obtained from firms and consultants specializing in analytical services.

- Data analysis services are offered by firms, also known as tab houses, that specialize in computer analysis of quantitative data such as those obtained in large surveys. Initially most data analysis firms supplied only tabulations (frequency counts) and cross tabulations (frequency counts that describe two or more variables simultaneously). With the proliferation of software, many firms now have the capability to analyze their own data, but, data analysis firms are still in demand.

- Branded marketing research products and services are specialized data collection and analysis procedures developed to address specific types of marketing research problems. These procedures are patented, given brand names, and marketed like any other branded product.

## Types

Marketing research techniques come in many forms, including:

- Ad Tracking – periodic or continuous in-market research to monitor a brand's performance using measures such as brand awareness, brand preference, and product usage. (Young, 2005)

- Advertising Research – used to predict copy testing or track the efficacy of advertisements for any medium, measured by the ad's ability to get attention (measured with Attention-Tracking), communicate the message, build the brand's image, and motivate the consumer to purchase the product or service. (Young, 2005)

- Brand awareness research — the extent to which consumers can recall or recognise a brand name or product name

- Brand association research — what do consumers associate with the brand?

- Brand attribute research — what are the key traits that describe the brand promise?

- Brand name testing - what do consumers feel about the names of the products?

- Buyer decision making process— to determine what motivates people to buy and what decision-making process they use; over the last decade, Neuromarketing emerged from the convergence of neuroscience and marketing, aiming to understand consumer decision making process

- Commercial eye tracking research — examine advertisements, package designs, websites, etc. by analyzing visual behavior of the consumer

- Concept testing - to test the acceptance of a concept by target consumers

- Coolhunting (also known as trendspotting) - to make observations and predictions in changes of new or existing cultural trends in areas such as fashion, music, films, television, youth culture and lifestyle

- Copy testing – predicts in-market performance of an ad before it airs by analyzing audience levels of attention, brand linkage, motivation, entertainment, and communication, as well as breaking down the ad's flow of attention and flow of emotion. (Young, p 213)

- Customer satisfaction research - quantitative or qualitative studies that yields an understanding of a customer's satisfaction with a transaction

- Demand estimation — to determine the approximate level of demand for the product

- Distribution channel audits — to assess distributors' and retailers' attitudes toward a product, brand, or company

- Internet strategic intelligence — searching for customer opinions in the Internet: chats, forums, web pages, blogs... where people express freely about their experiences with products, becoming strong opinion formers.

- Marketing effectiveness and analytics — Building models and measuring results to determine the effectiveness of individual marketing activities.

- Mystery consumer or mystery shopping - An employee or representative of the market research firm anonymously contacts a salesperson and indicates he or she is shopping for a product. The shopper then records the entire experience. This method is often used for quality control or for researching competitors' products.

- Positioning research — how does the target market see the brand relative to competitors? - what does the brand stand for?

- Price elasticity testing — to determine how sensitive customers are to price changes

- Sales forecasting — to determine the expected level of sales given the level of demand. With respect to other factors like Advertising expenditure, sales promotion etc.

- Segmentation research - to determine the demographic, psychographic, cultural, and behavioural characteristics of potential buyers

- Online panel - a group of individual who accepted to respond to marketing research online

- Store audit — to measure the sales of a product or product line at a statistically selected store sample in order to determine market share, or to determine whether a retail store provides adequate service

- Test marketing — a small-scale product launch used to determine the likely acceptance of the product when it is introduced into a wider market

- Viral Marketing Research - refers to marketing research designed to estimate the probability that specific communications will be transmitted throughout an individual's Social Network. Estimates of Social Networking Potential (SNP) are combined with estimates of selling effectiveness to estimate ROI on specific combinations of messages and media.

All of these forms of marketing research can be classified as either problem-identification research or as problem-solving research.

There are two main sources of data — primary and secondary. Primary research is conducted from scratch. It is original and collected to solve the problem in hand. Secondary research already exists since it has been collected for other purposes. It is conducted on data published previously and usually by someone else. Secondary research costs far less than primary research, but seldom comes in a form that exactly meets the needs of the researcher.

A similar distinction exists between exploratory research and conclusive research. Exploratory research provides insights into and comprehension of an issue or situation. It should draw definitive conclusions only with extreme caution. Conclusive research draws conclusions: the results of the study can be generalized to the whole population.

Exploratory research is conducted to explore a problem to get some basic idea about the solution at the preliminary stages of research. It may serve as the input to conclusive research. Exploratory research information is collected by focus group interviews, reviewing literature or books, discussing with experts, etc. This is unstructured and qualitative in nature. If a secondary source of data is unable to serve the purpose, a convenience sample of small size can be collected. Conclusive research is conducted to draw some conclusion about the problem. It is essentially, structured and quantitative research, and the output of this research is the input to management information systems (MIS).

Exploratory research is also conducted to simplify the findings of the conclusive or descriptive research, if the findings are very hard to interpret for the marketing managers.

## Methods

Methodologically, marketing research uses the following types of research designs:

Based on questioning

- Qualitative marketing research - generally used for exploratory purposes — small number of respondents — not generalizable to the whole population — statistical significance and confidence not calculated — examples include focus groups, in-depth interviews, and projective techniques

- Quantitative marketing research - generally used to draw conclusions — tests a specific hypothesis - uses random sampling techniques so as to infer from the sample to the population — involves a large number of respondents — examples include surveys and questionnaires. Techniques include choice modelling, maximum difference preference scaling, and covariance analysis.

Based on observations

- Ethnographic studies — by nature qualitative, the researcher observes social phenomena in their natural setting — observations can occur cross-sectionally (observations made at one time) or longitudinally (observations occur over several time-periods) - examples include product-use analysis and computer cookie traces.

- Experimental techniques - by nature quantitative, the researcher creates a quasi-artificial environment to try to control spurious factors, then manipulates at least one of the variables — examples include purchase laboratories and test markets

Researchers often use more than one research design. They may start with secondary research to get background information, then conduct a focus group (qualitative research design) to explore the issues. Finally they might do a full nationwide survey (quantitative research design) in order to devise specific recommendations for the client.

## Business to Business

Business to business (B2B) research is inevitably more complicated than consumer research. The researchers need to know what type of multi-faceted approach will answer the objectives, since seldom is it possible to find the answers using just one method. Finding the right respondents is crucial in B2B research since they are often busy, and may not want to participate. Encouraging them to "open up" is yet another skill required of the B2B researcher. Last, but not least, most business research leads to strategic decisions and this means that the business researcher must have expertise in developing strategies that are strongly rooted in the research findings and acceptable to the client.

There are four key factors that make B2B market research special and different from consumer markets:

- The decision making unit is far more complex in B2B markets than in consumer markets

- B2B products and their applications are more complex than consumer products

- B2B marketers address a much smaller number of customers who are very much larger in their consumption of products than is the case in consumer markets

- Personal relationships are of critical importance in B2B markets.

## Small Businesses and Nonprofits

Corporations with many employees and a large budget. Marketing information can be derived by observing the environment of their location and the competitions location. Small scale surveys and focus groups are low cost ways to gather information from potential and existing customers. Most secondary data (statistics, demographics, etc.) is available to the public in libraries or on the internet and can be easily accessed by a small business owner.

Below are some steps that could be done by SME (Small Medium Entreprise) to analyze the market:

1. Provide secondary and or primary data (if necessary);

2. Analyze Macro & Micro Economic data (e.g. Supply & Demand, GDP,Price change, Economic growth, Sales by sector/industries,interest rate, number of investment/ divestment, I/O, CPI, Social anlysis,etc.);

3. Implement the marketing mix concept, which is consist of: Place, Price, Product,Promotion, People, Process, Physical Evidence and also Political & social situation to analyze global market situation);

4. Analyze market trends, growth, market size, market share, market competition (e.g. SWOT analysis, B/C Analysis,channel mapping identities of key channels, drivers of customers loyalty and satisfaction, brand perception, satisfaction levels, current competitor-channel relationship analysis, etc.),etc.;

5. Determine market segment, market target, market forecast and market position;

6. Formulating market strategy & also investigating the possibility of partnership/ collaboration (e.g. Profiling & SWOT analysis of potential partners, evaluating business partnership.)

7. Combine those analysis with the SME's business plan/ business model analysis (e.g. Business description, Business process, Business strategy, Revenue model, Business expansion, Return of Investment, Financial analysis (Company History, Financial assumption, Cost/Benefit Analysis, Projected profit & Loss, Cashflow, Balance sheet & business Ratio,etc.).

Note as important : Overall analysis should be based on 6W+1H (What, When, Where, Which, Who, Why and How) question.

## International Plan

International Marketing Research follows the same path as domestic research, but there are a few more problems that may arise. Customers in international markets may have very different customs, cultures, and expectations from the same company. In this case, Marketing Research relies more on primary data rather than secondary information. Gathering the primary data can be hindered by language, literacy and access to technology. Basic Cultural and Market intelligence information will be needed to maximize the research effectiveness. Some of the steps that would help overcoming barriers include; 1. Collect secondary information on the country under study from reliable international source e.g. WHO and IMF 2. Collect secondary information on the product/service under study from available sources 3. Collect secondary information on product manufacturers and service providers under study in relevant country 4. Collect secondary information on culture and common business practices 5. Ask questions to get better understanding of reasons behind any recommendations for a specific methodology.

## Common Terms

Market research techniques resemble those used in political polling and social science research. Meta-analysis (also called the Schmidt-Hunter technique) refers to a statistical method of combining data from multiple studies or from several types of studies. Conceptualization means the process of converting vague mental images into definable concepts. Operationalization is the process of converting concepts into specific observable behaviors that a researcher can measure. Precision refers to the exactness of any given measure. Reliability refers to the likelihood that a given operationalized construct will yield the same results if re-measured. Validity refers to the extent to which a measure provides data that captures the meaning of the operationalized construct as defined in the study. It asks, "Are we measuring what we intended to measure?"

- Applied research sets out to prove a specific hypothesis of value to the clients paying for the research. For example, a cigarette company might commission research that attempts to show that cigarettes are good for one's health. Many researchers have ethical misgivings about doing applied research.

- Sugging (from SUG, for "selling under the guise" of market research) forms a sales technique in which sales people pretend to conduct marketing research, but with the real purpose of obtaining buyer motivation and buyer decision-making information to be used in a subsequent sales call.

- Frugging comprises the practice of soliciting funds under the pretense of being a research organization.

## Careers

Some of the positions available in marketing research include vice president of marketing research, research director, assistant director of research, project manager, field work director, statistician/data processing specialist, senior analyst, analyst, junior analyst and operational supervisor.

The most common entry-level position in marketing research for people with bachelor's degrees (e.g., BBA) is as operational supervisor. These people are responsible for supervising a well-defined set of operations, including field work, data editing, and coding, and may be involved in programming and data analysis. Another entry-level position for BBAs is assistant project manager. An assistant project manager will learn and assist in questionnaire design, review field instructions, and monitor timing and costs of studies. In the marketing research industry, however, there is a growing preference for people with master's degrees. Those with MBA or equivalent degrees are likely to be employed as project managers.

A small number of business schools also offer a more specialized Master of Marketing Research (MMR) degree. An MMR typically prepares students for a wide range of research methodologies and focuses on learning both in the classroom and the field.

The typical entry-level position in a business firm would be junior research analyst (for BBAs) or research analyst (for MBAs or MMRs). The junior analyst and the research analyst learn about the particular industry and receive training from a senior staff member, usually the marketing research manager. The junior analyst position includes a training program to prepare individuals for the responsibilities of a research analyst, including coordinating with the marketing department and sales force to develop goals for product exposure. The research analyst responsibilities include checking all data for accuracy, comparing and contrasting new research with established norms, and analyzing primary and secondary data for the purpose of market forecasting.

As these job titles indicate, people with a variety of backgrounds and skills are needed in marketing research. Technical specialists such as statisticians obviously need strong backgrounds in statistics and data analysis. Other positions, such as research director, call for managing the work of others and require more general skills. To prepare for a career in marketing research, students usually:

- Take all the marketing courses.

- Take courses in statistics and quantitative methods.

- Acquire computer skills.

- Take courses in psychology and consumer behavior.

- Acquire effective written and verbal communication skills.

- Think creatively.

## Corporate Hierarchy

1. Vice-President of Marketing Research: This is the senior position in marketing research. The VP is responsible for the entire marketing research operation of the company and serves on the top management team. Sets the objectives and goals of the marketing research department.

2. Research Director: Also a senior position, the director has the overall responsibility for the development and execution of all the marketing research projects.

3. Assistant Director of Research: Serves as an administrative assistant to the director and supervises some of the other marketing research staff members.

4. (Senior) Project Manager: Has overall responsibility for design, implementation, and management of research projects.

5. Statistician/Data Processing Specialist: Serves as an expert on theory and application of statistical techniques. Responsibilities include experimental design, data processing, and analysis.

6. Senior Analyst: Participates in the development of projects and directs the operational execution of the assigned projects. Works closely with the analyst, junior analyst, and other personnel in developing the research design and data collection. Prepares the final report. The primary responsibility for meeting time and cost constraints rests with the senior analyst.

7. Analyst: Handles the details involved in executing the project. Designs and pretests the questionnaires and conducts a preliminary analysis of the data.

8. Junior Analyst: Handles routine assignments such as secondary data analysis, editing and coding of questionnaires, and simple statistical analysis.

9. Field Work Director: Responsible for the selection, training, supervision, and evaluation of interviewers and other field workers.

## Advertising Management

Advertising refers to any paid form of communication designed to create interest in or stimulate
sales of products or services. Companies are constantly searching for novel media,
such as these human billboards, to get their message out to potential consumers

Advertising management is a planned managerial process designed to oversee and control the various advertising activities involved in a program to communicate with a firm's target market and which is ultimately designed to influence the consumer's purchase decisions. Advertising is just one element in a company's promotional mix and as such, must be integrated with the overall marketing communications program. Advertising is, however, the most expensive of all the promotional elements and therefore must be managed with care and accountability.

Marketers use different types of advertising. Brand advertising is defined as a non-personal communication message placed in a paid, mass medium designed to persuade target consumers of a product or service benefits in an effort to induce them to make a purchase. Corporate advertising refers to paid messages designed to that communicate the corporation's values in an effort to influence public opinion. Yet other types of advertising such as not-for-profit advertising and political advertising present special challenges that require different strategies and approaches.

Advertising management is a complex process that involves making many layered decisions including the developing the advertising strategy, setting the advertising budget, setting advertising objectives, determining the target market, media strategy (which involves media planning, developing the message strategy and evaluating the overall effectiveness of the advertising effort.) Advertising management may also involve media buying.

Advertising management is a complex process. However, at its simplest level, advertising management can be reduced to four key decision areas:

> Target audience definition: Who do we want to talk to?

> Message (or creative) strategy: What do we want to say to them?

> Media strategy: How will we reach them?

> Measuring advertising effectiveness: How do we know our messages were received in the form intended and with the desired outcomes?

## Advertising and Advertising Management: Definitions

Consumers tend to think that all forms of commercial promotion constitute advertising. However, in marketing and advertising, the term "advertising" has a very special meaning that reflects its status as a distinct type of promotion.

A key characteristic of advertising is that it utilises mass media channels
such as newspapers, magazines, radio or TV to reach potential customers

The marketing and advertising literature has many different definitions of advertising, but it is possible to identify common elements or themes within most of these definitions. The American Marketing Association (AMA) defines advertising as "the placement of announcements and persuasive messages in time or space purchased in any of the mass media by business firms, nonprofit organizations, government agencies, and individuals who seek to inform and/ or persuade members of a particular target market or audience about their products, services, organizations, or ideas". The *American Heritage Dictionary* defines advertising as "the activity of attracting public attention to a product or business, as by paid announcements in the print, broadcast, or electronic media." Selected marketing scholars have defined advertising in the following terms: "any non-personal communication that is paid for by an identified sponsor, and involves either mass communication viz newspapers, magazines, radio, television, and other media (e.g., billboards, bus stop signage) or direct to-consumer communication via direct mail" and "the element of the marketing communications mix that is non-personal, paid for by an identified sponsor, and disseminated through mass channels of communication to promote the adoption of goods, services, persons, or ideas. One of the shortest definitions is that advertising is "a paid, mass-mediated attempt to persuade."

Several common themes emerge in the various definitions of advertising:

- Firstly, advertising is a *paid* form of communication and is therefore commercial in nature.

- Secondly, advertising employs *non-personal channels* (i.e. commercial mass media) which implies that it is directed at a mass audience rather than at an individual consumer and is a one-way communication mode where the sponsor sends messages, but recipients cannot respond or ask questions about the message content.

- Thirdly, advertising has an *identified sponsor* .

Given that advertising is paid, it is one of the many controllable elements in the marketing program. Advertising is qualitatively different from publicity where the message sponsor is either not identified or ambiguously defined, and different to personal selling which occurs in real-time and involves some face-to-face contact between message sponsor and recipient allowing for two-way dialogue.

While advertising refers to the advertising message, per se, advertising management refers to the process of planning and executing an advertising campaign or campaigns; that is, it is a series of planned decisions that begins with market research continues through to setting advertising budgets, developing advertising objectives, executing the creative messages and follows up with efforts to measure the extent to which objectives were achieved and evaluate the cost-benefit of the overall advertising effort.

## Advertising and Organisational Responsibilities

In commercial organisations, advertising, along with other marketing communications activities, is the ultimate responsibility of the marketing department. Some companies outsource part or all of the work to specialists such as advertising agencies, creative design teams, web designers, media buyers, events management specialists or other relevant service providers. Another option is for a company to carry out most or all of the advertising functions within the marketing department in what is known as an *in-house agency*. By definition, an in-house agency is a "an advertising organization that is owned and operated by the corporation it serves". Its mission is to provide advertising services in support of its parent company's business and marketing objectives. Well-known brands that currently use in-house agencies include Google, Calvin Klein, Adobe, Dell, IBM, Kraft, Marriott and Wendy's.

Calvin Klein is one of a growing number of companies that uses an in-house agency for its advertising and promotion

Both in-house agencies and outsourcing models have advantages and disadvantages. Outsourcing to an external agency allows marketers to obtain highly specialised strategic, research and planning skills, access to top creative talent and provides an independent perspective on marketing or advertising problems. In-house agencies deliver cost advantages, time efficiencies and afford marketers greater control over the advertising effort. In addition, personnel who work within an in-house agency gain considerable creative experience which stays within the company. Recent trends suggest that the number of in-house agencies is rising.

Whether a company chooses to outsource advertising functions to an external agency or carry them out within the marketing department, marketers need a rich understanding of advertising principles so that they can prepare effective advertising plans, brief relevant agencies about their needs and expectations or develop their own creative solutions to marketing problems.

## Advertising's Role in the Promotional Mix

The promotional mix refers to the specific combination of promotional methods used for a brand, product or family of products. Advertising is best treated as a *multiplier* that can leverage other elements of the promotional mix and marketing program. Therefore, advertising must be considered as part of a broader marketing and promotional program.

The promotional mix includes a variety of tools such as:

> Advertising: messages paid for by those who send them and intended to inform or influence people who receive them

> Public relations (PR): the practice of maintaining goodwill between an organisation and its publics

Personal selling: face-to-face selling in which a seller attempts to persuade a buyer to make a purchase.

Direct marketing: contacting and influencing carefully chosen prospects with means such as telemarketing and direct mail

Sponsorship: the act of providing money for a television or radio program, website, sports event, or other activity usually in exchange for advertising or other form of promotion

Product placement: the practice of supplying a product or service for display in feature films or television programs

Sales promotion / merchandising: activities designed to stimulate sales normally at the point-of-sale; includes retail displays, product sampling, special price offers, shelf talkers, contests, give-aways, promotional items, competitions and other methods

Event marketing: a planned activity of designing or developing a themed activity, occasion, display, or exhibit (such as a sporting event, music festival, fair, or concert) to promote a product, cause, or organization.

Exhibitions/trade shows: events where companies can display their wares

The Vogue Fashion Show is a special event designed to promote top designers' seasonal collections

Advertising is just one of many elements that comprise the promotional mix. When marketers communicate with target markets across a broad range of different promotional types and media, the potential for contradictory or mixed messages is very real. Accordingly, it is important that advertising is treated as part of a total marketing communications program and that steps are taken to ensure that it is integrated with all other marketing communications, so that all communications messages speak with a 'single voice'. The process of ensuring message consistency across the entire marketing communications program is known as *integrated marketing communications*

Marketers need to be aware of the strengths and weaknesses of each of the elements in the promotional mix in order to select the right blend for a given situation. For instance, public relations allows for high credibility message delivery with relatively low costs, while advertising permits message repetition. The "right" promotional mix should consider both message impact and message consistency.

Mounting a display at a trade-fair or exhibition, such as the Hong Kong Food Show, is part of a company's total promotional mix

In terms of integrated communications, the literature identifies different types of integration: (1) *Image integration* refers to messages that have a consistent look and feel, regardless of the medium; (2) *Functional integration* refers to capacity of different promotional tools to complement each other and deliver a unified, coherent message; (3) *Coordinated integration* refers to the ways that different internal and external agencies (e.g. web designers, advertising agencies, PR consultants) coordinate to provide a consistent message; (4) *Stakeholder integration* refers to the way that all stakeholders such as employees, suppliers, customers and others cooperate to communicate a shared understanding of the company's key messages and values and (5) *Relationship integration* refers to the way that communications professionals contribute to the company's overall corporate goals and quality management.

Sales promotion includes a variety of activities such as special price offers designed to stimulate sales

On the surface, integrated marketing communications appear to be simple common sense. Yet, a survey of brand advertisers carried out by the Association of National Advertisers (ANA) revealed that while 67 per cent of marketers engage in integrated marketing communications, just one third are satisfied with their efforts. In practice, integrating communications messages across a broad range of promotional formats and media channels is very difficult to achieve.

## Theories of Advertising Effects

Advertising messages are all around us, yet the mechanism which leads from exposure to brand advertising through to sales is not entirely clear

Studies have repeatedly demonstrated a clear association between advertising and sales response. Yet the exact process that leads from the consumer being exposed to an advertising message through to a purchase or behavioral response is not entirely clear. Noting the difficulties in explaining how advertising works, one theorist wrote, "Only the brave or ignorant...can say exactly what advertising does in the market place."

The advertising and marketing literature suggests a variety of different models to explain how advertising works. These models are not competing theories, but rather explanations of how advertising persuades or influences different types of consumers in different purchase contexts. In a seminal paper, Vankratsas and Ambler surveyed more than 250 papers to develop a typology of advertising models. They identified four broad classes of model: *cognitive information models*, *pure affect models*, *hierarchy of effect models*, *integrative models* and *hierarchy-free models*.

## Cognitive Information Models

A directory such as *Yellow Pages* can eliminate the need for extensive store visits and the need to recall brand names

Cognitive information models assume that consumers are rational decision-makers and that advertising provides consumers with information utility by reducing the need to search for other information about a brand. For example, an advertisement in the *Yellow Pages* or an online directory means that the consumer does not have to travel from store to store in search of a product or service. Consumers process this information at a cognitive level before forming an attitude to the brand and purchase intent. A cognition is any thought that surfaces during the elaboration of the information. Cognitive information models are also known as the *central route to persuasion.*

In the cognitive information models, the general path to persuasion is as follows:

Ad cognition→ Attitude to ad ($A_{ad}$) → Brand cognition → Attitude to brand($A_b$) →Purchase Intention (PI)

Certain theoretical works, combined with empirical studies, suggest that advertising information is more useful for experience goods (experiential services) than for search goods (tangible products). Research studies also suggest that consumers who are involved in the purchase decision are more likely to actively seek out product information and actively process advertising messages while low-involvement consumers are more likely to respond at an emotional level.

## Pure Affect Models

Pure affect models suggest that consumers shape their preferences to a brand based on the feelings and attitudes elicited by exposure to an advertising message. When consumers view an advertisement, they not only develop attitudes towards the advertisement and the advertiser, but also develop feelings and beliefs about the brand being advertised.

Pure affect models help to explain the consumer's emotional responses to advertising and brands. These models suggest that simple exposure is to a brand is sufficient to generate purchase intention. Exposure in the form of advertising messages leads to an attitude to the advertisement ($A_{ad}$) which transfers to the attitude to the brand ($A_b$)without any further cognitive processing. Exposure it not restricted to physical contact; rather it can refer to any brand-related contact such as advertising, promotion or virtual brands on websites.

In pure affect models, the path to communication effectiveness is represented by the following:

Attitude to Ad ($A_{ad}$) → Attitude to Brand ($A_b$) → Purchase Intention (PI).

This path is also known as the *peripheral route to persuasion.* Empirical research in the pure affect sphere suggests that advertising messages do not need to be informative to be effective, however consumers must like the advertising execution for the message to be effective. In addition, ad liking and advertiser credibility, may be especially important for corporate image advertising (compared to product-related advertising).

## Hierarchy of Effects Models

Hierarchical models are linear sequential models built on an assumption that consumers move through a series of cognitive and affective stages culminating in the purchase decision. The common theme among these models is that advertising operates as a stimulus and the purchase decision is a response. A number of hierarchical models can be found in the literature including Lavidge's hierarchy of effects, DAGMAR and AIDA and other variants. Some authors have argued that, for advertising purposes, the hierarchical models have dominated advertising theory, and that, of these models, the AIDA model is one of the most widely applied.

The AIDA model proposes that advertising messages need to accomplish a number of tasks designed to move the consumer through a series of sequential steps from brand awareness through to action (purchase and consumption).

> Awareness - The consumer becomes aware of a category, product or brand (usually through advertising)
>
> ↓
>
> Interest - The consumer becomes interested by considering the brand's fit with the consumer's lifestyle
>
> ↓
>
> Desire - The consumer develops a favorable (or unfavorable) disposition towards the brand
>
> ↓
>
> Action - The consumer forms a purchase intention or actually makes a purchase

As consumers move through the hierarchy of effects they pass through both a cognitive processing stage and an affective processing stage before any action occurs. Thus the hierarchy of effects models all include Cognition (C)- Affect (A)- Behaviour (B) as the core steps in the underlying behavioral sequence. The underlying behavioral sequence for all hierarchy models is as follows:

> Cognition (Awareness/learning) → Affect (Feeling/ interest/ desire)→ Behavior (Action e.g. purchase/ consumption/ usage/ sharing information)

The literature offers numerous variations on the basic path to persuasion. The basic AIDA model is one of the longest serving models. Contemporary hierarchical models often modify or expand the basic AIDA model, resulting in additional steps, however, all follow the basic sequence which includes Cognition- Affect- Behaviour. Some of these newer models have been adapted to accommodate consumer's digital media habits. Selected hierarchical models follow:

> Basic AIDA model: Awareness→ Interest→ Desire→ Action
>
> Modified AIDA model: Awareness→ Interest→ Conviction →Desire→ Action
>
> AIDAS Model: Attention → Interest → Desire → Action → Satisfaction
>
> AISDALSLove model: Awareness→ Interest→ Search →Desire→ Action → Like/dislike→ Share → Love/ Hate
>
> Lavidge et al.'s Hierarchy of Effects: Awareness→ Knowledge→ Liking→ Preference→ Conviction→ Purchase
>
> DAGMAR Model: Awareness → Comprehension → Attitude/ Conviction → Action
>
> Rossiter and Percy's Communications Effects: Category Need → Brand Awareness → Brand Preference ($A_b$) → Purchase Intent→ Purchase Facilitation

The Purchase Funnel indicates that awareness is a necessary precondition for purchase

All hierarchical models indicate that brand awareness is a necessary precondition to brand attitude, brand preference or brand purchase intention. The process of moving consumers from purchase intention to actual sales is known as *conversion*. While advertising is an excellent tool for creating awareness, brand attitude and purchase intent, it usually requires support from other elements in the promotion mix and the marketing program to convert purchase intent into an actual sale. Many different techniques can be used to convert interest into sales including special price offers, special promotional offers, attractive trade-in terms, guarantees or a strong call-to-action as part of the advertising message.

In order to penetrate markets, it is essential that high levels of awareness are created as early as possible in a product or brand life-cycle. Hierarchical models provide marketers and advertisers with basic insights about the nature of the target audience, the optimal message and media strategy indicated at different junctures throughout a product's life cycle. For new products, the main advertising objective should be to create awareness with a broad cross-section of the potential market as quickly as practical. When the desired levels of awareness have been attained, the promotional effort should shift to stimulating interest, desire or conviction. The number of potential purchasers decreases as the product moves through the natural sales cycle in an effect likened to a funnel. Early in the campaign, the marketers should attempt to reach as many potential buyers as possible with high impact messages. Later in the cycle, and as the number of prospects becomes smaller, the marketer can employ more tightly targeted promotional activities such as personal selling, direct mail and email directed at those individuals or sub-segments more likely to exhibit a genuine interest in the product or brand.

## Integrative Models

Integrative models assume that consumers process advertising information via two paths - both cognitive (thinking) and affective (feeling) simultaneously. These models seek to combine the type of purchase with the consumer's dominant mode of processing. Integrative models are based on research findings indicating that congruence between personality and the way a persuasive message is framed. That is, aligning the message framing with the recipient's personality profile may play an important role in ensuring the success of that message. In a recent experiment, five advertisements (each designed to target one of the five personality traits) were constructed for a single product. Findings suggest that advertisements were evaluated more positively when they aligned with participants' motives. Tailoring persuasive messages to the personality traits of the targeted audience can be an effective way of enhancing the message's impact.

There are many integrative frameworks. Two of the more widely used models are the Foote, Cone, Belding (FCB) planning grid and Rossiter and Percy's planning grid which is an extension of the FCB approach.

## Foote, Cone, Belding (FCB) Planning Grid

The FCB planning grid was developed by Richard Vaughan, who was the Senior Vice President at advertising agency, Foote, Cone and Belding, in the 1980s. The planning grid has two dimensions, involvement and information processing. Each dimension has two values, representing extremes of a continuum, specifically involvement (high/low) and information processing (thinking/feeling). These form a 2 X 2 matrix with four cells representing the different types of advertising effects.

| The FCB Planning Grid | | |
|---|---|---|
| **Info processing**<br><br>**Type of Decision** | **Thinking** | **Feeling** |
| **High-involvement** | 1. Learn→Feel→Do | 2. Feel→Learn→Do |
| **Low-involvement** | 3. Do→Learn→Feel | 4. Do→Feel→ Learn |

The FCB planning grid gives rise to a number of implications for advertising and media strategy:

An expensive car is a high-involvement/ rational purchase (i.e., FCB Quadarant 1)

*Quadrant 1:* High-involvement/ rational purchases: In the first quadrant consumers learn about a product through advertising after which they develop a favourable (or unfavourable) disposition to the product which may or may not culminate in a purchase. This approach is considered optimal for advertising high ticket items such as cars and household furniture. When this is the dominant approach to purchasing, advertising messages should be information-rich and media strategy should be weighted towards media such as magazines and newspapers capable of delivering long-copy advertising.

*Quadrant 2*: High-involvement/ emotional purchases: In the second quadrant, audiences exhibit an emotional response to advertisements which transfers to products. This approach is used for products such as jewellery, expensive perfumes and designer fashion where consumers are emotionally involved in the purchase. When this mode of purchasing is evident, advertising should be designed to create a strong brand image and media should be selected to support the relevant image. For example, magazines such as *Vogue* can help to create an up-market image.

Impulse purchases are low-involvement/ emotional purchase
items that make consumers feel good

*Quadrant 3*: Low-involvement/ rational purchases: The third quadrant represents routine low-involvement purchases evident for many packaged goods such as detergents, tissues and other consumable household items. Consumers make habitual purchases, and after consumption the benefit of using the brand is reinforced which ideally results in long-term brand loyalty (re-purchase). Given that this is a rational purchase, consumers need to be informed or reminded of the product's benefits. Advertising messages should encourage repeat purchasing and brand loyalty while media strategy should be weighted towards media that can deliver high frequency required for reminder campaigns such as TV, radio and sales promotion.

*Quadrant 4*: Low-involvement/ emotional purchases: In the final quadrant, consumers make low-involvement, relatively inexpensive purchases that make them feel good. Impulse purchases and convenience goods fall into this category. The purchase leads to feelings of satisfaction which, in turn, reinforces the purchase behavior. When this approach is the dominant purchase mode, advertising messages should "congratulate" customers on their purchase choice and the media strategy should be weighted towards options that reach customers when they are close to the point-of-purchase such as billboards, sales promotion and point-of-sale displays. Examples of this approach include "McDonald's - You Deserve a Break Today" and "L'Oreal- Because You're Worth It".

## Hierarchy-free Models

Many authors have treated reason (rational processes) and emotion (affective processes) as entirely independent. Yet, other researchers have argued that both reason and emotion can be employed simultaneously, to process advertising information. Hierarchy-free models draw on evidence from psychology and consumer neuroscience which suggest that consumers process information via different pathways rather than in any linear/ sequential manner. Thus, hierarchy-free models do not employ any fixed processing sequence. These models treat advertising as part of the brand totality. Some hierarchy-free models treat brands as 'myth' and advertising as 'myth-making' while other models seek to tap into the consumer's memories of pleasant consumption experiences (e.g. the MAC- Memory-Affect-Cognition model). Hierarchy-free models are of increasing interest to academics and practitioners because they are more customer-centric and allow for the possibility of consumer co-creation of value.

## Advertising Planning

Advertising planning does not occur in a vacuum. Advertising objectives are derived from marketing objectives. Therefore, the first step in any advertising planning is to review to the objectives as set out in the marketing plan. This is designed to ensure that all promotional efforts, including advertising, are working towards achieving both short-term and long-term corporate and marketing goals and align with the company's values and vision.

## Review the Marketing Plan

A review of the marketing plan can be a relatively simple process or it can involve a formal review, known as an *audit*. The review or audit might consider such issues as prior marketing communications activity, an evaluation of what has been effective in the past, whether new market research studies are warranted, an outline of competitive advertising activity and a review of budgetary considerations.

The marketing plan can be expected to provide information about the company's long and short-term goals, competitive rivalry, a description of the target market, product(s) offered, positioning strategy, pricing strategy, distribution strategy and other promotional programs. All of this information has potential implications for developing the advertising program. The advertiser must study the marketing plan carefully and determine how to translate the marketing objectives into an advertising program. Each advertising campaign is unique, so that the review requires a great deal of analysis as well as judgement.

## Overall Communications Objectives

Communications objectives are derived from marketing objectives. However, communications objectives must be framed in terms of communications effects. For example, a company's short-term marketing objective might be to increase sales response for a given brand. However, this objective would require that a large number of consumers are aware of the brand and are favourably disposed towards it. Furthermore, consumers' purchase intentions may be dependent on other marketing activities such as access, price, the ability to trial the brand prior to final purchase and other marketing activities. It is unfair to hold marketing communications accountable for all sales when it is only one element in the total marketing effort.

While advertising is an excellent tool for creating awareness and interest in a brand, it is less effective at turning that awareness and interest into actual sales. To convert interest into sales, different promotional tools such as personal selling or sales promotion may be more useful. Many authors caution against using sales or market share objectives for marketing communications or advertising purposes.

Communications objectives might include such things as to:

- increase purchase

- encourage trial

- encourage loyalty

- position or re-position a brand

- educate customers

These will need to be translated into advertising objectives.

## Target Market and Target Audience

**Target Audience & Target Market**

Relationship between target market and target audience

The review should take note of the overall target market. However, this does not necessarily mean that the advertising campaign will be directed at the total target market. Marketers and advertisers make a distinction between the *target audience* for an advertising message and the *target market* for a product or brand. By definition, the target audience is the intended audience for a given advertisement or message in a publication or broadcast medium, while the target market consists of all existing and potential consumers of a product, service or brand. Companies often develop different advertising messages and media strategies to reach different target audiences. For example, McDonald's Restaurants uses the anthropomorphic brand characters, Ronald McDonald and Hamburgler, in its advertising directed at children who are important brand-choice influencers. However, for adult target audience members, McDonald's uses messages that emphasise convenience and quality. Thus the target audience for a given advertising message may comprise only a subset of the total market as defined in the marketing plan. Careful perusal of the marketing plan will assist marketers in the process of defining the optimal target audiences for specific advertising objectives.

## Push vs Pull Strategy

The communications objectives will, at least in part, depend on whether the marketer is using a push or pull strategy. In a *push strategy*, the marketer advertises intensively with retailers and wholesalers, with the expectation that they will stock the product or brand, and that consumers will purchase it when they see it in stores. In contrast, in a *pull strategy*, the marketer advertises directly to consumers hoping that they will put pressure on retailers to stock the product or brand, thereby pulling it through the distribution channel. Thus the media options in a push strategy will be weighted towards trade magazines, exhibitions and trade shows while a pull strategy would make more extensive use of consumer-oriented media.

## Devising Advertising Objectives

Setting advertising objectives provides the framework for the entire advertising plan. Therefore, it is important to specify precisely what is to be achieved and outline how advertising will be evaluated. Advertising objectives should be Specific, Measurable, Achievable and Time-dependent (SMART). Any statement of advertising objectives must include measurement benchmarks - that is the norms against which advertising effectiveness will be evaluated. One of the first approaches to setting communications-oriented objectives was the DAGMAR approach (Defining Advertising Goals for Measured Advertising Results) developed in the 1960s. While memorable, the DAGMAR approach fails to provide concrete guidance on how to link advertising objectives with communications effects.

In order to set realistic and achievable advertising objectives, most advertisers try to link advertising or communications objectives with the communications effects. Rossiter and Bellman have argued that, for advertising purposes, five communications effects should be considered, namely:

1. Category Need: The consumer's acceptance that the category (the product or service) is necessary to satisfy some need

2. Brand awareness (brand recognition and brand recall): The consumer's ability to recognise a brand or to recall a brand name from memory

3. Brand preference (or brand attitude): The extent to which a consumer will choose one brand over other competing brands in the category

4. Brand action intention (purchase intent): The consumer's self instruction to purchase a given brand

5. Purchase facilitation: The extent to which the consumer knows how and where to purchase the brand

| Managerial Options for Communications Objectives | | |
|---|---|---|
| **Target Consumer's State of Mind** | **Communication/ Advertising Objective** | **Advertising Message Example** |
| **Category Need**<br><br>• Category need already present<br><br>• Latent category need<br><br>• No or weak category need | • Omit category need as an objective of advertising or promotion<br><br>• Mention category need to remind customer of previously established need<br><br>• "Sell" category need using positive or negative motivations<br><br>(e.g. pain removal, pain avoidance, dissatisfaction, sensory gratification, social approval) | *Pain avoidance*: "For fast, sure pain relief, Anacin" |
| **Brand Awareness**<br><br>• *Brand recall*<br><br>• *Brand recognition* | • Use taglines, slogans, jingles to teach brand recall and strengthen learning<br><br>• Associate brand name with category<br><br>• Show product packaging or label in all advertising | *Paired category-brand association*: "When you think of chocolate, think of Cadbury" |
| **Brand Preference**<br><br>• Negative preference<br><br>• Unaware<br><br>• Moderate preference<br><br>• Strong preference | • Change to moderate preference<br><br>• Create strong preference<br><br>• Increase preference<br><br>• Reinforce strong preference | *Brand Preference*: "The burgers are better at Burger King (or Hungry Jack's)" |
| **Purchase Intention**<br><br>• Low-involvement decision<br><br>• High-involvement decision | • Omit purchase-intention<br><br>• Generate purchase-intention | *Purchase-intention*: "Hurry, hurry last days, offer must expire soon"; "Don't wait- limited stocks available" |
| **Purchase Facilitation**<br><br>• Customer knows where to purchase product or service and how much to pay for it<br><br>• Not obvious where to purchase or how to find retailer | • Omit purchase-facilitation<br><br>• Incorporate purchase-facilitation in all marketing communications | *Purchase-facilitation*: "Refer to website for nearest stockist" |

For many purchases, category need and purchase facilitation will be present in the customer's mind and can be omitted from the advertising objectives. However, for some purchases, the customer may not be aware of the product category or may not know how to access it, in which case these objectives will need to be addressed in the communications objectives. Brand awareness, brand preference and purchase intention are almost always included as advertising objectives.

## Setting Advertising Budgets

A firm's advertising budget is a sub-set of its overall budget. For many firms, the cost of advertising is one of the largest expenses, second only to wages and salaries. Advertising expenditure varies enormously according to firm size, market coverage, managerial expectations and even managerial style. Procter and Gamble, the top US advertiser, spent US$4.3 billion in 2015 on national media (exclusive of agency fees and production costs) while a small local advertiser might spend just a few thousand dollars in the same period.

The size of the budget has implications for the promotional mix, the media mix and market coverage. As a generalisation, very large budgets are required to sustain national television campaigns. Advertisers with tight budgets may forced to use less effective media alternatives. However, even advertisers with small budgets may be able to incorporate expensive main media, by focusing on narrow geographic markets, buying spots in non-peak time periods and carefully managing advertising schedules.

A number of different methods are used to develop the advertising (and/or marketing communications) budget. The most commonly used methods are: percentage-of-sales, objective and task, competitive parity method, market share method, unit sales method, all available funds method and the affordable method.

## Percentage-of-sales Method

Using the percentage-of-sales method, the advertiser allocates a fixed percentage (say 5% or 10%) of forecast sales value to the advertising budget. This method is predicated on the assumption that advertising causes future sales volume. The percentage of sales method is the easiest method to use and for this reason remains one of the most widely used methods for setting budgets.

A major problem with the %-of-sales method is that there is no consensus about the percentage value to apply. Some companies use industry averages as a guide to set their marcomms budget. The following table, based on industry averages, shows that the % value can vary from around 20% of sales to less than 1 percent.

| Ad-to-sales ratios for selected industries, 2004 | |
|---|---|
| **Industry** | **Ad-to-sales ratio** |
| Health services | 18.7 |
| Transportation services | 14.2 |
| Motion pictures and videotape production | 13.7 |
| Food | 11.9 |
| Computer & office equipment | 11.9 |
| Computer & software wholesale | 0.2 |

## Objective and Task Method

The objective and task method is the most rational and defensible of all budgeting methods. In this method, the advertiser determines the advertising objectives and then defines specific, measurable communication tasks that will need to be undertaken to achieve the desired objectives. Cost estimates are developed for each communication task in order to arrive at a total budget estimate.

This method is time-consuming and complex, and as a consequence has been less widely used in practice, however, recent research suggests that more marketers are taking up this approach.

## Competitive Parity Method

The competitive parity method allocates the advertising or promotional budget based on competitive spending for comparable activities. This approach is a defensive strategy used to protect a brand market position. It assumes that rival firms have similar objectives and is widely used in highly competitive markets. The main criticism of this method is that it assumes competitors know what they are doing in relation to advertising expenditure.

There are several approaches to using the competitive parity method:

a)  Allocate the same budget on advertising as a key rival;

b)  Allocate the budget based on the industry average expenditure levels;

c)  Allocate a similar percentage-of-sales as a key competitor;

d)  Allocate the same percentage-of-sales on advertising as the industry average;

e)  Use competitive activity as a benchmark to which sums are added or subtracted based on managerial judgement.

Competitive parity requires a detailed understanding of competitor's expenditure in key areas. Market intelligence used to inform this approach can be obtained by consulting company annual reports and also from commercial research service providers such as Nielsen's AdEx.

Other methods used to set advertising and promotional budgets include the *market share method, unit sales method, all available funds method, affordable method, marginal analysis* and others. Contemporary budgeting rarely relies on a single method, but instead uses a combination of methods to guide the marketer in determining the optimal expenditure levels.

## Devising the Creative Strategy

The creative strategy is also known as the *message strategy*. The creative strategy explains how the advertising campaign will address the advertising objectives. Developing the creative strategy typically begins by identifying the big idea (also known as the *creative concept* that will establish the intended product position in the minds of the customer. Another way of thinking about the creative concept is that it refers to the one thing that will make consumers respond. The creative concept should show how the product benefit meets the customer's needs or expectations in a unique way.

Laskey et al. developed a typology of nine creative strategies. Initially devised for television, this typology has been widely adopted for other media including print media  and social media.

Laskey, Day and Crask's typology first identifies two broad classes of creative strategy:

- Informational: rational appeals that typically provide information about the brand's benefits

- Transformational: emotional appeals that assist consumers to imagine an aspirational lifestyle

Informational appeals typically involve factual claims that list the product's benefits in a straight-forward manner and are more likely to be used with high involvement goods. Transformational appeals play on emotions and are designed to transform the consumer's perceptions of themselves or of the product. Transformational appeals are more likely to be indicated for low-involvement goods or services. Emotional appeals are often known as a *soft-sell* approach. Because they bypass rational cognitive processing, transformational appeals are less likely to result in counter-arguing in the consumer's mind.

| Typology of Creative Strategies | | |
|---|---|---|
| **Informational** | **Description** | **Uses** |
| Comparative | Explicit comparison of brand and rival(s) | Use with care in competitive markets |
| Unique Selling Proposition (USP) | Highlight a unique benefit that is meaningful to consumers | Use in categories with high levels of technological differentiation |
| Pre-emptive | Be the first to use a common attribute or benefit | Use when differentiation is difficult or impossible |
| Hyperbole | Gross exaggeration to highlight unique benefit | Use when brand has demonstrable point of difference |
| Generic informational | Focus on product category | Use for new categories, new products or repositioning |
| **Transformational** | | |
| User Image | Focus on the consumer's lifestyles e.g. activities, interests, work | |
| Brand Image | Claim of superiority based on extrinsic factors such as customer perceptions, designed to give the brand a 'personality' | Use with low-tech goods where differentiation is difficult e.g. coolness, prestige |
| Use Occasion | Focus on the brand experience, the ownership experience, the shopping experience or the consumption experience | Use with experiential goods where differentiation is difficult |
| Generic | Focus on product class with emotional appeal | Use for new categories, new products or repositioning |

In addition to determining the overall creative strategy, the advertiser also needs to consider the creative execution - which refers to the way that the message is presented. Examples of creative execution include: problem-solution formats, fear appeals, sex appeals, humour, parody, slogans or jingles, mnemonics, slice-of-life, guarantee, celebrity endorsement, testimonial, news style, scientific appeals, dramatisation and product demonstration.

## Media Planning

Strategic media planning consists of four key decision areas:

1) Setting media objectives (with reference to both marketing and advertising objectives);

2) Developing a media channel strategy for implementing media objectives - the broad vision of when and how to reach target audiences;

3) Designing media tactics - specific instructions about media vehicles, placement, preferred position;

4) Devising procedures for evaluating the effectiveness of the media plan.

Integrating the creative and the media can result in imaginative and powerful messages that grab attention and are noticed

The traditional approach to media strategy was primarily concerned with setting objectives for message reach, weight and frequency. The contemporary approach, however, often treats the media strategy as an extension of the creative strategy. For example, L'Oreal Men's Expert promoted its skincare range on dry-cleaner hangers. When customers picked up their shirt, they found a $2 coupon and a message, "Your shirt doesn't come with wrinkles, why should your face?" This novel execution shows how media and creative can be integrated to generate powerful advertising.

## Setting Media Objectives

In terms of setting media objectives, the planner needs to address several key decisions:

- Who do we want to talk to? [Target market/ audience definition]

- How often does an audience member need to hear our message before it is noticed or achieves the desired consumer response? [Effective frequency]

- When do audiences cease to notice the ad, or become tired of seeing the ad? [Advertising wear-out]

A number of key definitions are essential for media planning purposes:

> *Reach* is defined as the number of households (or people) exposed to an advertising message in a given time period.

*Frequency* is defined as the average number of times a household (or person) is exposed to an advertising message in a given time period.

*Effective frequency* refers refers to the minimum number of media exposures in order to achieve a specified communication goal

*Effective reach* refers to the reach (% of households or people) at the effective frequency level.

*Gross Ratings Points (GRPs)* is defined as reach multiplied by frequency and is a measure of overall campaign weight or intensity

With respect to reach objectives, planners must decide what proportion of the target market need to be exposed to the advertising message. It is not always be necessary to reach 100% of the target market. For new brands or brands with very low levels of awareness, it may be desirable to reach every member of the target market. However, for reminder type campaigns lower levels of reach may be all that is required. Reach objectives are normally framed in terms of a percentage of market. For example, a reach objective might read; *To reach 50% of women aged 18-25 years.*

With respect to frequency objectives, the planner must determine the optimal level of frequency in order to achieve the desired communications objective. Media planners often work with rules of thumb for setting frequency objectives that are based on an extensive body of evidence drawn from research findings. For example, empirical evidence suggests that the average consumer needs to be exposed to a message at least three times before they become aware of the brand information. This is sometimes known as the *3+ Rule.* To this basic benchmark of three exposures, media planners recognise that to achieve higher-level communication goals, such as persuasion and lead generation, higher levels of frequency are required. To achieve simple brand awareness, three exposures may be sufficient, but for consumers to act on that awareness, higher levels of exposure may be required. Some theorists have developed sophisticated decision models to assist with planning optimal frequency levels.

Planners also need to consider the combined effects of reach and frequency (GRPs). In an intensive campaign, the schedule will utilise both broad reach (expose more people to the message) and high frequency (expose people multiple times to the message). The overall campaign weight has implications for budgets and for media selection. In an intensive campaign (heavy weight campaign), the media strategy is normally skewed towards main media, which remains the most cost efficient means of reaching large audiences with the relatively high frequency needed to create stable brand awareness levels.

## Media Channel Strategy

The first channel decision that needs to be made is whether to use a *concentrated* channel strategy or a *dispersion* channel strategy:

Concentrated channel strategy

> In a concentrated approach the planner invests most of the media expenditure in a single medium or a narrow range or media.

Dispersion channel strategy

In a dispersion approach, the planner spends across a broad range of advertising media. The main advantage of a concentrated channel strategy is that the advertiser has the opportunity to achieve a high share-of- voice and can become the dominant advertiser in the selected channels. A dispersion approach allows the advertiser to reach a broader cross-section of the defined target market.

With reach and frequency objectives firmly in place, the planner turns to determining the media mix and selecting appropriate media vehicles to carry the message. The media planner must determine the way that the advertising budget is to be allocated across the relevant media options (e.g. 50% TV; 30% Mags; 15% Digital and 5% Out-of-home). To make these decisions, the planner requires a detailed understanding of the target market and its media usage habits. Accordingly, the design of the media channel strategy requires a rich understanding of the media options and what each type of media can accomplish in terms of audience reach and engagement.

| Overview of Main Advertising Media | | |
|---|---|---|
| Medium | Advantages | Disadvantages |
| | **Television**<br>• Excellent mass market coverage<br>• Low relative cost (i.e. cost per thousand exposures)<br>• Colour, sound and movement permit many creative possibilities<br>• Good attention | • Minimal geographic & demographic audience selectivity<br>• Cost of spots is high (in absolute terms)<br>• Production costs are high<br>• Clutter<br>• Short life; ephemeral<br>• Consumers can avoid exposure (via zapping) |
| | **Radio**<br>• Spots are relatively inexpensive<br>• High levels of reach and frequency<br>• Some geographic and demographic selectivity<br>• Message delivered in consumer's home or work environment<br>• Short life | • Lacks vision and movement - limited creative possibilities<br>• Non-standard rate structures |
| | **Newspapers**<br>• Broad coverage of national markets<br>• High level of frequency and immediacy<br>• Message delivered in home, car or work environment<br>• Often the last medium to be consulted before shopping<br>• Short lead times (for production and insertion) | • Short life<br>• Low attention<br>• Clutter<br>• Limited use of colour<br>• Poor production quality |

| | | |
|---|---|---|
| | **Magazines**<br>• Able to select targeted audiences<br>• Longer life - more opportunities to notice ads<br>• High quality production values<br>• Can add to brand prestige<br>• High pass-along effect | • Expensive<br>• Long lead times<br>• Limited frequency |
| | **Cinema**<br>• Some audience selectivity<br>• Able to reach youth audiences<br>• Captive audience - high attention<br>• High production values and big screen viewing<br>• Relatively low cost<br>• Minimal clutter | • Creativity can be challenging<br>• Minimal frequency<br>• Limited reach |
| | **Transit** (*bus, train, tram, cable-car, taxi*)<br>• Able to reach audiences when they are out shopping<br>• Relatively low cost | • Minimal audience selectivity<br>• Creativity can be a challenge |
| | **Out-of-home** (*billboards, posters, street furniture, signage, footpath art etc.*)<br>• Able to reach mobile audiences<br>• Good creative possibilities<br>• Some audience selectivity (e.g. billboards near sports venues) | • Static<br>• Creativity can be a challenge |
| | **Internet-based and digital**<br>• Immediacy<br>• Potential for two-way communications<br>• Relatively low cost<br>• Pay per number of views<br>• Able to reach global audiences<br>• Selective targeting | • Creativity can be a challenge<br>• Clutter |

## Media Audience Research

Media audience research is a central feature of media planning. The main purpose of media research is "to eliminate waste in advertising by objectively analysing the media available for promoting products and services." Identifying and profiling the audience for print media, broadcast media, cinema and online media magazine or newspaper is a specialized form of market research, often conducted on behalf of media owners. In most nations, the advertising industry, via its peak industry associations, endorses a single media research company as the official provider of audience measurement for main media. The methodology used by the official provider then becomes known as the *industry currency* in audience measurement. Industry members fund the audience research and share the findings. In a few countries, where the industry is more fragmented or where there is no clear peak industry association, two or more competing organisations may provide audience measurement services. In such countries, there is said to be no industry currency.

Research companies employ different methodologies depending on where and when media is used and the cost of data collection. All these methods involve sampling - that is taking a representative sample of the population and recording their media usage which is then extrapolated to the general population. Media owners typically share research findings with prospective advertisers, while selected findings are available to the general public via the media research company or an entity, such as a broadcast commission, established to administer the audience research process.

Media research acts as form of industry regulation and the legitimacy of research methodologies and provision of audience metrics. Media owners rely on metrics of both audience size and audience quality to set advertising rates.

Measures of media audience that are of especial interest to advertisers include:

Print Media

- *Circulation:* the number of copies of an issue sold (independently assessed via a circulation audit)

- *Readership:* the total number of people who have seen or looked into a current edition of the a publication (independently measured via survey)

- *Readership profiles:* Demographic/ psychographic and behavioural analysis of readership (sourced from Readership surveys)

Broadcast Media

- *Average audience:* The average number of people who tuned into the given time or given program, expressed in thousands or as a percentage. Also known as a *Rating* or T.A.R.P (Total Audience Rating Point).

- *Audience share:* The number of listeners (or viewers) for a given channel over a given time period, expressed as a percentage of the total audience potential for the total market. (The audience share is normally calculated by dividing a given channel's average audience by the average audience of all channels).

- *Audience potential:* The total number of people in a given geographical area who conform to a specific definition, such as the number of people with a television (or radio) set or the total number of people aged 6-12 years. Population potentials are normally derived from the census figures and are used to estimate the potential market reach.

- *Audience movement by session:* The number of listeners (or viewers) who switch channels during a given time period.

- *Audience profile:* Analysis of audience by selected demographic, psychographic or behavioural variables.

- *Cumulative audience (CUME):* The number of *different* listeners (or viewers) in a given time period; also known as *reach*.

- *People Using Television (PUT):* The number of people (or households) tuned to any channel during a given time period.

Out-of-home Media

- *Opportunities to see (OTS)* - a crude measure of the number of people who were exposed to the medium, For example, the number of cars that drive past an outdoor billboard in a given time period

Internet and Digital Media

- *Site traffic*: The number of visitors to a website within a given time period (e.g. a month)

- *Unique visitors*: The number of *different* visitors to a website within a given time period

- *Site stickiness*: The average length of time a person remains on a page (a measure of audience engagement)

- *Average page views per visit*: The number of different pages generated by a visitor to a site (a measure of engagement)

- *Click through rate (CTR)*: The number of people who clicked on an advertisement or advertising link

- *Cost per click* (CPS): The average cost of generating one click through

- *Rate of return visitors*: The number of unique visitors who return to a site

- *Bounce rate*: Number of site visitors who leave the site within a predetermined time (seconds)

Although much of the audience research data is only available to subscribers and prospective advertisers, basic information is published for the general public, often as topline survey findings. The type and depth of freely available information varies across geographic markets. The following table provides principal sources of information for main media audience research in English speaking markets.

| Sources of Broadcast Audience Data *( Main English speaking markets)* | | |
|---|---|---|
| **Country** | **Radio** | **Television** |
| Australia | Commercial Radio Australia | OZTAM |
| Britain | Radio Joint Audience Research | Broadcasters' Audience Research Board |
| Canada | Numeris* | Numeris* |
| India | Nielsen Media Research's RAM | TAM Media Research (a joint venture between AC Nielsen and Kantar Media) |
| Ireland | Broadcast Authority of Ireland | TAM Ireland |
| Malaysia** | Nielsen (Malaysia) | Nielsen Media (US) and Kantar Media *** |
| New Zealand | Radio NZ | Think TV **** |
| United States | Nielsen Audio | Nielsen ratings |
| South Africa | Broadcast Research Council | Broadcast Research Council |

## Media Buying

While it is certainly possible for advertisers to purchase advertising spots by dealing directly with media owners (e.g. newspapers, magazines or broadcast networks), in practice most media buying is purchased as part of broader negotiations. Prices depend on the advertiser's prior relationship with the network, the volume of inventory being purchased, the timing of the booking and whether the advertiser is using cross-media promotions such as product placements. Advertising spots purchased closer to air-time tend to be more expensive.

Many advertisers opt to centralise their media buying through large media agencies such as Zenith or Optimedia. These large media agencies are able to exert market power through volume purchasing by buying up space for an entire year. Media agencies benefit advertisers by providing advertising units at lower rates and also through the provision of added value services such as media planning services.

Buying advertising spots on national TV is very expensive. Given that most media outlets use dynamic pricing, rates vary from day to day, creating difficulties locating indicative rates. However, from time to time, trade magazines publish adrates which may be used as a general guide. The following table provides indicative advertising rates for selected popular programs on American national television networks, broadcast during prime time viewing hours.

| Advertising rates, selected US TV programs, 2010 | | | |
|---|---|---|---|
| **Program/ Network** | **Network** | **Broadcast Day / Time** | **Rate (per 30 second spot)** |
| *American Idol* * | Fox | Day not stated, prime-time | $360,000 - $490,000 |
| *Sunday Night Football* | NBC | Sunday, prime-time | $435,000 |
| *Family Guy* | Fox | Sunday, prime-time | $215,000 |
| *Saturday Night College Football* | ABC | Saturday, prime-time | $140,000 |

| *Survivor* | CBS | Thursday, prime-time | $152,000 |
| *The Biggest Loser* | NBC | Tuesday, prime-time | $128,000 |
| *Jay Leno* ** | NBC | Mon-Fri, Late-night | $48,800 - $65,000 |

## Pulling it all Together: Media Tactics and the Media Schedule

### Sample Media Schedule

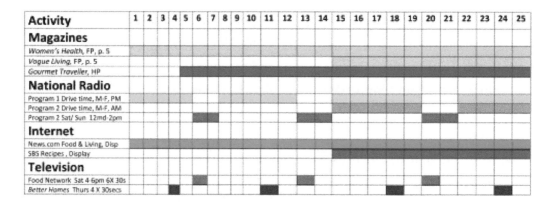

The media schedule includes specific detail such as dates, media, position, placement

A media schedule is a program or plan that "identifies the media channels used in an advertising campaign, and specifies insertion or broadcast dates, positions, and duration of the messages."

Broadly, there are four basic approaches to scheduling:

### Broad Approaches to Scheduling

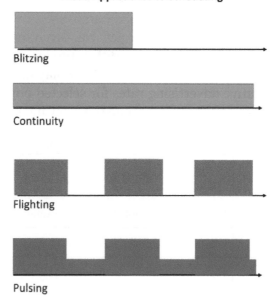

Blitzing, continuity, flighting and pulsing are the main schedule patterns

*Blitzing*: one concentrated burst of intense levels of advertising, normally during the initial period of the planning horizon

*Continuity*: a pattern of relatively constant levels throughout a given time period or campaign (i.e. a relatively expensive spending pattern)

*Flighting*: an intermittent pattern of bursts of advertising followed by no advertising (i.e. a moderate spending pattern)

*Pulsing*: a combination of both continuity and pulsing; low levels of continuous advertising followed by bursts of more intense levels of advertising; (i.e. alternates between a high spending pattern and a low spending pattern)

Empirical support for the effectiveness of pulsing is relatively weak. However, research suggests that continuous schedules and flighted schedules generally result in strong levels of consumer recall. With flighted schedules, the second and subsequent flights tend to build on the first flight, resulting in awareness levels similar to a continuous schedule, but often with reduced costs.

A major consideration in constructing media schedules is timing. The advertiser's main is to place the advertisement as close as practical to the point where consumers make their purchase decision. For example, an advertiser who knows that a grocery buyer does a main shop on Saturday afternoons and a top-up shop on Wednesday nights, may consider TV to achieve general brand awareness, supplemented with radio spots to reach the shopper while he or she is driving to the supermarket or regular place of purchase on the days when the majority of consumers carry out their shopping.

## Measuring Advertising Effectiveness

Advertising is a major expense for most firms. Improved advertising effectiveness can deliver strategic and tactical advantages. Advertising managers are expected to be accountable for advertising budgets. Hence, any campaign will invest in a number of measures to evaluate whether budgets are being well spent to assess whether the campaign requires improvement. The main aim of effectiveness testing is to improve consumer response rates.

Broadly, there are two classes of effectiveness testing:

- *Pre-testing*: qualitative and quantitative measures taken prior to running an advertisement with a view to gauging audience response and eliminating potential weaknesses

- *Post-testing*: qualitative and quantitative measures taken during or after the target audience has been exposed to the message or advertising campaign and used to track the extent to which advertising is achieving the desired communications objectives

## Pre-testing

Sound pre-testing exhibit the following characteristics:

(i)     relevant to the communications objectives;

(ii)   agree on how results are to be used;

(iii)  use multiple measures;

(iv)   be theoretically grounded - i.e. based on a model of human response (e.g. hierarchy of effects);

(v)    consider multiple exposures;

(vi)   test comparably finished executions;

(vii)  control the exposure context;

(viii) define the relevant sample;

(ix)   demonstrate reliability and validity;

(x)    take baseline (i.e., pre-exposure) measurements and/or use control groups

Specific types of pre-testing include copy tests, projective techniques and increasingly, a diverse range of physiological and/or biometric testing methods.

## Copy Testing

Copy testing is a general term used to describe tests that evaluate advertising copy and creative executions.

## Mock-ups

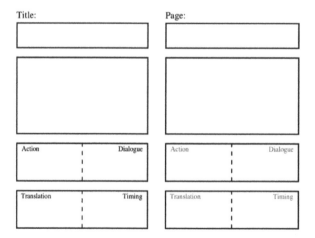

Researchers often use mock-ups of the final creative with varying degrees of finished artwork. A sample of respondents is invited to look at the mock-ups and subsequently asked a series of questions designed to capture advertising effects that are of interest for the given campaign. Mock-ups are useful for gauging audience response to the proposed advertising copy. Mock-ups can be used in face-to-face interviews, small focus groups or theatre tests.

Types of advertising mock-ups that are used in copy testing, both print and broadcast advertising, include:

To pre-test advertisements, researchers might use face-to-face interviews,
small focus groups or theatre tests for larger audiences

*Rough art* refers to very rough drawings of the creative concept

*Comps* (abbreviation of "composition art") refers to rough art included along with copy,
slogans and campaign strategy

*Ripomatics* are very rough versions of a TV commercial that include stock images and film
footage designed to emulate the look and feel of the final creative execution.

*Photomatics* include photographs along with the intended audio

*Storyboards* are a sequence of drawings or photographs accompanied by relevant copy and
designed to resemble the final creative execution of a film or digital TV commercial.

*Animatics* are a more elaborate version of a storyboard and include dialogue, sound tracks
and voice overs that are intended to represent a more polished version of the final creative
execution.

## Projective Techniques

In projective techniques, the respondent is invited to project themselves into the advertisement. There are many projective techniques including word association, sentence completion
and story completion. These techniques assume that when exposed to incomplete stimuli, respondents use underlying attitudes or motivations to complete the storyline, thereby revealing
their fears and aspirations that may not surface under more direct questioning. Projective
techniques have been found to be very useful for evaluating concepts and generating new
concepts.

## Phsysiological Measures

For decades, researchers have been using physiological measures to study such responses to advertising. These measures include such things as pupil response, electrode mal response (GSR) and
heart rate. These measures have been shown to be effective measures of attention and the strength

of emotional response. With the rise of consumer neuroscience, researchers have begun to use a much wider range of measures to investigate cognitive responses as well as emotional responses.

Some of the techniques used to measure consumer responses to advertising stimuli include:

## Pupil Dilation

The amount of pupil dilation (also known as *pupillometry*) is believed to provide a relatively precise measure of the amount of mental effort associated with a task. Pupil dilation tests became a staple of advertising copy testing during the 1970s as a way to test consumers' responses to television commercials  Pupil dilation suggests a stronger interest in the stimuli and can be associated with arousal and action. Pupil dilation is not only used to study advertising, but also used to investigate product and package design.

## Eye Tracking

While viewing an advertisement, a sensor aims a beam of infrared light at the eye and follows the movement to show the spot on which the viewer is focusing. This shows the length of time the viewer focuses on each element of the image and the general sequence used to interpret the image. Eye tracking is often used to fine tune advertising executions. Research studies suggest that eye tracking is associated with brand recognition, but less useful for brand recall.

## Galvanic Skin Response (GSR)

Galvanic skin response uses a device, called a galvanometer, which is very similar to a lie detector, designed to measure minute amounts of skin perspiration and electrical activity in the skin. Changes in skin response are associated with arousal and are an indicator of the advertisement's ability to capture attention.

## Electro-encephelograph (EEG)

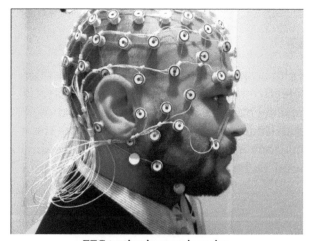

EEG testing is more invasive

An electro-encephelograph (EEG) is a device that measures changes in brain-wave activity. EEG testing can detect emotional arousal which is difficult to detect using alternative testing methods.

Arousal is an indicator of the advertisement's ability to grab attention and engage the consumer in the message. EEG testing is a cumbersome and invasive testing method which militates against routine use in advertising testing.

## Functional Magnetic Resonance Imaging (FmRI)

FmRI is a technique that enables researchers to monitor activity in specific areas of the brain. This techique has been used to identify specific brain networks associated with pleasure and arousal associated with advertising.

## Post-testing

The aim of post-testing is to provide indicators of how well a given campaign is achieving the desired communications objectives, so that corrective action and fine-tuning can occur during the campaign as well as to evaluate the effectiveness of advertising expenditure in order to provide benchmarks for future advertising programs. Techiques used in post-testing depend on the media employed, and may include such tests as Starch scores, day-after recall tests (DAR), campaign tracking, advertising ROI and other measures.

## Starch Scores

Starch scores were developed by Daniel Starch in the 1920s to evaluate the copy effectiveness of print advertisements, and are still in use today. A consumer is shown a magazine page by page and subsequently asked whether they had noticed any part an advertisement. If they answer, 'Yes', the interviewer asks the respondent to indicate which parts of the ad were noticed. For each advertisement, three scores are calculated:

(1) *Noted* - the percentage of readers who recognize the advertisement as one they previously saw in the magazine issue (designed to capture the advertisement's ability to grab attention)

(2) *Associated* - the percentage of readers who saw or read any part of the advertisement that clearly indicated the brand advertised (designed to indicate the level of brand processing)

(3) *Read most* - the percentage of readers who read half or more of the ad's written material (an indicator of reader involvement or engagement)

## Day-after-Recall Tests (DARs)

Day-after-recall (DAR) tests were developed by George Gallup in the 1940s and are still used. DAR tests provide a measure of the percentage of the people who recall something specific about an ad (e.g., sales message or a visual) the day following exposure. Interviewers ask questions designed to elicit:

(a) *Unaided recall* - when respondents remember any commercials for the product category in question

(b) *Aided recall* - when respondents remember seeing a commercial for Brand X

(c) *Copy points* - when respondents can recall what the brand showed, looked like and the main points of the commercial

## Tracking

Ad tracking or campaign tracking refers to techniques used to monitor the "in-market perfor-mance" of advertising. A particular area of concern during an advertising campaign is the problem of advertising *wear-out*. When audiences are repeatedly exposed to the same message, the level of attention begins to plateau and eventually decays. Any further repetitions may cease to be noticed or may alienate target audiences. When wear-out occurs, additional advertising expenditure is simply wasted. One way that advertisers avoid wear-out is to use *repetition with variation* - that is, the use of different executions of the same message. Campaign tracking can assist advertisers to determine when to introduce a new execution of the same advertising message.

## Advertising Return on Investment (ROI)

Advertising return on investment (advertising ROI) is designed to ensure that the right advertising tactics were employed. Good measures of advertising ROI should consider both short term and long term measures. Online campaigns and co-operative advertising are useful for building sales, while television and PR are essential to long-term brand building and customer loyalty.

## Careers in Advertising Management

Advertising management is a career path in the advertising or marketing industries. Advertising and promotions managers may work for an agency, a public relations firm, a media outlet, or may be hired directly by a company to work in their in-house agency where they would take responsi-bility for communications designed to develop the company's brands or group of brands. In the agency environment, advertising managers are often known as *account managers* and their role involves working closely with client firms. In a marketing department, the advertising manager's position can include supervising employees, acting as a liaison between multiple agencies working on a project, or creating and implementing promotional campaigns.

## Target Market

### Total Available Market, Served Available Market, Target Market

Euler diagram showing the relationship among Target Market, Served Available Market (SAM), and Total Available Market (TAM)

A target market is a group of customers a business has decided to aim its marketing efforts and ultimately its merchandise towards. A well-defined target market is the first element of a marketing strategy. Product, price, promotion, and place are the four elements of a marketing mix strategy that determine the success of a product or service in the marketplace. It is proven that businesses must have a clear definition of their target market as this can help reach its target consumers and analyze what their needs and suitability are.

A target market is a group of people considered likely to buy a product or service. A target market consists of customers that share similar characteristics, such as age, location, income and lifestyle, to which a business directs its marketing efforts and sells its products. As marketing efforts are becoming increasingly online based, the need to find the right market for marketing campaigns is essential. One of the first steps in developing an effective marketing campaign is determining an appropriate target market so that marketing goals can be set and implemented.

Target markets can be separated into primary and secondary target markets. Primary target markets are those market segments to which marketing efforts are primarily directed and secondary markets are smaller or less important. For instance, the primary target market for a jewellery store might be middle aged women who care about fashion, and their secondary target market could be middle aged men who may want to buy gifts for the women in their lives.

It is important for a business to identify and select a target market so it can direct its marketing efforts to that group of customers and better satisfy their needs and wants. This enables the business to use its marketing resources more efficiently, resulting in more cost and time efficient marketing efforts. It allows for better understanding of customers and therefore enables the creation of promotional materials that are more relevant to customer needs. Also, targeting makes it possible to collect more precise data about customer needs and behaviors and then analyze that information over time in order to refine market strategies effectively.

Target markets or also known as target consumers are certain clusters of consumers with similar or the same needs that most businesses target their marketing efforts in order to sell their products and services. Market segmentation including the following:

- Geographic - Addresses, Location, Climate, Region

- Demographic/socioeconomic segmentation - Gender, age, wage, career, education.

- Psychographic - Attitudes, values, religion, and lifestyles

- Behavioral segmentation - (occasions, degree of loyalty)

- Product-related segmentation - (relationship to a product)

Market segmentation divides the market into four main sub categories – demographic, geographic, psychographic and behavioural segmentation. After doing market segmentation the subdivision market will be much more specific and it is relatively easy to understand consumer demand, enterprises can determine their own service objects according to their business ideology, principles and production technology and marketing power. To aim at the small target market, which is easy to formulate the special marketing strategy. At the same time, in the segments of the market, the information is easy to understand and feedback, once the consumer demand changes, enterprises can rapidly change marketing strategy formulated corresponding countermeasures, in order to adapt to the change of market demand, improve the flexibility and competitiveness of enterprises. Through market segmentation, the enterprise will be able to notice every subdivision market purchasing potential, satisfying degree, competition and comparative analysis, to better meet market needs. Meanwhile, the manpower, material resources and funds of any enterprise are limited. Through market segments, after select the suitable target market, enterprises can focus more on human, financial, and material resources, to fight for the advantages of local market, and then to occupy their own target market. Segmenting the market allows marketers to better understand the group they are aiming their message at, which is more efficient than aiming at a broad group of people. Segmentation has been an essential part of marketing since industrial development induced mass production, particularly in manufacturing. This caused the focus to shift from customer satisfaction to reduction of production costs. However, as manufacturing processes became more variable, and consumer demand diversified, businesses needed to respond by segmenting the market. Businesses who were able to identify specific consumer needs were able to develop the right message for consumers within particular segments, which gave them a competitive advantage (Wedel & Kamakura, 2012). Since being introduced by Wendell R. Smith in 1956, the theory has become a key concept in marketing. Smith stated: "market segmentation involves viewing a heterogeneous market as a number of smaller homogeneous markets, in response to differing preferences, attributable to the desires of consumers for more precise satisfaction of their varying wants." (Wedel & Kamakura, 2012). Not establishing a target market will often result in a poor response from consumers, or no response at all. The aim of market segmentation for businesses is to gain a competitive advantage by having a better understanding of a specific segment than its competitors. Hunt and Arnett (2004) use the example of Black and Decker power tools, and the way the company segmented the market into three main groups. After identifying each different group, Black and Decker then designed one separate power tool range for each segment, based on their characteristics. "To target each segment, B&D uses specific products lines with different brand names" (Hunt & Arnett, 2004).

Demographic segmentation refers to aspects of a market such as age, gender, race, occupation and education. Creating a message aimed at a particular demographic allows the sender to reach a wide range of receivers, while still staying within the confines of a specific segment. "Demographic segmentation almost always plays some role in a segmentation strategy" (Thomas, 1980), and is often paired with other segments to create a slightly more specific segment. A luxury good or service may be marketed to high income earners if the marketer believes that it would be relevant across a large enough portion of the segment to make it profitable for the sender, or create the awareness intended. Certain brands only target working professionals whereas others might only target people who are at high school.

Geographic segmentation divides the market by location. This could be divided into countries, cities, towns and neighborhoods etc. Different geographic locations usually have different aspects to their environment, which allows marketers to appeal to the specific needs of each location. For example, marketers could target tractors specifically towards rural areas where there are likely to be a number of farmers who operate tractors. In contrast, it would not make sense to market those same tractors in an urban area where people are not likely to find them as useful (Thomas, 1980).

Psychographic segmentation relates to dividing a market based on how they live their everyday lives. This could encompass their values, as well as their personality, attitudes and general interests (A. S. Boote, 1984). According to Boote (1984), a popular psychographic segment in marketing is personal values. In the example used, a segment categorised by how much money a consumer is willing to spend on a product could be defined by certain inclinations when shopping. One being – "spending no more money than is necessary...even if it means not buying the best." Another orientation being – "shopping around to get the best price once I have decided on the kind of product I want to buy." By learning about these orientations, the marketer is able to gauge different attitudes of the consumers potentially being targeted.

Behavioural segmentation subdivides the market depending on how consumers behave towards a product. Consumers behave differently depending on occasions and the frequency of usage of a product. For example, a spouse may not usually spend money on flowers for their significant other, but might on Valentine's Day, as it is a special occasion. "Many Marketers believe that behaviour variables are the best starting points for building market segments" (Tatum, 2007).

Market segmentation involves subdividing the total market into groups of people who share common characteristics, to which the business can direct specific marketing efforts. Segmenting markets aims to increase sales, market share and profits by better responding to the desires of the different target customer groups. A segmentation variable is a characteristic of individuals or groups used by marketers to divide a total market into segments. Markets can generally be segmented according to four main variables: demographic, geographic, psychographic and behavioural characteristics.

One key to identifying the best target market is assessing brand loyalty involving attitudes and behaviors toward the brand. Buyer groups can be divided into the following: those loyal to the brand, those who buy your brand but also buy from competing brands, those who buy more than one competing brand, those who are regularly loyal to another brand, and new users who are entering for the first time or re-entering. Loyalty, which concerns consumer attitudes in terms of interest in competitive alternatives, overall satisfaction, involvement, and intensity, has become increasingly important in competitive markets.

## Demographic

Demographic segmentation is the process of dividing the total market according to particular characteristics such as age, gender, family size, family life cycle, income, occupation, education, religion, race, and nationality. Age and gender are two of the most commonly used demographic variables used to segment markets. Demographics are useful and widely used but should be coupled with other segmentation variables to effectively define a target market.

Gender: Due to physiological differences, males and females have very different product demands and preferences, for example, in clothing, hair care, and other lifestyle items.

Age: Consumers of different ages have different demand characteristics. Young people, for example, might demand bright, fashionable clothing, while the elderly prefer dignified and simple but elegant dress.

Income: Lower income and higher income consumers will be quite different in product selection, leisure time arrangement, social communication and communication and so on.

Occupation and education: Consumers with different occupations education levels desire different products. For example, farmers prefer to buy load-carrying bicycles while students and teachers love light, beautiful style bikes.

Family life cycle: Families can be divided into five stages based on age, marital status, and children. These are newly married, full nest, empty nest and lonely. In different stages, family purchasing power and interest in particular goods and services vary greatly.

## Geographic

Geographic segmentation is the process of dividing the total market according to geographic location, for instance region (urban, suburban, rural, city size), climate and land type. Businesses may do this because different regions may present different needs and provide different commercial opportunities. For instance, an ice cream shop would be more likely to start up in a hot location than a cold climate. Identifying regional preferences and attitudes can help campaigns to be better targeted for particular geographic areas.

## Psychographic

Psychographic segmentation is based on personality characteristics, mainly includes the consumer's personality, the life style, the social class, the motive, the value orientation. Businesses can do this by researching consumer's preferences, likes and dislikes, habits, interests, hobbies, values and socioeconomic group. These variables are concerned with why people behave the way they do and are often used effectively in conjunction with other segmentation variables. Psychographics also relates to attitudes toward certain activities like fitness, willingness to take risks, concern for the environment, political opinions, concern with fashion, and innovativeness. Values and culture are strongly linked to how people think and behave and are important aspects of segmentation variables, especially in global campaigns. Personality traits such as self-esteem, intelligence, and introversion/extroversion also affect the processing and persuasiveness of communication.

Lifestyle: Lifestyle is a particular habit of individuals or groups in the consumption, work and entertainment. Different lifestyles tend to produce different consumer demand and purchase behavior, even on the same kind of goods, there will be different needs in the quality, appearance, style, and specifications. Today, many consumers does not only buy goods to meet the material needs, it is more important to show the performance of their lifestyle, to meet the psychological needs, such as identity, status, and the pursuit of fashion.

Social class: Due to the different social class have a different social environment, different backgrounds, and different characteristics of different consumer preferences, demand for goods or services are quite different. Philip Kotler divided American society into six classes.

Upper uppers: Inheritance property, family background has famous celebrities.

Lower uppers: The extraordinary vitality in the occupation or business and get higher income or wealth.

Upper middles: They are extremely concerned about their careers,they are doing special occupations, independent entrepreneurs and managers.

Lower middles: Middle-income white-collar and blue collar workers.

Upper lowers: Low wages, life is just at the poverty line, the pursuit of wealth but no skills.

Lower lowers: The poor, often rely on long-term unemployment, or public charity relief to the people. People in different social classes, the demand for cars, clothing, furniture, entertainment, reading, there is a big difference.

Personality: Personality refers to the individual's unique psychological characteristics, this psychological characteristics of individuals and their environment to maintain a relatively consistent and lasting response. Everyone has a unique personality affecting their buying behavior. To distinguish between different personality, there is a strong correlation between the premise and specific personality with the product or brand choice, so personality can become the market segments of the psychological variables.

## Behavioural

Behavioral segmentation relates to customers' knowledge, attitude, use of product and the purchase occasion, such as special one-off or regular loyal buying. Identifying what customers want from products and the benefits they seek are important to behavioural segmentation to allow marketers to better design and select products that satisfy these needs . Many marketers believe that behavioral variables are the best starting point for market segmentation.

Opportunity: It is the time consumers buy and use the product. these opportunities include marriage, divorce, purchase, moving, demolition, admission, study, retirement, travel, tourism, holidays,and so on. It will help improve brand usage and marketing targeted. Such as travel agencies can provide specialized travel services at Christmas, stationery enterprises can begin to provide more learning supplies before new semester.

Benefit: Benefit segmentation is a kind of classification method based on the different interests of consumers from the brand products.Using the benefit segmentation method, what must be determined is the benefit people are seeking for, who are seeking these benefits, how important to them these benefits are, what brand can offer these benefits, what benefits have not been met.

User status: According to the state of use, consumers can be classified into once users, nonusers, potential users, the primary user, occasionally users and often user type, for different type of consumers the brand should use different marketing strategies and methods. The brand who has a high market share can focus more on the potential users to change them to the actual users, such as leading brands; some small businesses can only be used as an often user services.

Brand loyalty: Consumer loyalty is the most valuable wealth of enterprises. Consumers can be divided into four types according to their brand loyalty: True Friends, Butterflies, Barnacles and Strangers.

True Friends: They are the highest level of the four types and the most important part of the customer group. For example, a fan of a Swiss knife, they will keep telling their friends and neighbors the benefits of this knife, their frequency of use. These loyal customers will be free of charge to the brand, and continue to recommend to others. For any business, this is the most popular type of customer.

Butterflies: Butterflies are not particularly loyal, but have spent money on your products and brought in good revenue. An example of a butterfly would be someone that supports Microsoft in general, but buys the iPhone since it happened to be the best available phone on the market.

Barnacles: Here is where some companies, especially B2B companies, find a surprising amount of their customer base falls into. Barnacles are loyal customers, but they are loyal customers that rarely make a purchase, and may not bring in much of a profit. A great example would be a customer that buys one cup of coffee at your coffee shop, and then comes in every day for the next month to use your free WiFi without making a purchase.

Strangers: Due to different reasons, some customers are not loyal to certain brands. Generally speaking, enterprises should avoid targeting strangers, because they will never become a sincere customer, they have little contribution to the development of enterprises.

Market segmentation is a marketing strategy that categorises or segments the market based on their characteristics. These categories or segments are demographic, geographic, psychographic, psychological and behavioural (market segmentatio n). Market segmentation is an effective tool for marketers and is said to be a fundamental concept in modern marketing. It realises that individuals have different motivations, desires, lifestyles and tastes. Market segmentation's effectiveness is in ability to divide a market into segments which management can then use to effectively make further informed decisions. By targeting individuals with similar characteristics, management can create an effective marketing plan for their targeted buyers. They can market their brand and develop and advertise products that relate at deeper and personal level with their targeted customers (market segmentationi).

## Demographic

Demographic segmentation is the division of the market based on an individual's sex, age, income and life style. Demographic segmentation is used the most frequently by businesses in comparison to the other market segments. This is possibly because of the ability to easily collect this kind of information. The national census of a country collects this kind of information. Demographic segmentation has been challenged with scholars stating that demographic segmentations such as age and sex are poor behaviour predictors. However, other studies have showed that demographic segmentation is accurate and effective when analysed as a group rather than looking at an individual's behaviour.

## Geographic

Geographic segmentation is the division of the market based on an individual's location. This can be either nationally, regionally or locally and was said to be the first kind of segmentation used practically. Geographic segmentation can be used to compare certain habits and characteristics of different locations. UK's National Food survey showed that Scotland's consumption of vegetables and beverages was much lower than England and Wales.

## Psychological

Psychological segmentation is the division of the market based on an individual's personality, attitudes and interests. This type of segmentation is based around understanding an individual's traits, habits and reason. Segmenting the market based on personality has been met with controversy. Some scholars state that personality is too complex of a segment and shows disappointing results. Psychological studies have seen trends in certain traits displayed by individuals. Mothers who were difficult to persuade to buy products for their child displayed high-esteem personality traits. In contrast, those portraying low self-esteem were easily influenced. Studies have also shown a correlation between aggression and cigarette smokers in men. This kind of research can prove beneficial to a company segmenting their target market psychologically.

## Behavioural

Behavioural segmentation is the division of the market based on how individuals react or respond to a product. Behavioural segmentation relates to a consumer's brand loyalty, usage rate and usage situation, to name a few. Consumer's purchase products primarily for their value or benefits and this is the basic element of this segmentation. Many marketers believe the best starting point for constructing market segmentation is behavioural segmentation. This is understandable as this segment deals an individual's reaction to the product exclusively. Businesses can use an individual's reaction to price drops, technology changes and product status to determine how to market their product or service effectively.

## Marketing Mix (4 P's)

The 4p's, also widely known in the market as the Marketing Mix, is a business tool commonly used in marketing that covers four pieces to help a particular business successfully reach and deliver its products to target consumers. This four piece includes Product, Price Promotion, and Place. It is proven to be known that marketing mix is a crucial part that must be implemented in marketing as it has the ability to determine a group of a particular target consumer's needs, likes, and most importantly suitability.

## Marketing Mix

Marketing mix is a combination of all of the factors at the command of a marketing manager to satisfy the target market McCarthy (1964). The Marketing mix can also be commonly known as the 4P's (product, price, place and promotion) these are the main parts of the marketing mix and can be distinguished in the real world. 'Product', is the item or service that is being offered, through there features and benefits to the consumer these can ether be high or low quality products. 'Price', is a combination of the price of the item, payment methods and the price changes, changes in price can give one company have a competitive advantage. 'Place' is where the service or item is sold; it also includes the distribution channels in which the company received the service or item. Finally 'Promotion' is the market communication achieved by, personal selling, advertising, public and customer relations etc. (Cengiz & Yayla (2007); Shahhosseini & Ardahaey (2011) and Suprihanti (2011))

## The First Signs of the Marketing Mix

The fist emergence of the 'marketing mix' was claimed to be in 1965 by Borden, at this stage it wasn't split into the 4P's but instead it was just a few things that helped make up marketing (Rafiq & Ahmed, 1995). The 4P's were debated at length and then the theory of 8P's was suggested by Goldsmith (1999), the eight included product, price, place, promotion, participants, physical evidence, process and personalization.

## Price

Price is the most important factor in determining customer satisfaction; the customer weighs up the price of the item or service and then work out if it will benefit them (Virvilaite et al., 2009). The value of the item to consumers will be different for each individual and therefore the amount that the customer is willing to pay to get the item or service also changes (Nakhleh, 2012). Price is the only one of the 4P's that is required to be set at a certain amount after the other 3 P's have been set. This means that the price of an item can fluctuate dramatically. Out of the 4P's price is also the most important for a business due to the fact that it is the only way that a company can make profit and therefore making sure that the price is right is the most important thing that a company can do. The 3 remaining P's are what are called the variable costs for an organization. The company has to use money to promote, design and distribute a product and the price of the item means has to allow the company to make a profit. The price of the item or service must reflect the supply and demand so that the company is losing out on possible profits from having the price too low or losing sales due to the price being too high. Price can be very influential, a high price may be the best way to gain large short term profits it may not be suitable to keep it at this high price as time goes on. Price can also be used as a means to advertise, short stints of lower prices increase sales for a short time promoting the company.

## Product

A 'Product' is either a good or service, which is offered to the market by a company. The definition is "something or anything that can be offered to the customers for attention, acquisition, or consumption and satisfies some want or need" (Riaz & Tanveer (n.d); Goi (2011) and Muala & Qurneh (2012)). The product is the main part of the marketing mix where the company can show the different parts of their product compared to that of another product created by another company. The differences can include quality, look, brand name or size. By creating a unique product it allows for a gap in the market to be filled or a new market to be created increasing profits for the company.

## Place

Riaz & Tanveer (n.d) wrote that Place refers to the availability of the product to the targeted customers. So a product or company doesn't have to be close to where its customer base is but instead they just have to make their product as available as possible. This improves efficiency and therefore price can be dropped intern increasing sales and profit. For max profits a company's distribution channels must be effective in enticing the customer.

## Promotion

Promotion refers to "the marketing communication used to make the offer known to potential customers and persuade them to investigate it further ". May comprise elements such as: advertising, PR, direct marketing and sales promotion.

## Strategies for Reaching Target Markets

Marketers have outlined four basic strategies to satisfy target markets: undifferentiated marketing or mass marketing, differentiated marketing, concentrated marketing, and micromarketing/ nichemarketing.

## Mass Marketing (Undifferentiated Marketing)

Undifferentiated marketing/Mass marketing is a method which is used to target as many people as possible to advertise one message that marketers want the target market to know (Ramya & Subasakthi). When television first came out, undifferentiated marketing was used in almost all commercial campaigns to spread one message across to a mass of people. The types of commercials that played on the television back then would often be similar to one another that would often try to make the viewers laugh, These same commercials would play on air for multiple weeks/months to target as many viewers as possible which is one of the positive aspects of undifferentiated marketing. However, there are also negative aspects to mass marketing as not everyone thinks the same so it would be extremely difficult to get the same message across to a huge number of people (Ramya & Subasakthi).

## Differentiated Marketing Strategy

Differentiated marketing is a practice at which different messages is advertised to appeal to certain groups of people within the target market (Ramya & Subasakthi). Differentiated marketing however is a method which requires a lot of money to pull off. Due to messages being changed each time to advertise different messages it is extremely expensive to do as it would cost every time to promote a different message. Differentiated marketing also requires a lot time and energy as it takes time to come up with ideas and presentation to market the many different messages, it also requires a lot of resources to use this method. But investing all the time, money and resources into differentiated marketing can be worth it if done correctly, as the different messages can successfully reach the targeted group of people and successfully motivate the targeted group of people to follow the messages that are being advertised (Ramya & Subasakthi).

## Concentrated Marketing Or Niche Marketing

Niche marketing is a term used in business that focuses on selling its products and services solely on a specific target market. Despite being attractive for small businesses, niche marketing is highly considered to be a difficult marketing strategy as businesses may need thorough and in-depth research to reach its specific target market in order to succeed.

According to (Caragher, 2008), niche marketing is when a firm/ company focuses on a particular aspect or group of consumers to deliver their product and marketing to. Niche marketing, is also primarily known as concentrated marketing, which means that firms are using all their resources and skills on one particular niche. Niche marketing has become one of the most successful marketing strategies for many firms as it identifies key resources and gives the marketer a specific category to focus on and present information to. This allows companies to have a competitive advantage over other larger firms targeting the same group; as a result, it generates higher profit margins. Smaller firms usually implement this method, so that they are able to concentrate on one particular aspect and give full priority to that segment, which helps them compete with larger firms.

Some specialities of niche marketing help the marketing team determine marketing programs and provide clear and specific establishments for marketing plans and goal setting. According to, (Hamlin, Knight and Cuthbert, 2015), niche marketing is usually when firms react to an existing situation.

There are different ways for firms to identify their niche market, but the most common method applied for finding out a niche is by using a marketing audit. This is where a firm evaluates multiple internal and external factors. Factors applied in the audit identify the company's weaknesses and strengths, company's current client base and current marketing techniques. This would then help determine which marketing approach would best fit their niche.

There are 5 key aspects or steps, which are required to achieve successful niche marketing. 1: develop a marketing plan; 2: focus your marketing program; 3: niche to compete against larger firms; 4: niche based upon expertise; 5: develop niches through mergers.

Develop A Marketing Plan: Developing a market plan is when a firms marketing team evaluates the firms current condition, what niches the company would want to target and any potential competition. A market plan can consist of elements such as, target market, consumer interests, and resources; it must be specific and key to that group of consumers as that is the speciality of niche marketing.

Focus Your Marketing Program: Focusing your marketing program is when employees are using marketing tools and skills to best of their abilities to maximise market awareness for the company. Niche marketing is not only used for remaining at a competitive advantage in the industry but is also used as a way to attract more consumers and enlarge their client database. By using these tools and skills the company is then able to implement their strategy consistently.

Niche To Compete Against Larger Firms: Smaller and medium-sized firms are able to compete against niche marketing, as they are able to focus on one primary niche, which really helps the niche to grow. Smaller firms can focus on finding out their clients problems within their niche and can then provide different marketing to appeal to consumer interest.

Niche Based Upon Expertise: When new companies are formed, different people bring different forms of experience to the company. This is another form of niche marketing, known as niche based on expertise, where someone with a lot of experience in a specific niche may continue market for that niche as they know that niche will produce positive results for the company.

Developing Niches Through Mergers: A company may have found their potential niche but are unable to market their product/ service across to the niche. This is where merging industry specialist are utilised. As one company may have the tools and skills to market to the niche and the other may have the skills to gather all the necessary information required to conduct this marketing. According to (Caragher, 2008), niche marketing, if done effectively, can be a very powerful concept.

Overall, niche marketing is a great marketing strategy for firms, mainly small and medium-sized firms, as it is a specific and straightforward marketing approach. Once a firm's niche is identified, a team or marketers can then apply relevant marketing to satisfy that niche's wants and demands.

Niche marketing also closely interlinks with direct marketing as direct marketing can easily be implemented on niches within target markets for a more effective marketing approach.

## Direct Marketing

Direct marketing is a method which firms are able to market directly to their customers needs and wants, it focuses on consumer spending habits and their potential interests. Firms use direct marketing a communication channel to interact and reach out to their existing consumers (Asllani & Halstead, 2015). Direct marketing is done by collecting consumer data through various means. An example is the internet and social media platforms like Facebook, Twitter and Snapchat. Those were a few online methods of which organisations gather their data to know what their consumers like and want allowing organisations to cater to what their target markets wants and their interest (Lund & Marinova, 2014). This method of marketing is becoming increasingly popular as the data allows organisations to come up with more effective promotional strategies and come up with better customize promotional offers that are more accurate to what the customers like, it will also allows organisations to uses their resources more effectively and efficiently and improve customer management relationships. An important tool that organisations use in direct marketing is the RFM model (recency-frequency-monetary value) (Asllani & Halstead, 2015). Despite all the benefits this method can bring, it can be extremely costly which means organisation with low budget constraints would have trouble using this method of marketing.

## The Psychology of Target Marketing

A principal concept in target marketing is that those who are targeted show a strong affinity or brand loyalty to that particular brand. Target Marketing allows the marketer or sales team to customize their message to the targeted group of consumers in a focused manner. Research has shown that racial similarity, role congruence, labeling intensity of ethnic identification, shared knowledge and ethnic salience all promote positive effects on the target market. Research has generally shown that target marketing strategies are constructed from consumer inferences of similarities between some aspects of the advertisement (e.g., source pictured, language used, lifestyle represented) and characteristics of the consumer (e.g. reality or desire of having the represented style). Consumers are persuaded by the characteristics in the advertisement and those of the consumer.

## Online Targeting

Targeting in online advertising is when advertisers use a series of methods in order to showcase a particular advertisement to a specific group of people. Advertisers use these techniques in order to find distinct individuals that would be most interested in their product or service. With the social media practices of today, advertising has become a very profitable industry. People are constantly exposed to advertisements and their content, which is key to its success. In the past, advertisers had tried to build brand names with television and magazines; however, advertisers have been using audience targeting as a new form of medium. The rise of internet users and its wide availability has made this possible for advertisers. Targeting specific audiences has allowed for advertisers to constantly change the content of the advertisements to fit the needs and interests of the individual viewer. The content of different advertisements are presented to each consumer to fit their individual needs.

The first forms of online advertising targeting came with the implementation of the personal email message The implementation of the internet in the 1990s had created a new advertising medium; until marketers realized that the internet was a multibillion-dollar industry, most advertising was limited or illicit

Many argue that the largest disadvantage to this new age of advertising is lack of privacy and the lack of transparency between the consumer and the marketers. Much of the information collected is used without the knowledge of the consumer or their consent Those who oppose online targeting are worried that personal information will be leaked online such as their personal finances, health records, and personal identification information.

Advertisers use three basic steps in order to target a specific audience: data collection, data analysis, and implementation. They use these steps to accurately gather information from different internet users. The data they collect includes information such as the internet user's age, gender, race, and many other contributing factors. Advertisers need to use different methods in order to capture this information to target audiences. Many new methods have been implemented in internet advertising in order to gather this information. These methods include demographic targeting, behavioral targeting, retargeting, and location-based targeting.

Much of the information gathered is collected as the consumers are browsing the web. Many internet users are unaware of the amount of information being taken from them as they browse the internet. They don't know how it is being collected and what it is being used for. Cookies are used, along with other online tracking systems, in order to monitor the internet behaviors of consumers.

Many of these implemented methods have proven to be extremely profitable. This has been beneficial for all three parties involved: the advertiser, the producer of the good or service, and the consumer. Those who are opposed of targeting in online advertising are still doubtful of its productivity, often arguing the lack of privacy given to internet users. Many regulations have been in place to combat this issue throughout the United States.

## Media Planning

Media planning is generally outsourced to a media agency and entails sourcing and selecting optimal media platforms for a client's brand or product to use. The job of media planning is to determine the best combination of media to achieve the marketing campaign objectives.

In the process of planning, the media planner needs to answer questions such as:

- How many of the audience can be reached through the various media?

- On which media (and ad vehicles) should the ads be placed?

- How frequent should the ads be placed?

- How much money should be spent in each medium?

Choosing which media or type of advertising to use can be especially challenging for small firms with limited budgets and know-how. Large-market television and newspapers are often too expensive for a company that services only a small area (although local newspapers can be used). Magazines, unless local, usually cover too much territory to be cost-efficient for a small firm, although some national publications offer regional or city editions.

## Developing a Media Plan

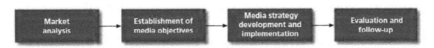

Developing a Media Plan

The fundamental purpose of a media plan is to determine the best way to convey a message to the target audience. A media plan sets out a systematic process that synchronizes all contributing elements in order to achieve this specific goal. The media plan is broken down into four stages; market analysis, establishment of media objectives, media strategy development and implementation, and evaluation and follow-up.

Similarities can be made to other marketing concepts such as the consumer decision-making process with comparisons such as, increasing brand awareness and knowledge, improving brand image, and the maximization of customer satisfaction.

The first phase of any media plan is the initial market analysis, which consists of a situation analysis and the marketing strategy plan. These form the basis of information which the rest of the media plan is reliant on. The purpose of a situation analysis is to understand the marketing problem, in relation to their competitors. For example, undertaking an internal and external review or competitive strategy evaluation.

The marketing strategy plan should establish specific objectives and goals that will solve the marketing problems that developed. Once the market analysis is complete the improved knowledge gained should indicate a proffered target market. Enabling the marketers to understand where the prime advertising space would be to gain sufficient exposure, what factors effect that certain demographic, and how to promote to the audience effectively.

The second phase in the media plan is the establishment of media objectives. Just as the marketing analysis lead to specific marketing objectives, this phase will result in explicit media objectives; such as creating a positive brand image through stimulating creativity. These objectives should be limited to those that can only be obtained through media strategies.

Media strategy development and implementation is the third phase and is the point in the process that is directly influenced by the actions from previously determined objectives. Actions that meet these objectives are taken into consideration with following criteria; media mix, target market, coverage consideration, geographic coverage, scheduling, reach & frequency, creative aspects & mood, flexibility, or budget considerations. Each of these criteria are explained briefly below:

- Media Mix – A combination of communication and media channels use that is utilized to meet marketing objectives, such as social media platforms and magazines.

- Target Market – A specific group of consumers that has been identified to aim it's marketing and advertising campaigns towards, as they are the most likely to purchase the particular product.

- Coverage Consideration – To alter the level of exposure of media to the target market, whilst minimizing the amount of overexposure and saturation into other demographics.

- Geographic Coverage – Increased emphasis of exposure to a certain area where interest may thrive, whilst reducing exposure to areas they have less relevance.

- Scheduling – The concept of aligning communication activity to coincide with peak potential consumer exposure times, such as around a big sports game on television.

- Reach & Frequency – The decision to have a certain message seen / heard by a large number (reach) or expose the same message to a smaller group more often (frequency).

- Creative Aspects & Mood – Different mediums for communication should be considered when developing a campaign. Social media might be more effective to generate emotion than a billboard poster on a main road.

- Flexibility – In order to adapt to rapidly changing marketing environments it is important for strategies to be flexible. Such as unique opportunities in the market, media availability or brand threats.

- Budget Considerations – The relationship between the effectiveness of a media campaign and the cost involved needs to be carefully managed. There should be an optimal level of response from the consumer for the price for the exposure.

The final phase in the media plan is to evaluate the effectiveness of the plan and determine what follow-up is required. It is important to assess whether each individual marketing and media objective was met, as if they were successful it will be beneficial to use a similar model in future plans.

## Components of a Media Plan

- Define the marketing problem. Where is the business coming from and where is the potential for increased business? Does the ad need to reach everybody or only a select group of consumers? How often is the product used? How much product loyalty exists? How to build awareness or drive consideration through use of optimized contextual based material?

- Translate the marketing requirements into media objectives. Must the ad reach people in a wide area? Then mass media, like newspaper and radio, might work. If the target market is a select group in a defined geographic area, then direct mail could be best.

- Define a media solution by formulating media strategies. For example, the rule of thumb is that a print ad must run three times before it gets noticed. Radio advertising is most effective when run at certain times of the day or around certain programs, depending on what market is being reached.

Media planning's major steps include:

- 1 - Targeting,
- 2 - Environmental scan,
- 3 - Understanding the audience,
- 4 - Determination of content,
- 5 - Control.

## Advertising Media Includes

- Social (Facebook, Twitter, Instagram, Pinterest, etc.)
- Television ( TVC, television commercial)
- Radio (AM, FM, XM, Pandora, Spotify)
- Newspapers
- Magazines (consumer and trade)
- Outdoor billboards
- Ambient experiential
- Public transportation
- Direct Media (DM)
- Digital advertising (such as web-based, mobile and mobile applications)
- Search Engine Marketing (SEM, keyword marketing in search engines)
- Specialty advertising (on items such as matchbooks, pencils, calendars, telephone pads, shopping bags and so on)
- Other media (catalogs, samples, handouts, brochures, newsletters and so on)

## Factors to Consider When Comparing Various Advertising Media

- Reach - expressed as a percentage, reach is the number of individuals (or homes) to expose the product to through media scheduled over a period of time.

- Frequency - using specific media, how many times, on average, should the individuals in the target audience be exposed to the advertising message? It takes an average of three or more exposures to an advertising message before consumers take action.

- Cost per thousand - How much will it cost to reach a thousand prospective customers (a method used in comparing print media)? To determine a publication's cost per thousand, also known as CPM, divide the cost of the advertising by the publication's circulation in thousands.

- Cost per point - how much will it cost to buy one rating point of your target audience, a method used in comparing broadcast media. One rating point equals 1 percent of the target audience. Divide the cost of the schedule being considered by the number of rating points it delivers.

- Impact - does the medium in question offer full opportunities for appealing to the appropriate senses, such as sight and hearing, in its graphic design and production quality?

- Selectivity - to what degree can the message be restricted to those people who are known to be the most logical prospects?

Reach and frequency are important aspects of an advertising plan and are used to analyze alternative advertising schedules to determine which produce the best results relative to the media plan's objectives.

Calculate reach and frequency and then compare the two on the basis of how many people will be reached with each schedule and the number of times the ad will connect with the average person. Let's say the ad appeared in each of four television programs (A, B, C, D), and each program has a 20 rating, resulting in a total of 80 gross rating points. It's possible that some viewers will see more than one announcement—some viewers of program A might also see program B, C, or D, or any combination of them.

For example, in a population of 100 TV homes, a total of 40 are exposed to one or more TV programs. The reach of the four programs combined is therefore 40 percent (40 homes reached divided by the 100 TV-home population).

Researchers have charted the reach achieved with different media schedules. These tabulations are put into formulas from which the level of delivery (reach) for any given schedule can be estimated. A reach curve is the technical term describing how reach changes with increasing use of a medium.

Now assume the same schedule of one commercial in each of four TV programs (A, B, C, D) to determine reach versus frequency. In our example, 17 homes viewed only one program, 11 homes viewed two programs, seven viewed three programs, and five homes viewed all four programs. If we add the number of programs each home viewed, the 40 homes in total viewed the equivalent of 80 programs and therefore were exposed to the equivalent of 80 commercials. By dividing 80 by 40, we establish that any one home was exposed to an average of two commercials.

To increase reach, include additional media in the plan or expand the timing of the message. For example, if purchasing "drive time" on the radio, some daytime and evening spots will increase the audience. To increase frequency, add spots or insertions to the schedule. For example, if running three insertions in a local magazine, increase that to six insertions so that the audience would be exposed to the ad more often.

Gross rating points (GRPs) are used to estimate broadcast reach and frequency from tabulations and formulas. Once the schedule delivery has been determined from reach curves, obtain the average frequency by dividing the GRPs by the reach. For example, 200 GRPs divided by an 80 percent reach equals a 2.5 average frequency.

## Reach and Frequency

In media planning, reach is one of the most important factors, as the whole media planning is all about reach. The Purpose of the reach is exposure of brand (Belch & Belch, 2012). The higher the reach; the higher the brand exposure (Belch & Belch, 2012). And of course, higher exposure means high chances of new customers. When it comes to media planning most of the businesses decide well in advanced what their target market would be (Belch & Belch, 2012). They Choose their target market on the assumption that they already know who their customers would be (Ossi, 2015). Even though, choosing a target market for reach in media planning could be a very successful way to get to the potential customers of the brand, but this method leaves out potential customers outside of the target market; Customers the brand thought were not important to reach to (Ossi, 2015). Smart businesses also reach outside of their targeted market in order to know other segments that could be targeted (Ossi, 2015). Therefore, starting with a broader reach and then choosing target markets would be a much informed decision; derived from actual data rather than just assumption. A broader reach is also beneficial for general brand awareness, otherwise many people outside of the targeted market never even get to hear about the brand.

In media planning, frequency is also a very important factor to consider. Most small businesses say "We just want to see what happens", which just wastes their money leading to disappointment on media planning ("The importance of frequency," n.d.). In Advertisement, once is just not enough ("The importance of frequency," n.d.). The biggest problem in media planning is; advertisers assume that someone would see their advertisement, would walk in their store and just buy something!!That is definitely not how it happens. There are five different steps for buying cycle a consumer goes through before actually purchasing something (Euan, 2013). These are Awareness, interest, need, Comparison and purchase ("The importance of frequency," n.d.). Frequency is important as it pushes a consumer towards the actual step of purchasing something. The understanding of how exactly a consumer goes through the buying cycle is very essential to grasp the importance of frequency in media planning. Initially, the idea of reach is there to increase the awareness and exposure, but people forget. 80% of people forget the advertisement they see within 24 hours or even sooner ("The importance of frequency when advertising," 2016). So, frequency is also important for awareness - deceasing the chances for forgetfulness. Secondly, frequency builds familiarity, familiarity builds trust ("The importance of frequency," n.d.) and trust builds interest. In need, it is absolute that the consumer is aware of the company and have somewhat trust/ interest. And again, frequency plays essential role is remembrance, trust and interest. Higher frequency also helps to beat the competition ("The importance of frequency when advertising," 2016). And finally, the consumer is on the final step of buying cycle the purchase, with the help of frequent advertisement. Without the good amount of frequency, a consumer would be very unlikely to get to the purchasing step. Thus, frequency is important because consistence advertisement reinforces top of mind brand awareness, brand favor-ability and brand loyalty among the current and potential consumers. Patience and effective frequency plays a great role in a business's long term success.

## Models of Consumers

Consumers approach the marketplaces differently; they go though the buying decision process differently as it gets impacted by internal and external forces. Researchers have attempted to understand the dynamics of consumer decision making and they have classified *four varying views* and perspectives, the underlying forces operating within consumers that could be employed to approach the marketplace. These are i) Economic ii) Cognitive iii) Passive iv) Emotional.

i)   *Economic view:* According to the economic perspective of studying consumers, the consumer is regarded as being rational. The model assumes that there exists in the market a state of perfect competition; the consumer is aware of the various alternatives; he has the knowledge and ability to rank all of these; and he finally takes a rational decision. He takes a decision and makes a choice as after taking into account the cost and benefit, and the overall value in economic terms.

ii)  *Cognitive view:* The consumer is regarded as being a problem solver, who searches for products to fulfill his needs/wants. Consumer decisions are based on information gathering and processing. The consumer is believed to take decisions after a lot of thought and deliberation, so as to get maximum benefit and value.

iii) *Passive view:*  Here, the consumer is regarded as irrational and impulsive, who easily succumbs to the selling and promotional efforts of the marketer. It is assumed that the consumers are submissive to the self-serving interests of the marketer and the salespersons are powerful.

iv)  *Emotional view:* The consumer is regarded as being emotional and impulsive who takes decisions based on moods and emotions. Marketers must put in efforts and create positive mood and emotions.

## Models of Consumer Behavior

The consumer models refer to *varying orientations and perspectives with which consumers approach the marketplace and how/why they behave as they do.* They refer to *how the varying orientations impact the buying decision process and overall buyer behavior.*

Various models have been proposed by researchers; these models can be classified as (a) General models (b) Specific models. This session deals with the General Models. The Specific Models are dealt with in the next session.

*General Models:* There are four models that fall under this category, viz. *Economic model, Psychological model, Psychoanalytic model and Sociological model*

i)   *The Economic model:* The economic model explains buying behavior from an economic perspective; The assumption is that resources are scarce viz. a viz unlimited needs; a consumer seeks value: he wants maximum benefit at minimum cost. The economic models showed concern as to how scarce resources were allotted to satisfy the unlimited needs and wants. Economic models can be further classified into *Micro economic models* and *Macro economic models.*

*Micro economic models:* The micro economic models focus on the act of purchasing; they focus on what an average consumer would purchase and in what quantity; they also ignore why and how the needs/wants get prioritized, and how the behavior is underpinned.

According to the micro economic view, consumers are rational in nature and value utility. With resources being scarce, they would allocate money on their purchases in a way that satisfies them maximally. The consumer decisions are thus based on benefit to cost ratio; the consumer would settle on an alternative that provides the highest ratio in terms of marginal utility.

The limitations of studying consumer behavior with this orientation is that consumers are not always rational, and they seek average /adequate satisfaction and not total satisfaction. Also, consumers assess the benefit to cost ratio differently; they define the two variables "cost" and " benefit" variedly; the issue is subjective. The view is also silent about other forces that operate during the buying process.

*Macro economic models*: The macro economic models focus on the overall trend in the economy that has an impact and is also impacted upon by buying patterns. They focus on the aggregate flows in the economy. Conclusion about consumer behavior are made after analyzing such flows. This approach could also be studied with two orientations:

a) Relative income hypothesis: A persons' expenses is influenced by his social surrounding and group. With his income being constant, the relative expenses and the resultant savings will not change, until and unless, there is a big change in the total income. The hypothesis holds that what and how much a consumer spends is not solely dependent on income, but is influenced by peers.

b) Permanent income hypothesis: Even if the total income increases, people initially exhibit inertia towards spending as they want to accumulate wealth; so purchasing pattern does not change immediately.

The limitations of studying consumer behavior with this orientation is that the view is silent about other forces that operate during the buying process.

ii) The Psychological model: The psychological model, also called the Learning Model or the Pavlovian Learning Model, was proposed by classical psychologists led by Pavlov. According to this model, consumption behavior and decision making is a function of interactions between human needs and drives, stimuli and cues, responses and reinforcements.

People have needs and wants; They are driven towards products and services (stimuli and cues), which they purchase (response), and they expect a satisfying experience (rewards and reinforcements); Repeat behavior would depend on reinforcement received.

The model believes that behavior is deeply affected by the learning experiences of the buyers; and learning is a product of information search, information processing, reasoning and perception. Reinforcement leads to a habit formation and the decision process for an individual becomes routinized, leading to brand loyalty. Consumers also learn through trial and error and resultant experiences that get stored in our memory.

The limitations of studying consumer behavior with this approach is that the model seems incomplete. Learning is not the only determinant in the buying process and the decision making. The model totally ignores the role played by (a) other individual determinants like perception, personality (the sub-conscious), attitudes; as well as (b) interpersonal and group influences.

iii) Psychoanalytic model: The psychoanalytic model was proposed by Sigmund Freud. The model tries to explain consumer behavior as a resultant of forces that operate at subconscious level. The individual consumer has a set of deep seated motives which drive him towards certain buying decisions.

According to the model, buyers needs and desires operate at several levels of consciousness. Not all of the behavior is understandable and explainable by the person. Also not all of human behavior is overtly visible and explainable. Sometimes, the behavior may not be realized and understood by the person himself. Such causes can be understood by drawing inferences from observation and casual probing.

There have been two more contributions that have been made to the psychoanalytic approach, these are *a) Gestalt model  b) Cognitive theory*

*Gestalt model:* The model based on Gestalt principles (meaning "patterns and configuration") lays emphasis on the perceptual processes that impact buying behavior.  According to this model, consumption behavior and decision making is based on how a consumer perceives a stimuli ( the product and the service offering and the 4 Ps) viz a viz. the external environment and his own prior experiences.

*Cognitive theory*: The model proposed by Leon Festinger, views the consumer as one who faces a feeling of anxiety (dissonance), while he is making a purchase; this is because he is faced with many alternatives, all of which seem desirable. Post-purchase, this dissonance increases even further. There is an imbalance in the cognitive structure; and the consumer tries to get out of this state as soon as he can. So a buyer gathers information that supports his choice and avoids information that goes against it.

iv) Sociological model: The model is based on findings of Thorstien Veblen, and focuses on the role played by social groups and social forces. A person's consumption pattern and buying behavior is affected by social factors; his family, friends, peers, social groups, reference group and culture have a major role to play. According to the model, man is perceived as a "social animal", and thus he conforms to norms of its culture, sub culture and groups amongst which he operates. Emulative factors and social influences have a big role to play in consumer decision making.

Table: MARKETING IMPLICATIONS OF MODELS

| MODEL | IMPLICATION |
|---|---|
| **Economic model:** | - Consumers' are price sensitive; they look out for a value proposition and thus buy those offerings that give them more benefit vis a vis cost. |
|  | - As a marketer, this implies that he should offer to customers a Value proposition. |
| a) Micro economic | - Deals and sales promotion can also impact buying decisions to his favor. |
| b) Macro economic | Consumer purchases are affected by fluctuations in the economy. |

| Psychological model | - Consumers learn from experiences of self and others. |
| | - They would buy products and services that are rewarding and would bring positive reinforcement. |
| | - Marketers should arrange for product demonstrations. |
| | - They should also encourage trials: free samples, testing and sales promotion can help elicit trials. |
| | - If the consumer finds the product usage satisfying, he would go for a repeat purchase. |
| **Psychoanalytic model:** | - While consumers may look for functional benefits while buying a product, they are also affected by hedonic elements. The marketer also needs to understand the consumer psyche and design the 4Ps accordingly; this has implications on pricing and promotion. |
| a) Gestalt | This has implications for brand management; branding, brand associations and imagery. |
| b) Cognitive | - This is related to post-purchase behavior; the marketer needs to help minimize the consumer's post-purchase dissonance. |
| **Sociological model** | - A persons' purchase behavior is affected by his culture, sub culture and social group; |
| | - Opinion leadership and social group appeals. |

## Model of Consumer Buying

The consumer market is defined as end user markets. Also called Business to Consumer markets, or B2C markets, the product and service offering is bought by the consumer for his personal use. The decision making process in consumer markets is different from the one that takes place in business or industrial markets.

According to Kotler and Armstrong, the basic model of consumer decision making process comprises three major components, viz., *marketing and other stimuli* (these act as influences), *the buyer's black box* (these are related to the consumer) *and the buyer responses* (this is the response part). The components/processes as well as the working dynamics are explained as follows:

1. Marketing and other stimuli: A consumer is confroned with a stimulus in the environment. This stimulus could be of two kinds;

a) One that is presented by the marketer through the *marketing mix or the 4Ps*, product, price, place and promotion;

- product: attributes, features, appearance, packaging etc.

- price: cost, value, esteem (prestige)

- place: location and convenience, accessibility

- promotion: advertising, sales promotion, personal selling, publicity, direct marketing.

b) The other that is presented by the *environment*, and could be economic, technological, political and cultural.

2. Buyer's black box: The stimuli that is presented to the consumer by the marketer and the environment is then dealt with by the buyer's black box. The buyer's black box, comprises two sub components, viz., the buyer's characteristics and the buyer decision process.

The *buyers characteristics* could be personal, psychological, cultural and social.

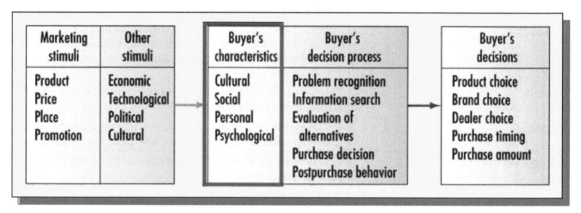

Model of Buyer Behavior

a) *Personal*:

- age & life-cycle stage (family life cycle: single, newly married couples, full nest I, full nest II, full nest III, empty nest I, empty nest II, solitary survivor

- occupation (occupation affects consumption patterns)

- economic situation

- lifestyle (pattern of living as Activities, Interest, Opinions, AIOs)

- personality (personality is defined in terms of traits; these are psychological characteristics which lead to relatively consistent patterns of behavior towards the environment) & self-concept (self-concept is reflective of identity; how a person perceives himself including attitudes, perceptions, beliefs etc). Products and brands also have a personality; consumers are likely to choose such brands whose personalities match their own self.

b) *Psychological*:

- motivation (motives; urge to act to fulfil a goal or satisfy a need/want)

- perception (ability to sense the environment and give meaning to it through the mechanisms of selection, organization and interpretation).

- learning (a relatively permanent change in behavior as a result of ones' experience; relates to memory; learning could be experiential based on direct experience or conceptual based on indirect experience; consumer learning could be based on marketing communication/seller provided information, personal word of mouth and/or experiential).

- beliefs (thoughts that a person holds about something; these are subjective perceptions about how a person feels towards an object/person/situation) and attitudes (a favorable or unfavorable disposition/feeling towards an object, person or a situation).

c) *Cultural*:

- culture (a sum total of values, knowledge, beliefs, myths, language, customs, rituals and traditions that govern a society). Culture exerts the broadest and the deepest influence; eg. Influences on our eating patterns, clothing, day to day living etc. Cultural influences are handed down from one generation to the next and are learned and acquired).

- sub-culture (subset of culture: smaller groups of people within culture with shared value systems within the group but different from other groups; identifiable through demographics).

- social class: ordered and relatively permanent divisions/startifications in the society into upper, middle lower classes; members in a  class share similar values, interests, lifestyles and behaviors; the division is based on combination of occupation, income, education, wealth, and other variables.

d) *Social*:

- family: most important influence; (there occurs in a family what is referred to as socialization; family of orientation: parents and siblings; family of procreation: spouse and children; further some decisions are husband dominated, some are wife dominated and some are joint; roles played by family members), family life cycle (stages through which a family evolves; People's consumption priorities change and they buy different goods and services over a lifetime).

- friends and peers, colleagues.

- groups: reference groups {these are people to whom an individual looks as a basis for personal standards; they are formal and informal groups that influence buying behavior; reference groups could be direct (membership groups) or indirect (aspirational groups); reference groups serve as information sources, influence perceptions, affect an individual's aspiration levels; they could stimulate or constrain a person's behavior}.

- opinion leaders (they influence the opinion of others based on skills, expertise, status or personality).

- roles & status: the role refers to the expected activities and status is the esteem given to role by society.

Research and studies into these factors can provide a marketer with knowledge that can help him serve the consumers more effectively. These characteristics affect the *buying decision process*, which comprises five steps:

a) *Problem recognition*: This is the first stage where a person recognizes that there is a problem or a need to fulfill. This may either be an actual state (AS Type), where a problem has arisen and needs to be sorted out; the product is failing, or the consumer is running short of it, and thus needs a replacement. A problem could also be a desired state (DS Type), where there is an imbalance between the actual state and the desired state; another product seems better and superior to the one that is being currently used, and so the consumer wants to buy it.

A need could be triggered off by an internal stimulus or an external stimulus. Marketers need to identify what could trigger a particular need.

b)  *Information search*: After a need is recognized, the consumer goes for an information search, so as to be able to make the right purchase decision. He gathers information about the product category and the variations, various alternatives and the various brands. Such a search could be ongoing, specific or incidental.

The consumer could recalls information that is stored in his memory (comprising information gathered and stored, as well as his experiences, direct and indirect). He could also seek information from the external environment.

The sources of information search could be *personal* (family, friends, peers and colleagues), *commercial* (marketers' communication in the form of advertising, salespersons, publicity etc), *public* (mass media, consumer forums, government rating agencies) and *experiential* (self and others' experiences). Personal contacts are highly influential sources, public sources are highly credible.

c)  *Evaluation of alternatives*: Once the consumer has gathered information and identified the alternatives, he compares the different alternatives available on certain features. These are those features that a consumer considers in choosing among alternatives; these could be functional/utilitarian in nature (benefits, attributes, features), or subjective/emotional/ hedonic (emotions, prestige etc.).The consumer also uses decision rules that help a consumer simplify the decision process. At the end of the evaluation, purchase intentions are formed.

d)  *Purchase decision*: After the consumer has evaluated the various alternatives, he selects a particular brand. Consumer purchases may be trials/first purchases or repeat purchases. The consumer may further have to make decisions on where to buy from, how much to buy, whom to buy from, when to buy and how to pay. It is noteworthy that a purchase intention(desire to buy the most preferred brand)may not always result in a purchase decision in favor of the brand; it could get moderated by attitudes of others and unexpected situational factors.

e)  *Post purchase behavior*: After the purchase, the consumer uses the product and re evaluates the chosen alternative in light of its performance viz. a viz. the expectations. He could be experience feelings of neutrality (Performance meets expectations), satisfaction (Performance exceeds expectations) or dissatisfaction (Performance falls short of expectations). This phase is significant as it (i) acts as an experience and gets stored in the memory; (ii) affects future purchase decisions; (iii) acts as a feedback.

3.  Buyer responses: While in the black box, the buyer also takes a decision with respect to the product, brand, dealer, timing and amount.

# Model of Industrial Buying

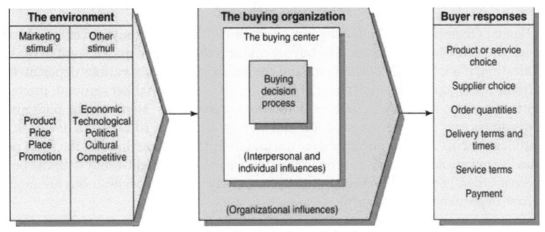

Model of Business Buyer Behavior

The business/industrial market is defined as a market that buys, transforms/processes and sells further, either for further transformation/processing or, for consumer use. The business market consists of all the organizations, that buy goods and services for further use in the production and supply of other goods and services that are sold to others. Also called Business to Business markets, or B2B markets, the product and service offering is bought by one business organization and further processed/transformed/assembled consumer for further sale either to another business consumer or a personal consumer. The business markets are very different from consumer markets; they are huge in terms of size and investment; contain fewer but larger and bulkier buyers; they are geographically concentrated; it's a derived demand and there is more inelasticity; demand also fluctuates very rapidly. The buying situation that an industrial buyer faces could range between a straight rebuy, a modified-rebuy and a new-task. These situations are based on the complexity of the problem being solved, the newness of the product requirement, the risk involved, the number of people involved in the buying process, the time available in hand.

With business markets being different than industrial markets, the decision making process in business/industrial markets is also different from the one that takes place in consumer markets. The buying decision is taken in a very formal and professional manner by a group of people who are referred to as the buying center. It is highly formalized, bureauctartic and very complex. The buyers and sellers work very closely and try to build long term alliances and partnerships.

According to Kotler and Armstrong, the basic model of business consumer decision making process comprises three major components, viz., *the environment* (these act as influences), *the buying organization* (these are related to the buying center, the decision process and the influences) *and the buyer responses* (this is the response part). The components/processes as well as the working dynamics are explained as follows:

1. The Environment: The environment surrounding the business organization comprises the *marketing stimuli* in terms of the marketing mix or the 4Ps, product, price, place and

promotion; It also comprises the *other stimuli* in terms of economic, technological, political, cultural and competitive environment. They environment acts as a stimulus to act; it provides strengths and opportunities and also helps identify weaknesses and threats.

2.  The Buying Organization: The buying organization comprises the buying center which goes through the entire buying process. The buying center is the decision making unit of the buying organization; it is a formally defined unit and comprises people from various departments and functional areas; the various members of the unit, vary in personal background, interest and preferences as also their buying motives, habits and orientations. Membership, power balance and dynamics vary for different products and buying situations. In case of a new-task, when the product/service is being purchased for the first time, the engineering and the R&D person-nel have a major role to play and act powerful; In cases of the straight-rebuy (routine purchas-es; repeat orders) and modified-rebuy situations (where product specifications are modified), purchase department acts powerful.

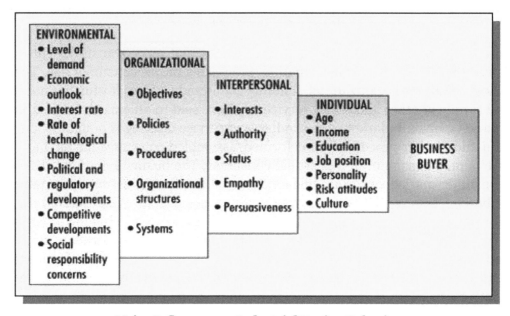

**Major Influences on Industrial Buying Behavior**

There are various factors that influence the buying decision in industrial buying behavior, viz, en-vironmental, organizational, interpersonal and individual.

a) *Environmental*:

*   Economic: Various stages in the business cycle (inflation, depression, recession etc) and their resultant impact on money flows in the economy, level of demand , government ori-entation towards economy and monetary policies (interest rates etc).

*   Technological: Rate of technological change; Technology transfer and adoption; Technolo-gy versus environment; Kind of technology adopted.

*   Competitive: Amount of competition (number of competitors); Nature of competition; Dy-namics of competition.

- Political: Political stability/instability; Governmental philosophy and orientation towards investment, growth and development.

- Natural environment: Availability of natural resources; Impact of industry on the environment; Environmental depletion; Environmental pollution; Waste and disposal etc.

b) *Organizational*:

- Philosophy and orientation of the founder, directors and executives.

- Company vision, mission and strategy.

- Objectives of the company.

- Policies and procedures for purchase (Centralized versus decentralized; Quality versus price; Short term versus long term contracts; Intranet and extranet; Supply chain management; Partnership management).

- Structures, systems for purchase: Buying center constituents, power dynamics and balances.

c) *Interpersonal and Individual:* The buying center comprises people from various departments and functional areas. Every constituent is an individual in himself. He is different from others in terms of demographic and psychographic backgrounds in terms of age, income, personality, risk attitude, culture etc. The buying centre is diverse in terms of varying interests and orientations towards buying, as well as varying interests, authority, status, empathy, and persuasiveness.

The decision making process in industrial buying is much more elaborate and complex than consumer buying. Robinson and Associates have identified eight stages and called each of the stages as buyphases.

a) *Problem recognition*: The buying process begins when someone in the organization identifies a need. A need could be triggered off by an internal stimulus or an external stimulus.

b) *General need description*: The product/service requirement is laid out in very broad terms.

c) *Product specification*: Then the concerned department/person specifies the product's characteristics and requirements.

d) *Supplier search*: Business organizations generate for themselves a list of vendors. This list is drawn up from trade directories, websites, trade shows etc. In case of a straight rebuy or a modified rebuy, the buyer can refer to such a database. In cases of a new-task, he would have to search for new vendors.

e) *Proposal solicitation*: Thereafter, the buyer would invite suppliers to submit their trade proposals; such an invitation could be placed in the newspapers, trade journals and company websites. The vendors are asked to submit details related to the product specifications, features, price, delivery time and period etc,

f) *Supplier selection*: After the proposals have been submitted by the vendors, the buyer would go in for an evaluation of the suppliers. The buying center would establish the evaluative criteria, i.e. the basis on which the vendors would be evaluated. These criteria would vary across products/services, buying situations etc. In cases of government organization, the prime consideration while evaluating suppliers is the price. The buying center needs to take decisions on:

- how many suppliers to use.

- whether quality is a major determinant or price is a major determinant.

- total evaluation of the supplier, including his reputation.

g) *Order-routine specification*: Once the busying center has taken a decision on the selection of the vendor, the formal requisition is made in terms of listing the technical specifications, quantity required, delivery terms, negotiated price, payment terms, damages, return policies etc.

h) *Performance review*: The buyer reviews the performance of the chosen supplier(s) on a regular basis. This evaluation helps the buyer later in cases of straight rebuy and modified rebuy. On the basis of an evaluation, the relationship/contract with the supplier is continued or terminated.

3. Buyer responses: While in the black box, the buyer also takes a decision with respect to the product/service choice, supplier choice, order quantity, delivery terms and times, service terms and payment.

## Working Relationships between Constructs and the Model

Through their model, Howard and Sheth explain the buying decision process that a buyer undergoes, and the factors that affect his choice decision towards a brand. The process starts when the buyer is exposed to a stimulus. As a result of the exposure, stimulus ambiguity occurs, which leads to an overt search for information. The information that is received is contingent upon the interplay between the attitudes and the motives. In other words, the search for information and the conclusions drawn would be filtered by perceptual bias (that would be a result of attitude, confidence, search and motives). It may alter the existing patterns of motives and choice criteria, thereby leading to a change in the attitude towards the brand, brand comprehension, motives, purchase intention and/or action. The final purchase decision is based on the interaction between brand comprehension, strength of attitudes towards the brand, confidence in the purchase decision and purchase intention. The actual purchase is influenced by the buyer's intentions and inhibitors, which he confronts. The entire process is impacted by various exogenous variables like the importance of purchase, price, time available to make the purchase, social and cultural influences etc. After the purchase, the buyer experiences satisfaction if the performance matches and exceeds expectation; this satisfaction would strengthen brand comprehension, reinforce the confidence associated with the buying situations, and strengthen the intention to repeat purchase of the brand. With a satisfying purchase decision, the buyer learns about buying in similar situations and the behavior tends to get routinized. The purchase feedback thus influences the consumers' attitudes and intention.

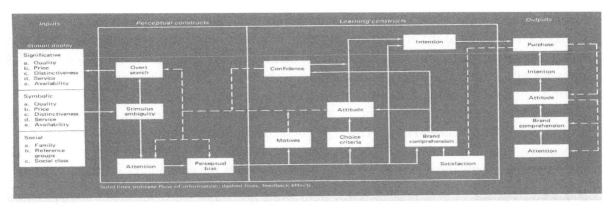

Howard-Sheth Model of Buyer Behavior

*An Assessment of the Model:* The model is an integrative model that incorporates many of the aspects of consumer behavior; it links together the various constructs/variables which may influence the decision making process and explains their relationship that leads to a purchase decision. It highlights the importance of inputs to the consumer buying process. It was one of the first models to divulge as to what constitutes loyalty towards a specific product. It helped gain insights in to the processes as to how consumers' process information. The model is user friendly and is one of the few models which has been used most commonly and tested in depth. However, the limitation lies in the fact that the various constructs cannot be realistically tested; some of the constructs are inadequately defined, and thus do not lend to reliable measurements.

i) *Nicosia's model of Consumer Decision Process* (1966): The model proposed by Francesco Nicosia in the 1970s, was one of the first models of consumer behavior to explain the complex decision process that consumers engage in during purchase of new products. Instead of following a traditional approach where the focus lay on the act of purchase, Nicosia tried to explain the dynamics involved in decision making. Presenting his model as a flow-chart, he illustrated the decision making steps that the consumers adopt before buying goods or services; decision aiming was presented as a series of decisions, which follow one another. The various components of the model are seen as interacting with each other, with none being essentially dependent or independent; they are all connected through direct loops as well as feedback loops. Thus, the model describes a flow of influences where each component acts as an input to the next. The consumer decision process focuses on the relationship between the marketing organization and its consumers; the marketing organization through its marketing program affects its customers; the customers through their response to the marketer's action, affects the subsequent decisions of the marketer; the cycle continues.

The various components that are further distinguished into main fields and subfields of the model are *marketer's communication affecting consumer's attitude, consumer's search and evaluation, purchase action, consumption experience and feedback.* The first field ranges from the marketer (source of message) to the consumer (attitude); the second from the search for to the evaluation of means/end(s) relation(s) which forms the preaction field; the third field relates to the act of purchase; and the fourth to feedback. The output from one field acts as the input for the next. These are explained as follows:

1.  Marketer's communication affecting consumers' attitude: This comprises Field 1 (i.e."from the source of a message to the consumers' attitude").The consumer is exposed to the firm's attributes through the marketing communication; this marketing communication could take place impersonally via mass media (TV, newspaper, websites, etc) as well as personally. The information could relate to the firm attributes as well as the product, price and distribution. This message relating to the firm's attributes affects the consumers' perception, predisposition and attitude toward the firm and its offering. Of course, the impact on perception and attitude is also dependent upon the consumer's personal characteristics, values, experiences, culture, social influences etc. Thus, the marketer's communication affects the consumers' attitude.

2.  Consumer's search and evaluation: After an attitude is formed, the consumer moves to Field 2 of the model, i.e. the consumer's search for and evaluation of means/end(s) relation(s) which forms the preaction field. The consumer searches for information about the product category and the varying alternatives, and thereafter evaluates the various brands on criteria like attributes, benefits, features etc. These criteria could be based on his learning and past experiences as well as the marketer's inputs. This step creates a motive in the mind of the consumer to purchase the product.

3.  Purchase action: The motivated state leads to Field 3 of the model, i.e. the decision making on the part of the consumer and the act of purchase. The consumer finally gets into action and buys the product from a chosen retailer.

4.  Consumption experience and feedback: The purchase action leads a consumer to Field 4 of the model which is consumption experience and feedback. After purchasing the product, and the resultant consumption, the consumer may have two kinds of experiences. A positive experience in terms of customer satisfaction may reinforce his predisposition with the product/brand and make him loyal towards it. A negative experience on the other hand, implying consumer dissatisfaction would affect his attitude negatively, lower down evaluations about the product/brand and even block his future purchases. This Filed provides feedback to the marketer, who can modify its mix accordingly.

In the first field, the marketer communicates with the customer and promotes an unfamiliar product to him; depending upon the existing predispositions and his evaluation, the consumer develops an attitude.  In the second field, the consumer searches for information and evaluates it based on his attitudes; thereafter, he develops a motivation to act. In the third field, he makes and purchase and in the fourth field, he would provide feedback and also memorize his experience and learning for future use. Thus, the firm communicates with consumers through its marketing messages and the consumers react through an act of purchase. Both the firm and the consumer influence each other.

*An Assessment of the Model:* Nicosia's model is an integrative model that tries to integrate the body of knowledge that existed at the time of its formulation in the area of consumer behavior. It was a pioneering attempt to focus on the conscious decision-making behavior of consumers, where the act of purchase was only one stage in the entire ongoing decision process of consumers. The flowcharting approach proposed by Nicosia, simplifies and systemizes the variables that affect consumer decision making. It contributes to the step by step "funnel approach" which views consumers' movement from general product knowledge toward specific brand knowledge and from a passive position to an active state which is motivated toward a particular brand.

However, the model suffers from limitations in the sense that the model proposes assumptions, boundaries and constraints that need not be realistic. It has been argued that attitude, motivation and experience may not occur in the same sequence. Variables in the model have not been clearly defined. Factors internal to the consumer have not been defined and dealt with completely. The mathematical testing of the model and its validity are questionable.

## References

- Mudzanani, T., "A review and analysis of the role of integrated marketing communication message typology in the development of communication strategies," African Journal of Marketing Management, Vol. 7, no 8, 2015, pp. 90-97

- Krause, Tatum. "Target Marketing." Encyclopedia of Business and Finance, 2nd ed.. 2007. Retrieved March 30, 2016 from

- Corkindale, D., "Setting objectives for advertising ", European Journal of Marketing, Vol. 10, No. 3, 1976 pp.109–126

- McDonald, Malcolm (2007), Marketing Plans (6th ed.), Oxford, England: Butterworth-Heinemann, ISBN 978-0-7506-8386-9

- Percy, Rossiter, Elliott (2001). "Target Audience Considerations, in Strategic Advertising Management 2001"

- J. Scott Armstrong and Randall L. Schultz (1993). "Principles Involving Marketing Policies: An Empirical Assessment" (PDF). Marketing Letters. 4 (3): 253–265. doi:10.1007/bf00999231

- Malhotra, Naresha K. (2002), Basic Marketing Research: A Decision-Making Approach, Upper Saddle River, NJ: Prentice Hall, ISBN 978-0-13-376856-5, ISBN 0-13-376856-2. ISBN 0-13-009048-4. ISBN 978-0-13-009048-5

- Sherlock, Tracie (25 November 2014). "3 Keys to Identifying Your Target Audience". Database: Business Source Complete. Retrieved 23 March 2016

- MacKenzie, S.B. and Lutz, R.J., "An Empirical Examination of the Structural Antecedents of Attitude toward the Ad in an Advertising Pretesting Context," Journal of Marketing Vol. 53, No. 2, 1989, pp. 48-65

- Hirsh, J. B.; Kang, S. K.; Bodenhausen, G. V. (2012). "Personalized persuasion: Tailoring persuasive appeals to recipient personality traits". Psychological Science. 23: 578–581. doi:10.1177/0956797611436349

- Harrison, T.P., Lee, H.L. and Neale., J. J., The Practice of Supply Chain Management, Springer, 2003, ISBN 0-387-24099-3

- Kaleikini, Michael. "Why is it important to define a target market for your business?". Entrepreneur. Retrieved 2016-03-31

- Bharadwaj, S.G., Varadarajan, P.R. and Fahy,J., "Sustainable competitive advantage in service industries: a conceptual model and research propositions," Journal of Marketing, vol. 57, no. 3, 1993, pp 83-94

- Petty, R. E, Cacioppo, J. T., and Schumann, D., "Central and Peripheral Routes to Advertising Effectiveness: The Moderating Role of Involvement," Journal of Consumer Research, vol 10, 1983, 135-146

- J. Scott Armstrong, Roderick J. Brodie and Andrew G. Parsons (2001). "Hypotheses in Marketing Science: Literature Review and Publication Audit" (PDF). Marketing Letters. 12 (2): 171–187. doi:10.1023/a:1011169104290

- Credo (2011). "Profiling your target market. in Business: The ultimate resource". Credo. Retrieved 25 March 2016

# Consumer Groups: An Integrated Study

Consumer groups are groups who possess a need to purchase a good or service in order to satisfy them. These groups are mainly classified on the basis of number and size, regularity of contact, and structure and hierarchy. Moreover, a consumer group feels the need to take reference or compare itself with another group. The group to which a consumer group compares itself to is called a reference group. The aspects elucidated in this section are of vital importance, and provide a better understanding of consumer groups and communications.

## Consumer Groups

The term "group", may be defined as two or more people who interact with each in order to achieve mutually agreed upon goals; such goals may relate to an individual or to the many who get together for the achievement of such goals. When we speak of *consumer groups*, we refer to individuals or group of individuals or the family who have a need and desire purchasing a good or service so as to fulfill the need and derive satisfaction.

While speaking of groups, it becomes necessary to understand the various kinds of groups. Groups may be i) small or large; ii) formal or informal (based on purpose of formation, legitimacy and structure of reporting relationships). So far as consumer behavior is concerned, the focus lies on small informal groups. This is because small groups are more cohesive in nature, there is more of interaction and the members can influence the purchase patterns and consumption behavior of each other.

### Consumer Organization

Consumer organizations are advocacy groups that seek to protect people from corporate abuse like unsafe products, predatory lending, false advertising, astroturfing and pollution.

Consumer organizations may operate via protests, litigation, campaigning, or lobbying. They may engage in single-issue advocacy (e.g., the British Campaign for Real Ale (CAMRA), which campaigned against keg beer and for cask ale) or they may set themselves up as more general consumer watchdogs, such as the Consumers' Association in the UK.

One common means of providing consumers useful information is the independent comparative survey or test of products or services, involving different manufacturers or companies (e.g., *Which?*, *Consumer Reports*, etcetera).

Another arena where consumer organizations have operated is food safety. The needs for campaigning in this area are less easy to reconcile with their traditional methods, since the scientific, dietary or medical evidence is normally more complex than in other arenas, such as the electric safety of white goods. The current standards on mandatory labelling, in developed countries, have in part been shaped by past lobbying by consumer groups.

The aim of consumer organizations may be to establish and to attempt to enforce consumer rights. Effective work has also been done, however, simply by using the threat of bad publicity to keep companies' focus on the consumers' point of view.

Consumer organizations may attempt to serve consumer interests by relatively direct actions such as creating and/or disseminating market information, and prohibiting specific acts or practices,or by promoting competitive forces in the markets which directly or indirectly affect consumers (such as transport, electricity, communications, etc.).

## History

Two precursor organizations to the modern consumer organization are standards organizations and consumers leagues. Both of these appeared in the United States around 1900.

Trade associations and professional societies began to establish standards organizations to reduce industry waste and increase productivity. Consumers leagues modeled themselves after trade unions in their attempts to improve the marketplace with boycotts in the same way that trade unions sought to improve working conditions with strike action.

## Consumer Organizations in Some Countries

## International Organization

- Consumers International - International NGO
- ANEC (Europe; focus on standardization)
- BEUC (Europe; French: *Bureau Européen des Unions de Consommateurs*)
- ICRT The only independent international organization for consumer research and testing

## National Organization

## Australia

- Consumers' Federation of Australia
- Australian Consumers Association
- Australian Communications Consumer Action Network

## Belgium

- Test-Aankoop / Test-Achats

## Botswana

- Consumer Watchdog

## Brazil

- IDEC - Instituto Brasileiro de Defesa do Consumidor
- Proteste

## Canada

- Consumers' Association of Canada
- Consumers Council of Canada
- Option consommateurs

## China

- MingJian

## Denmark

- Forbrugerrådet Tænk

## Fiji

- Consumer Council of Fiji
- Fiji Consumers Association

## France

- UFC Que Choisir
- 60 Millions de Consommateurs

## Germany

- Stiftung Warentest
- Öko-Test
- Verbraucherzentrale Bundesverband (vzbv)

## India

- Consumer Guidance Society of India
- All India Consumer Protection Organization
- The Consumers Eye India
- United India Consumer's Association

- "Grahak Shakti"-Bengaluru-Karnataka-Non profit Non Political Voluntary Consumer Organisation working for the empowerment of Consumer for over Three decades.Very dedicated and doing yeomen service to the society. They have a large membership base with about 21 Life Timers who contribute their time and energy honorarily. It is driven by a passionate Managing Trustee who leads from front and puts in his money to steer the organisation. They are very principled and have earned Consumer Confidence. They have faced several crisis for being bold and uncompromising in their outlook. Remarkable indeed.

- "CONSUMER AWARENESS, PROTECTION and EDUCATION COUNCIL (CAPE COUNCIL)" is also a Major Voluntary Consumer Organization based in Bangalore. This organization has been continuously working for the welfare of Consumers.

- "Coordinated Action of Consumer & Voluntary Organisations of Karnataka"-A network of various Voluntary Consumer Organisations in the State of Karnataka with presence in 22 districts out of 30 at present.

- "Consortium of South India Consumer Organisations (COSICO)" spread out in 6 States of Southern India Viz: Karnataka, Tamil Nadu, Andhra, Telangana, Puduchery and Kerala. The idea is to share, work together and plan joint action in strengthening the Consumer Movement in these States.

## Italy

- AltroConsumo

- Unione nazionale consumatori

- Federconsumatori

- Movimento Consumatori

## Japan

- Consumers Union of Japan (founded in 1969)

- Japan Offspring Fund (founded in 1984)

## Korea

- Korea Consumer Agency (founded in 1987)

## The Netherlands

- De Consumentenbond (founded in 1953)

## Pakistan

- The Consumers Eye Pakistan (founded in 2005)  The Consumers Eye Pakistan (TCEP) is a non profit registered social welfare organization (NGO), for the protection of

Consumer rights in Pakistan since 2005. The Consumers Eye Pakistan's vision is a world where everyone has access to safe and sustainable goods and services, where the strength of the collective power is used for the good of consumers throughout Pakistan. TCEP's is working to put the rights of consumers at the heart of decision-making. TCEP host seminars and events especially on occasion of World Consumer Rights Day & World Standards Day every year with the collaboration of PSQCA and other organizations related to consumer rights protection, to create consumer awareness against unregistered, Substandard and counterfeit Products and Services. The Consumers Eye Pakistan cooperates with PSQCA to promote Quality Standard Culture in Pakistan. TCEP is actively involved with PSQCA in improving quality and standards of the citizens by advocating accountability and code of conduct in government and society to promote standardization and Quality consciousness culture in Pakistan for the benefit of consumers. TCEP's representatives have been going with the PSQCA raiding Task force team to open markets as an independent observer. TCEP represent consumers as member in different technical Committees of Standardization in PSQCA. The Consumers Eye Pakistan campaigns on the domestic and international issues that matter to consumers. TCEP seeks to hold corporations to account and demands government action to put consumer concerns first, acting as a global watchdog: campaigning against any behaviour that threatens, ignores or abuses the principles of consumer protection. The Consumers Eye Pakistan also organizes workshops, seminars and colloquiums throughout the Pakistan, bringing together people from different sections of the society, including politicians, economists, and experts from related fields, to create awareness and build opinion on nationally important issues. Carrying out studies and researches on various issues related to Consumers and consumables. TCEP publish material for consumer awareness in Pakistan. The Consumers Eye Pakistan have introduced an annual series of awards "Quality-Standard Award" in 2010 to appreciate for the highly valuable Products/Brands and services in Pakistan. This program has the official collaboration of Pakistan Standards and Quality Control Authority Ministry of Science and technology (Government of Pakistan) also have support of other organizations. Quality Standard Award is a new concept to develop a relationship of trust among consumers, producers and service providers in Pakistan. The Consumer Eye Pakistan is working to build a better Pakistan. We believe that better work with commitment and honesty can improve people's lives."

- Consumer Voice Pakistan (CVP) (founded in 2002) Consumers Voice (Pakistan) CVP is a non-profit Voluntary Social Welfare organization NGO; Working Since 2002 to empower consumers in Pakistan, with the aim of getting Pakistani consumers a fairer deal to put the rights of consumers at the heart of decision-making. CVP's vision is a world where everyone access to safe and sustainable goods and services, where the strength of the collective power is used for the good of consumers. CVP's objective is to protect the interests of the consumer, making the consumer conscious of the malpractices perpetuated in the marketplace. Consumers Voice (Pakistan) CVP formed to protect and educate consumers, represent them on all forums, and make sure that consumer goods and services are given highest priority for the benefits of consumers. Consumers Voice (Pakistan) CVP campaigns on the domestic and international issues that matter to consumers in Pakistan. This means achieving real changes in government policy and corporate behaviour while raising Voice for awareness of rights and responsibilities CVP seeks to hold corporations to account and demands government action to put consumer concerns first, acting as a watchdog: campaigning against any behaviour that threatens, ignores or abuses the principles of consumer protection. This modern movement is essential to secure a fair safe and sustainable future for consumers in a marketplace increasingly dominated by international corporations. In Pakistan, the consumer is left at the sympathy of shopkeepers and manufacturers. The markets are full of substandard and forged products are widely available for general public or consumers and these foods are semi expired, low standard and hazard for healthy lives. CVP campaign to end the menace and create awareness among the people regarding the consumer rights; it includes adequate food, clothing, shelter, health care, education and safe drinking water in Pakistan. Consumer VOICE Pakistan (CVP) publishes monthly Consumer VOICE magazine in Pakistan.

## Poland

- Federacja Konsumentów

- Stowarzyszenie Konsumentów Polskich (founded in 1995)

## Portugal

- DECO.ProTeste

## Republic of Ireland

- The National Consumer Agency (NCA) is a statutory body that defends consumer interests in the Republic of Ireland

## Romania

- Asociatia Nationala pentru Protectia Consumatorilor si Promovarea Programelor si Strategiilor din Romania/ National Association for Consumers Protection and Promotion of Programs and Strategies from Romania

## South Africa

- The National Consumer Commission

- SA National Consumer Union

## Spain

- Organización de Consumidores y Usuarios (OCU)

- ADICAE

## Switzerland

The Swiss Alliance of Consumer Organisations is the umbrella organisation of the three Swiss consumer organisations (the Stiftung für Konsumentenschutz (SKS) of German-speaking Switzerland, the Fédération romande des consommateurs (FRC) of French-speaking Switzerland and the Associazione consumatrici e consumatori della Svizzera italiana (ACSI) of Italian-speaking Switzerland).

## Uganda

- Uganda Consumer Action Network (U-CAN) is a non-government, not-for profit organisation founded in 2007 and registered as a company limited by guarantee. It works towards ensuring that consumers, especially the most vulnerable (rural poor, disabled, elderly and women) get value for their money through quick, easy, accessible and affordable alternate dispute resolution mechanisms.

## United Kingdom

In the United Kingdom, the Enterprise Act 2002 allows consumer bodies that have been approved by the Secretary of State for Trade and Industry to be designated as "super-complainants" to the Competition and Markets Authority. These super-complainants are intended to, "strengthen the voice of consumers," who are "unlikely to have access individually to the kind of information necessary to judge whether markets are failing for them." Eight have been designated as of 2007:

- CAMRA - a lobbying group concerned with the tradition and quality of beer.

- The Citizens Advice Bureau, a free service that provides legal advice, practical help and information on consumer rights across the country.

- Consumer Council for Water (formerly known as Watervoice)

- Consumer Direct (abolished per 31 March 2012 with its functions being passed to local trading standards departments and Citizens Advice Bureaux)

- Consumer Focus (formerly National Consumer Council). The Government announced as part of the October 2010 spending review that Consumer Focus will be abolished, with the Consumer Direct helpline taken over by Citizens Advice. Some of Consumer Focus' functions would transfer to Citizens Advice Bureaux, Citizens Advice Scotland and the General Consumer Council for Northern Ireland following the Public Bodies Act 2011 and any necessary secondary legislation. The transfer is expected to begin April 2013 and be complete by April 2014.

- General Consumer Council of Northern Ireland

- Good Garage Scheme, an automobile repair shop motoring scheme

- Postwatch

- Which? - formerly the Consumers Association - a consumer advocacy organisation which has substantial powers (for example to take representative actions under the Competition Act 1998) but which is primarily a lobbying organisation funded entirely by subscriptions to its regular consumer information magazine.

## United States

- Alliance for Justice

- Better Business Bureau

- Consumer Action

- Consumer Federation of California

- Consumers Union, publishers of *Consumer Reports*

- Consumer Watchdog, formerly the Foundation for Taxpayer and Consumer Rights

- FlyersRights.org

- Public Citizen

- Consumer Federation of America

- Center for Science in the Public Interest (food/nutrition)

- National Consumers League

- U.S. Public Interest Research Group

- HGRBS - Honor Guard Residential Business Services (advocacy for private home decision makers getting true results from contractors)

## Types of Consumer Groups

Groups may be classified on various bases like i) number and size; ii) regularity of contact; and iii) structure and hierarchy. The various types of consumer groups are as follows:

i) *Primary and Secondary Groups*: The distinction between *primary and secondary groups* is based on the significance/relevance of the group to an individual, and the frequency of interaction between group members.

Based on the regularity of contact and the importance given to subsequent interaction, groups may be classified as primary and secondary. When people interact with each other on a regular basis, and regard each others' opinions as valuable and significant, they are said to constitute a primary group; an individual who interacts with others regularly, is said to be a member of that primary group. For example, family, neighbours, work peers, co-workers and colleagues. Secondary groups, on the other hand, are those, where the level of interaction is infrequent, irregular and occasional, and not much of value is given to other's judgments and beliefs. When a person interacts with others on an occasional basis, he is said to be a constituent of a secondary group. So far as consumer behavior is concerned, the focus lies on primary groups.

# Consumer Reference Groups

It is a natural tendency on the part of an individual to look up to another as with comparison; each one of us looks towards another individual or a group as a point of comparison. This group to which a person looks up as a point of comparison is known as a *reference group*. A reference group may be a person or a group to which an individual looks up as a frame of reference for his general and specific acts of behavior, values, opinions, attitudes etc. The reference person or the reference group exercises tremendous influence on an individual. This is true for consumer behavior as well. A consumer always has with him in his conscious and sub-conscious state, a person or a group that he looks up to as a reference point. Consumer actually look up to reference groups because:

a) He desires information before he actually decides to go in for the purchase of a product and service offering. As reference groups are regarded as impartial and have no hidden agenda like salespersons, consumers trust the former more than the latter.

b) He wants social approval for the product/services purchased or the brands bought, and he feels that once he has this approval from the reference group, he would not face any kind of social embarrassment .

c) He feels that he would be much at ease if he does something that others approve of.

The reference group exercises impact on the manner in which a consumer selects, purchases and uses a product or service offerings and/or brands. He influences the purchase decision making process as also the purchase decisions, consumption patterns and resultant behavior. It is noteworthy that consumers have different reference groups; he may look towards one for guidance and advice of one product, and he may look towards another for purchase of another product. Gradually, the consumer begins to adopt the standards and norms used by the reference group(s) and behaves like them. Thus, marketers make effective use of reference groups in bringing about changes in a consumer's thinking and purchasing pattern.

## Types of Reference Groups

Broadly speaking, based on the *kind of contact* (regularity, frequency, direct/indirect), reference groups could be of two kinds, viz., *primary* reference groups and *secondary* reference groups. Such group(s) with which a person has a direct (face-to-face) contact and where a direct influence occurs, is known as a primary reference group(s). For example, family, friends, neighbours, superiors, peers, colleagues etc. At the time of its origin, reference groups were narrowly defined so as to include only such groups. Gradually the concept broadened to include both direct and indirect influences. So such group(s) with which a person has an indirect contact and where an indirect influence occurs, is known as a secondary reference group. For example, movie stars and celebrities, sportsmen, successful business men, political leaders, religious leaders etc.

Based on the *kind of influence* that they have, reference groups can also be classified as *normative* reference groups and *comparative* reference groups. Those groups that influence general or broadly defined values, attitudes and/or behavior are known as *normative reference groups*. For example, for a child the family acts as a normative reference group; the parents (as family of orientation) have a big role to play in making us understand our value system as well as our acts of good and bad behavior. The parents teach the child his mannerisms, as well as what he should eat, how he should dress, and how he should behave. On the other hand, those groups that influence and serve as standards for specific or narrowly defined values, attitudes and/or behavior are known as *comparative reference groups*. For example, for the same child, his friend's family or a neighbor may constitute a comparative reference group. The child desires emulating their lifestyles, customs, traditions etc, which he finds exciting, admirable and praiseworthy (and something which may be very different from his own). In terms of consumer behavior, the normative reference group may exert influence on the kinds of products that should be bought e.g. hygienic food, clean clothes, fresh fruits and vegetables etc. The comparative reference group may exert influence in terms of the things like junk food versus traditional food, fashion and fad as also the latest styles etc. Both normative and comparative reference groups have relevance for a marketer. While the former set the basic norms of behavior in terms of products to purchase, the latter is more specific in terms of brands to buy; in fact the latter depends on the former; i.e. the specific acts of behavior are governed by the general.

Based on i) membership and level of involvement; as well as ii) the kind of influence (positive or negative) they have on values, attitudes, and behavior, reference groups may be classified into four categories, viz., contactual groups, aspirational groups, disclaimant groups, and avoidance groups.

Table: Types of Reference Groups based on Cross-Classification

|  | Membership | Non-membership |
| --- | --- | --- |
| **Positive Influence** | Contactual group | Aspirational group |
| **Negative Influence** | Disclaimant group | Avoidance group |

a) *Contactual Group*: A contactual group is defined as a group where people hold membership, meet face-to-face and have interaction, and where people abide by the values, norms, opinions and judgments that the group entails. This kind of a primary group has the maximum influence on a person, and his behavior. This has implications for a marketer in the sense that such groups impact purchase patterns and consumption behavior.

b) *Aspirational Group*: An aspirational group is one in which a person does not have a membership, and does not interact face-to-face, but he aspires to become a member. The group values and norms have a positive impact on the person, who desires membership to such a group. In terms of consumer behavior, these are secondary groups and impact a consumer's ideal self or desired self-concept.

c) *Disclaimant Group*: Here, a person holds membership with the group, but does not believe in the values, norms, attitudes and behavior of the group and its members. So the person acts as a deviant and behaves in a manner that is in opposition to how others in the group behave. In terms of consumer behavior, such people are referred to as inner- directed (an also detached), who want to set their own norms and patterns of behavior. These people could also act as innovators.

d) *Avoidance Group*: As the term denotes, this group is one where a person does not have membership, and he also disapproves of the values, norms, attitudes and behavior. He adopts such values and behavior that are in opposition to those that the group believes in.

## Factors Affecting Impact of Reference Groups

The impact of reference groups on the behavior of a person is subjective in nature; it varies across a) people; b) product and service offerings; as also c) situational factors. Nevertheless there are certain factors that affect the impact that a reference group generates on people. The factors that impact reference group influence on consumption behavior are explained as follows:

i)   *Information and Experience:* The amount of knowledge and experience an individual possesses or has the capacity to possess determines the impact that the reference group can generate. A person who has information about a product and service offering, the brand, and the 4 Ps, and also possess some experience, would not look for advice from his reference groups, and it is unlikely that he would be carried away by advice from others. On the other hand, a person who is little or no knowledge and also lacks experience, would look towards primary and secondary reference groups for help and advice.

ii)  *Power, credibility, and trustworthiness:* The impact that a reference group can generate also depends upon how powerful, credible and trustworthy the reference group is. When a reference group is powerful, and regarded as credible and trustworthy, there is greater probability of it being able to influence people. A person who looks towards reference groups for information and advice about product and service offerings as also brands, always examines the credibility and trustworthiness of the group. He may also be fearful of the power of the reference group and would go by group-say out of fear or to avoid any undesirable consequences. He may also be looking for social approval and acceptance of others in his reference group. The probability of he being persuaded by such reference groups is high.

iii) *Conformance with group and social approval:* When a consumer is other- directed or socially-directed, and looks towards others for social approval, he generally conforms to the advice given by members of his reference groups. This is because he wants to be identified with people whom he likes or whom he wants to be associated with. Thus he would conform to the product and service and/or brand suggested by members of their reference group.

iv)  *Visibility and Conspicuousness of the Product:* The impact of reference groups also depends on the visibility and conspicuousness of a product. When a product offering is visible and conspicuous, such that it relates to esteem and is status revealing (fashion apparel, carpets and upholstery, jewellery and other luxurious items), the consumer tends to be conscious while purchasing it especially because of reaction of others (fear of social disapproval, social embarrassment). Thus he would buy such keeping in mind the advice, likes and dislikes of reference group. When the product is low on public visibility and conspicuousness, one is less likely to be influenced by the reference group.

## Reference Group Appeals

While designing the messages, marketers may use various kinds of appeals so that the consumer can identify himself with the spokesperson (from the reference group) in the advertisement. The commonly used reference group appeals are: i) celebrity appeals; ii) expert appeals; iii) common man appeals; iv) executive appeals, trade or spokes-character appeals.

i) *Celebrity appeals:* Celebrity appeals are the most commonly used kind of appeal. The public admires film stars, TV personalities and sportspersons. They represent a lifestyle that people aspire to be in. People idolize them and aspire to become like them. Thus, marketer's use of celebrities particularly for FMCG products.

Celebrities in advertisements could be used in a variety of forms; they could be used as a spokesperson (educating the consumers about the company, and the brand); or as a celebrity giving a testimonial and endorsement (statement in support of claim or a fact about the brand); or as an actor/model. Whatever form it may be in, commercials with celebrity appeals have major impact on the consumers' minds. Nevertheless the marketer must be careful about the credibility of the celebrity, in terms of expertise (regarding the product or service and/or the brand) as well as trustworthiness (honesty about what he/she says).

Research has indicated that the credibility of the celebrity also depends upon the number of brands he/she advertises for; where a celebrity advertises for only one or few brands, he/she is looked up with credibility as against another who advertises for many, where he/she is looked up with less credibility primarily because of the monetary benefit associated with the advertisement.

Marketers make regular use of celebrities for their advertisements; they presume that the image that is associated with the celebrity passes on to the product or service offering that they are advertising for. This phenomenon is known as prototypical bonding where a spokesperson's traits, personality, image etc. gets associated with a particular service or product. For example, Aishwarya Rai advertising for Lux or Sachin Tendulkar for Boost.

ii) *Expert appeals*: Another reference group appeal that is used by marketers is the expert appeal. People who are experts in a particular field are used in the advertisement. Because of the knowledge, expertise and experience that they possess in a particular field, they are in a position to give advice that would help potential consumers to evaluate the various product alternatives, and finally make a choice. For example, a health nutritionist or a dietician advertising for Complan.

iii) *Common man appeals*: As a common man appeal, the advertisement relates to individuals, who find parity in such advertisements with real life situation; thus they are able to identify better with the situation portrayed in the advertisement. As they relate to realities of life and real-life problems, they are also known as slice-of-the life commercials.

A common man appeal may also include testimonials from a satisfied customer, so as to portray to potential consumers, that another commoner like them uses the product and/or brand and is satisfied with it. Advertisements depict how day to day problems are solved through purchase of products and service offerings and/or brands. Examples where such appeals are used are agony and pain (Amrutanjan Balm), Bad breath (Close-Up), Insurance (LIC) etc.

iv) *Executive appeals, trade or spokes-character appeals*: Companies may also use their spokespersons or their top executives in their advertisements. Such people are often used at product launch and also relates to a publicity exercise. The spokespersons address the consumers and provide information about the product or service offering. Due to the popularity that they hold, people and their consumption behaviors are impacted by them. For example, Ratan Tata for Nano, Nita Ambani for Reliance Fresh stores etc.

v) *Other appeals*: Other appeals that impact consumption behavior include print media and editorial content, promotional strategies from dealers and retailers and seals of approval from recognized and reputed agencies and organizations.

## Usefulness of Reference Group Appeals

Reference group appeals are useful for a marketer in two ways; firstly they provide information and increase consumer awareness and knowledge; two, they reduce perceived risk amongst consumers, with respect to market offerings.

i) *Increase consumer awareness*: Reference group appeals help in providing information about product and service offerings, as also brands. This helps increase consumer awareness and knowledge about the various offerings and alternative brands. The most effective appeal is a celebrity appeal that attracts customer attention, and aids retention and retrieval during time of purchase. Celebrities are particularly useful as they are familiar and popular with customers and thus draw the latter's attention. Other appeals (experts, spokesperson's etc.) are useful too and because of the conviction with which they endorse the various brands, they create a huge impact in favor of the product and service and/or brand being advertised.

ii) *Reduce Perceived Risk:* Reference group appeals help in reducing the fear and apprehensions consumers have when buying a product and service and/or brand. This is particularly true for new product offerings. The manner in which reference groups endorse a product or provide testimonials, help in reducing the uncertainty and consumer's perceived risk in purchasing product offerings. Mention may particularly be made of expert appeals or trade or spokes-character appeals, where the manner in which an endorsement is made, helps provide confidence to the consumer that his intention to buy is a correct one.

## Reference Group and Implications for Marketers

Reference groups have relevance for the marketer in the sense that reference groups help impact consumer values, attitudes and behavior; reference groups inform and educate the consumers (potential) about a product/service offering. By acting as a standard and as a frame of reference, they also influence potential consumers towards adoption and usage of such product and service offerings. Marketers often use them in advertisements to communicate with the masses, for example, celebrities, sportsperson and leaders are often used in advertisements to influences the masses. They are admired by the consumers who desire to identify with them and even aspire to become or behave like members of such secondary reference groups. Further they not only provide information and increase consumer awareness but they also reduce perceived risk amongst consumers with respect a product and service and/or brand.

# Impact of Culture on Consumer Behavior

Consumerism is an ideology that propagates the idea to buy goods and services in an ever-increasing manner. After the Industrial Revolution, this idea led to overproduction, which in turn gave birth to planned advertising. This section also deals with consumer socialization, which puts focus on how early year experiences pave way for future consumer behavior.

## Culture

Culture may be defined as the "personality of a society". It is broad and all pervasive in nature, inclusive of language, customs and traditions, norms and laws, religion, art and music, etc. It also includes the interests of people, the work practices and orientations, as also their attitudes towards general and specific issues.

Culture delineates precisely, the do's and dont's of a society, and specifies all that is acceptable and all that is not. It is reflective of values and beliefs that are widely accepted by members of a society. The members of a society subscribe to the various values, beliefs and norms, and this gives strength to a society's culture. This does not imply that cultures are truly rigid; in fact, they evolve and adapt to changing situations and times.

Culture is a society's personality, unique in itself and differentiated from others; it is further divided into various sub-cultures. Culture is also trans-generational, and is passed on from one generation to another. A study on our culture requires an elaborate and detailed inquiry into the very character and personality of the society that we live in.

The culture of a society also has a bearing on buying patterns and consumption behavior. In terms of consumer behavior, Schiffman defines culture as *"the sum total of learned beliefs, values, and customs that serve to direct the consumer behavior of members of a particular society"*. The kinds of products and services and/or brands that consumers' buy and use, are all based on their cultures and sub-cultures. For example, the food they eat and the kinds of clothes they buy and wear, are all impacted by their culture, their customs, traditions, norms and values.

### Characteristics of Culture

Culture and its impact on consumption behavior can be better explained by understanding the nature and characteristics of culture:

a) *Culture is natural and permeates naturally into the social system.* Its inbreds into the members of a social system and is all-pervasive. It influences the manner in which a person behaves, as consciously or sub-consciously, we are all governed by culture. Not only do people use their values and beliefs to govern their behavior, but they also except that others' behavior would also be similar and consistent (as culture is shared). Culture unites the members of a social system.

In terms of consumer behavior, the kinds of food we buy and eat or the clothes that we purchase and wear, are all governed by the socialization process. Similar is with respect to other purchases that we make. Culture encompasses the general and specific patterns of consumption behavior.

b) *Culture helps in satisfaction of needs.* In fact, it exists as it helps satisfy the needs of people. Beliefs, values, customs and tradition, help govern the social system, and specify the manner in which people in a social system should behave; they delineate the do's and don't's, and thereby create boundaries of acceptable behavior in the social system. However, such values, beliefs, customs and traditions continue to exist as long as they meet the needs of the people in the society. That is why culture evolves with passage of time. As the needs of the people evolve, beliefs, values, customs and tradition also undergo change so as to meet and match with newer needs and wants.

For example, in earlier times, people preferred eating their whole meals at home. In fact, eating out was considered unhealthy and undesirable. With a change in society, and the emergence of dual income households, people have begun eating out of home; the fast food culture is in. This has given a boost to the fast food and restaurant industry. Thus, we see that when a value system fails to satisfy the members of a social system, it is adapted, changed and/or modified to suit newer social patterns and trends. Marketers must be conscious of newly developed and embraced values, customs and traditions, so as to be able to take advantage of the situation. For example, lately developed consciousness of people towards i) fashion, has given boost to the apparel and accessories business; ii) fitness, has given boost to the gymnasium and sports business; iii) health, has given a boost to natural products like fruit juices, honey, aloe vera, etc.

c) *Culture is not inborn; it is learnt as a result of the socialization process.* There occurs a socialization process right from one's childhood, a process that continues throughout life. Culture is imparted by this socialization process. This learning of culture could be of two kinds; viz., enculturation and acculturation. The process of learning one's native culture is known as enculturation, while the process of learning a new or a foreign culture is known as acculturation.

We are impacted by our family (family of orientation and family of procreation), as well as our friends throughout our life. People learn from family and friends about what are acceptable and what is not in terms of our values and beliefs. Cultural learning could take place in three forms, viz., formal learning, informal learning and technical learning.

- formal learning: when a child is taught how to behave by family, viz., grandparents, parents and siblings; they tell him about the right's and wrong's in behavior.

- informal learning: when the child learns by imitating the behavior of others, be it members in the family, or friends, or celebrities, or characters.

- technical learning: when the child is taught how to behave in a formal educational environment by a teacher.

As consumers, it is through our culture learning that we are taught what is regarded as a desirable purchase and what is not. Similar is with respect to brands. Our perception about brands is influenced i) informally by views and opinions from family, friends, and colleagues, and ii) formally by the marketer, the dealer and the sales people. Thus, both general and specific consumption behavior is indicative of the culture that we live in. The kind of products/services consumers buy are ultimately determined by culture as well. For example, in certain cultures, eating pork and beef is a taboo; thus, when McDonalds came to India, they had to introduce the chicken burger, instead of the normal beef burger sold in the US. They could not disregard the vegetarian population of the country and so introduced the veg-tikki burger. MNC's who desire to enter foreign markets, and wish to introduce their products and services there, should carefully study and understand the cultures of such countries. They need to go through an elaborate process of acculturation so that they can understand the inhabitants of such cultures and their needs, so as to assess whether such potential markets could be profitable target segments. They should design the product and service offerings (including the 4Ps), in line with the culture so as to be bale to gain quicker acceptance. The colors, language and symbols, should all be kept in mind. The marketer could use all the three forms of cultural learning through designing appropriate promotional messages and using an appropriate channel.

d) *Culture is shared.* It is accepted and imbibed by all the members of the social system. In fact, it ties together the people that form a social system. Social institutions (family), educational institutions (schools, colleges and universities), political institutions (law, public policy, leaders and government), and religious institutions (like places of worship, artifacts, and religious leaders) etc., all help in transmitting this culture to the members of the society. The mass media, print and audio-visual, also has a role to play in the transmitting of culture.

Also today, cultures and sub-cultures are shared by people within, and outside. Needless to say, the mass media has a big role to play. With the various satellite channels vying for viewer ship across India, and higher TRP ratings, the various soaps and serials reflect cultures of all kinds; they portray all kinds of families, all types of cultures and sub-cultures. We get to see stories on families from Gujarati, Bengali,Punjabi and Tamilian cultures; the dressing patterns, the favorite dishes, the customs and rituals etc. With the various national and vernacular channels that we have in India, we have begun to share sub-cultures too. Sub-cultures are no longer restricted to geographical boundaries today. As consumers, we are also impacted most by such institutions, and primarily by mass media. As discussed in the above paragraph, with the advent of satellite channels, there is growing awareness of other cultures and sub-cultures. An important role on spread of culture is also through advertisements. Today there is demand for dhokla and khakra (Gujarati food) in North India, or mishti doi and hilsa fish (Bengali food) in South India. This trend is also increasing because people are crossing borders of their states and moving elsewhere for jobs and assignments. d) Culture is dynamic in nature, and evolves constantly with time. It adapts itself to the changing environment. As said above, values, beliefs, customs and traditions continue to exist as long as they satisfy the needs and wants of the people. Once they cease to satisfy people's needs, they change. Thus, culture changes and adapts to the environment. Marketers need to continually assess the environment so as to identify changing need patterns, and change/modify/adapt existing products and services, and even come up with new ones. One such example, i.e. dual income households and the need for eating out, resulting in demand for fast food and restaurants, has already been discussed above. With changes in culture, we can also witness its impact on the buying roles. The marketers have to identify the initiators, influencers, deciders, buyers and users, and approach them accordingly, either personally or impersonally via media. Marketers who continually assess the environment can identify opportunities and exploit them to their advantage.

## Consumer Culture

Malls have been a huge impact on the consumer culture. Shown in the picture is the Mall of America, one of the largest malls in the USA.

Consumer Culture focuses on the spending of the customers money on material goods to attain a lifestyle in a capitalist economy. One country that has a large consumer culture is the United States of America.

### Types of Culture

According to Berger, "Social scientists Aaron Wildavsky and Mary Douglas suggest that there are four political cultures, which also function as consumer cultures: hierarchical or elitist, individualist, egalitarian, and fatalist."

1.  An elitist, is a person who believes that a system or society should be ruled or dominated by an elite.

2.  An individualist, is a person who does things without being concerned about what other people will think.

3.  An egalitarian, believes in the principle that all people are equal and deserve equal rights and opportunities.

4.  A fatalist, is someone who feels that no matter what he or she does, the outcome will be the same because it's predetermined.

Consumer culture is based on the idea of demographics, which is targeting a large group of people with similar interests, traits or cultural attributes.

## Strategies

Over the years, people of different age groups are employed by marketing companies to help understand the beliefs, attitudes, values, and past behaviors of the targeted consumers. This creates a more effective advertisement than the normal data gathering strategy that is used.

## Advertising

Over the years, people of different age groups are employed by marketing companies to help understand the beliefs, attitudes, values, and past behaviors of the targeted consumers. This creates a more effective advertisement than the normal data gathering strategy that is used.

A quote by Shah states that, "The sophistication of advertising methods and techniques has advanced, enticing and shaping and even creating consumerism and needs where there has been non before."

## Labor

After this consumer culture developed, the life of workers changed forever.

## Wage Work

Both men and women working in the factory together.

Before the Industrial Revolution, home was a place where men and women produced, consumed, and worked. The men were high valued workers, such as barbers, butchers, farmers, and lumbermen who brought income into the house. The wives of these men completed various tasks to save money which included, churning butter, fixing clothes, and tending the garden. This system created an equal value to all of the jobs and tasks in a community.Once the Industrial Revolution began, there was no such thing as an equal and high valued work(er) in a mass production industry. The only value these workers had were the wage they made. That meant the wives lost their value at home and had to start working for a living. This new system created the thought of everyone being replaceable.

### Life of a Worker

The life of a worker was a challenging one. Working 12-14 hour days, 6 days a week, and in a dangerous environment. The worst part was the infrequency of pay or not being paid at all. At times, employers paid their workers in script pay, or non-U.S. currency, or even in-store credit.

### Outcome

Now that we understand the basics of consumer culture let's talk about the benefits and drawbacks listed by Augustine.

### Benefits

Consumer culture helps grows our economy through supply and demand, thus causes the economy to be self-regulating and self-sustaining since money is constantly flowing. This also drives the workforce up because people need a way to retain this lifestyle. In return, people are much happier when they can buy the items that they want or need.

### Drawbacks

This culture causes our country to become greedy, materialistic, and wasteful. The people of our country start to become shallow and acquire status symbols through buying expensive things. In order to feed this materialistic lifestyle, loans are given, thus accumulating our nations debt. People now work for a living instead of living to work.

### Consumer Choice

The theory of consumer choice is the branch of microeconomics that relates preferences to consumption expenditures and to consumer demand curves. It analyzes how consumers maximize the desirability of their consumption as measured by their preferences subject to limitations on their expenditures, by maximizing utility subject to a consumer budget constraint.

Consumption is separated from production, logically, because two different economic agents are involved. In the first case consumption is by the primary individual; in the second case, a producer might make something that he would not consume himself. Therefore, different motivations and abilities are involved. The models that make up consumer theory are used to represent prospectively observable demand patterns for an individual buyer on the hypothesis of constrained optimization. Prominent variables used to explain the rate at which the good is purchased (demanded) are the price per unit of that good, prices of related goods, and wealth of the consumer.

The law of demand states that the rate of consumption falls as the price of the good rises, even when the consumer is monetarily compensated for the effect of the higher price; this is called the substitution effect. As the price of a good rises, consumers will substitute away from that good, choosing more of other alternatives. If no compensation for the price rise occurs, as is usual, then the decline in overall purchasing power due to the price rise leads, for most goods, to a further decline in the quantity demanded; this is called the income effect.

In addition, as the wealth of the individual rises, demand for most products increases, shifting the demand curve higher at all possible prices.

The basic problem of consumer theory takes the following inputs:

- The consumption set $C$ – the set of all bundles that the consumer could conceivably consume.

- A preference relation over the bundles of $C$. This preference relation can be described as an ordinal utility function, describing the utility that the consumer derives from each bundle.

- A price system, which is a function assigning a price to each bundle.

- An initial endowment, which is a bundle from $C$ that the consumer initially holds. The consumer can sell all or some of his initial bundle in the given prices, and can buy another bundle in the given prices. He has to decide which bundle to buy, under the given prices and budget, in order to maximize his utility.

## Example: Homogeneous Divisible Goods

Consider an economy with two types of homogeneous divisible goods, traditionally called X and Y.

- The consumption set is $R_+^2$, i.e. the set of all pairs $(x, y)$ where $x \geq 0$ and $y \geq 0$. Each bundle contains a non-negative quantity of good X and a non-negative quantity of good Y.

- A typical preference relation in this universe can be represented by a set of indifference curves. Each curve represents a set of bundles that give the consumer the same utility. A typical utility function is the Cobb-Douglas function: $u(x, y) = x^a \cdot y^a$, whose indifference curves look like in the figure below.

- A typical price system assigns a price to each type of good, such that the cost of bundle $(x, y)$ is $xp_X + yp_Y$.

- A typical initial endowment is just a fixed income, which along with the prices implies a budget constraint. The consumer can choose any point on or below the budget constraint line BC In the diagram. This line is downward sloped and linear since it represents the boundary of the inequality $xp_X + yp_Y \leq \text{income}$. In other words, the amount spent on both goods together is less than or equal to the income of the consumer.

The consumer will choose the indifference curve with the highest utility that is attainable within his budget constraint. Every point on indifference curve I3 is outside his budget constraint so the best that he can do is the single point on I2 where the latter is tangent to his budget constraint. He will purchase X* of good X and Y* of good Y.

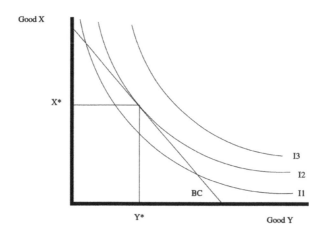

Indifference curve analysis begins with the utility function. The utility function is treated as an index of utility. All that is necessary is that the utility index change as more preferred bundles are consumed.

Indifference curves are typically numbered with the number increasing as more preferred bundles are consumed. The numbers have no cardinal significance; for example if three indifference curves are labeled 1, 4, and 16 respectively that means nothing more than the bundles "on" indifference curve 4 are more preferred than the bundles "on" indifference curve 1.

Income effect and price effect deal with how the change in price of a commodity changes the consumption of the good. The theory of consumer choice examines the trade-offs and decisions people make in their role as consumers as prices and their income changes.

## Example: Land

As a second example, consider an economy which consists of a large land-estate L.

- The consumption set is $P(L)$, i.e. the set of all subsets of L (all land parcels).

- A typical preference relation in this universe can be represented by a utility function which assigns, to each land parcel, its total "fertility" (the total amount of grain that can be grown in that land).

- A typical price system assigns a price to each land parcel, based on its area.

- A typical initial endowment is either a fixed income, or an initial parcel which the consumer can sell and buy another parcel.

## Effect of a Price Change

The indifference curves and budget constraint can be used to predict the effect of changes to the budget constraint. The graph below shows the effect of a price increase for good Y. If the price of Y increases, the budget constraint will pivot from BC2 to BC1. Notice that because the price of X does not change, the consumer can still buy the same amount of X if he or she chooses to buy only good X. On the other hand, if the consumer chooses to buy only good Y, he or she will be able to buy less of good Y because its price has increased.

To maximize the utility with the reduced budget constraint, BC1, the consumer will re-allocate consumption to reach the highest available indifference curve which BC1 is tangent to. As shown on the diagram below, that curve is I1, and therefore the amount of good Y bought will shift from Y2 to Y1, and the amount of good X bought to shift from X2 to X1. The opposite effect will occur if the price of Y decreases causing the shift from BC2 to BC3, and I2 to I3.

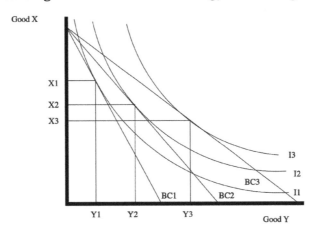

If these curves are plotted for many different prices of good Y, a demand curve for good Y can be constructed. The diagram below shows the demand curve for good Y as its price varies. Alternatively, if the price for good Y is fixed and the price for good X is varied, a demand curve for good X can be constructed.

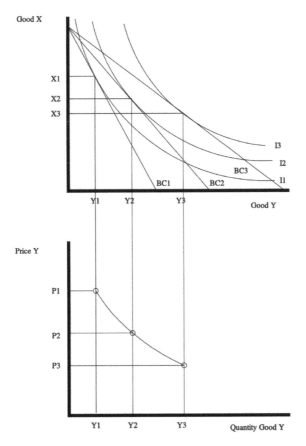

## Income Effect

Another important item that can change is the money income of the consumer. The income effect is the phenomenon observed through changes in purchasing power. It reveals the change in quantity demanded brought by a change in real income. Graphically, as long as the prices remain constant, changing income will create a parallel shift of the budget constraint. Increasing the income will shift the budget constraint right since more of both can be bought, and decreasing income will shift it left.

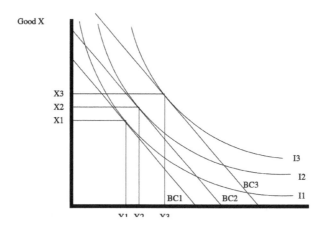

Depending on the indifference curves, as income increases, the amount purchased of a good can either increase, decrease or stay the same. In the diagram below, good Y is a normal good since the amount purchased increased as the budget constraint shifted from BC1 to the higher income BC2. Good X is an inferior good since the amount bought decreased as the income increases.

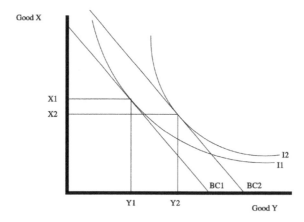

$\Delta y_1^n$ is the change in the demand for good 1 when we change income from $m'$ to $m$, holding the price of good 1 fixed at $p_1'$:

$$y_1^n = y_1(p_1', m) - y_1(p_1', m').$$

## Price Effect as Sum of Substitution and Income Effects

Every price change can be decomposed into an income effect and a substitution effect; the price effect is the sum of substitution and income effects.

The substitution effect is the change in demands resulting from a price change that alters the slope of the budget constraint but leaves the consumer on the same indifference curve. In other words, it illustrates the consumer's new consumption basket after the price change while being compensated as to allow the consumer to be as happy as he or she was previously. By this effect, the consumer is posited to substitute toward the good that becomes comparatively less expensive. In the illustration below this corresponds to an imaginary budget constraint denoted SC being tangent to the indifference curve I1. Then the income effect from the rise in purchasing power from a price fall reinforces the substitution effect. If the good is an *inferior good*, then the income effect will offset in some degree the substitution effect. If the income effect for an inferior good is sufficiently strong, the consumer will buy less of the good when it becomes less expensive, a Giffen good (commonly believed to be a rarity).

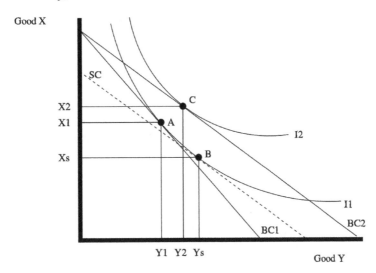

The substitution effect, $\Delta y_1^s$, is the change in the amount demanded for $Y$ when the price of good $Y$ falls from $p_1$ to $p_{1'}$ (represented by the budget constraint shifting from BC1 to BC2 and thus increasing purchasing power) and, at the same time, the money income falls from $m$ to $m'$ to keep the consumer at the same level of utility on $I1$:

$$\Delta y_1^s = y_1(p_1', m') - y_1(p_1, m) = Ys - Y1.$$

The substitution effect increases the amount demanded of good $Y$ from $Y_1$ to $Y_s$ in the diagram. In the example shown, the income effect of the fall in $p_1$ partly offsets the substitution effect as the amount demanded of $Y$ in the absence of an offsetting income change ends up at $Y_2$ thus the income effect from the rise in purchasing power due to the price drop is that the quantity demanded of $Y$ goes from $Y_s$ to $Y_2$. The total effect of the price drop on quantity demanded is the sum of the substitution effect and the income effect.

## Assumptions

The behavioral assumption of the consumer theory proposed herein is that all consumers seek to maximize utility. In the mainstream economics tradition, this activity of maximizing utility has been deemed as the "rational" behavior of decision makers. More specifically, in the eyes of economists, all consumers seek to maximize a utility function subject to a budgetary constraint. In other words, economists assume that consumers will always choose the "best" bundle of goods they can afford. Consumer theory is therefore based around the problem of generate refutable hypotheses about the nature of consumer demand from this behavioral postulate.

In order to reason from the central postulate towards a useful model of consumer choice, it is necessary to make additional assumptions about the certain preferences that consumers employ when selecting their preferred "bundle" of goods. These are relatively strict, allowing for the model to generate more useful hypotheses with regard to consumer behaviour than weaker assumptions, which would allow any empirical data to be explained in terms of stupidity, ignorance, or some other factor, and hence would not be able to generate any predictions about future demand at all. For the most part, however, they represent statements which would only be contradicted if a consumer was acting in (what was widely regarded as) a strange manner. In this vein, the modern form of consumer choice theory assumes:

### Preferences are complete

Consumer choice theory is based on the assumption that the consumer fully understands his or her own preferences, allowing for a simple but accurate comparison between any two bundles of good presented. That is to say, it is assumed that if a consumer is presented with two consumption bundles A and B each containing different combinations of $n$ goods, the consumer can unambiguously decide if (s)he prefers A to B, B to A, or is indifferent to both. The few scenarios where it is possible to imagine that decision-making would be very difficult are thus placed "outside the domain of economic analysis". However, discoveries in behavioral economics has found that actual decision making is affected by various factors, such as whether choices are presented together or separately through the distinction bias.

### Preferences are reflexive

Means that if A and B are in all respect identical the consumer will consider A to be at least as good as (i.e. weakly preferred to) B. Alternatively, the axiom can be modified to read that the consumer is indifferent with regard to A and B.

### Preference are transitive

If A is preferred to B and B is preferred to C then A must be preferred to C.

This also means that if the consumer is indifferent between A and B and is indifferent between B and C she will be indifferent between A and C.

This is the consistency assumption. This assumption eliminates the possibility of intersecting indifference curves.

### Preferences exhibit non-satiation

This is the "more is always better" assumption; that in general if a consumer is offered two almost identical bundles A and B, but where B includes more of one particular good, the consumer will choose B.

Among other things this assumption precludes circular indifference curves. Non-satiation in this sense is not a necessary but a convenient assumption. It avoids unnecessary complications in the mathematical models.

Indifference curves exhibit diminishing marginal rates of substitution

This assumption assures that indifference curves are smooth and convex to the origin.

This assumption is implicit in the last assumption.

This assumption also set the stage for using techniques of constrained optimization. Because the shape of the curve assures that the first derivative is negative and the second is positive.

The MRS tells how much y a person is willing to sacrifice to get one more unit of x.

This assumption incorporates the theory of diminishing marginal utility.

Goods are available in all quantities

It is assumed that a consumer may choose to purchase any quantity of a good (s)he desires, for example, 2.6 eggs and 4.23 loaves of bread. Whilst this makes the model less precise, it is generally acknowledged to provide a useful simplification to the calculations involved in consumer choice theory, especially since consumer demand is often examined over a considerable period of time. The more spending rounds are offered, the better approximation the continuous, differentiable function is for its discrete counterpart. (Whilst the purchase of 2.6 eggs sounds impossible, an average consumption of 2.6 eggs per day over a month does not.)

Note the assumptions do not guarantee that the demand curve will be negatively sloped. A positively sloped curve is not inconsistent with the assumptions.

## Use Value

In Marx's critique of political economy, any labor-product has a value and a use value, and if it is traded as a commodity in markets, it additionally has an exchange value, most often expressed as a money-price. Marx acknowledges that commodities being traded also have a general utility, implied by the fact that people want them, but he argues that this by itself tells us nothing about the specific character of the economy in which they are produced and sold.

## Labor-leisure Tradeoff

One can also use consumer theory to analyze a consumer's choice between leisure and labor. Leisure is considered one good (often put on the horizontal axis) and consumption is considered the other good. Since a consumer has a finite amount of time, he must make a choice between leisure (which earns no income for consumption) and labor (which does earn income for consumption).

The previous model of consumer choice theory is applicable with only slight modifications. First, the total amount of time that an individual has to allocate is known as his "time endowment", and is often denoted as $T$. The amount an individual allocates to labor (denoted $L$) and leisure ($l$) is constrained by $T$ such that

$$l + L = T.$$

A person's consumption is the amount of labor they choose multiplied by the amount they are paid per hour of labor (their wage, often denoted $w$). Thus, the amount that a person consumes is:

$$C = w(T - l).$$

When a consumer chooses no leisure $(l = 0)$ then $T - l = T$ and $C = wT$.

From this labor-leisure tradeoff model, the substitution effect and income effect from various changes caused by welfare benefits, labor taxation, or tax credits can be analyzed.

# Consumer Culture Theory

Consumer culture theory is the study of consumption choices and behaviors from a social and cultural point of view, as opposed to an economic or psychological one. It does not offer a grand unifying theory but "refers to a family of theoretical perspectives that address the dynamic relationships between consumer actions, the marketplace, and cultural meanings". Reflective of a post-modernist society, it views cultural meanings as being numerous and fragmented and hence view culture as an amalgamation of different groups and shared meanings, rather than an homogenous construct (such as the American culture). Consumer culture is viewed as "social arrangement in which the relations between lived culture and social resources, between meaningful ways of life and the symbolic and material resources on which they depend, are mediated through markets" and consumers as part of an interconnected system of commercially produced products and images which they use to construct their identity and orient their relationships with others.

## Methodology

There is a widely held misperception by people outside CCT researchers that this field is oriented toward the study of consumption contexts. Memorable study contexts, such as the Harley-Davidson subculture or the Burning Man festival probably fueled this perspective, which is far from the theory development aim of this school of thought.

While CCT is often associated with qualitative methodologies, such as interviews, case studies, ethnographic, as well as 'netnographic' methods which are well adapted to study the experiential, sociological and cultural aspects of consumption, these are not a prerequisite to CCT contribution (Arnould & Thompson 2005).

## Fields of Study

Arnould & Thompson identifies four research programs in CCT:

- Consumer identity projects, such as Schau & Gilly study on personal web space, which studied how consumers create a coherent self through marketer-produced materials

- Marketplace culture, such as Schouten & McAlexander study on the Harley-Davidson sub-culture, which looked at consumers as culture producers. This research program builds particularly on Maffesoli's concept of neo-tribes Studies of consumer tribes have focused, for example, on clubbing culture and surf culture.

- Mass-mediated marketplace ideologies and consumers' interpretive strategies, such as Kozinets study of the Burning Man Festival, which looked at consumer ideologies and identities are influenced by economic and cultural globalisation and how cultural product systems orient consumers toward certain ideologies or identity projects.

- Sociohistoric patterning of consumption, such as Holt study which looked at the influence of social capital on consumption choices.

## Consumer Confusion

Consumer confusion is a state of mind that leads to consumers making imperfect purchasing decisions or lacking confidence in the correctness of their purchasing decisions.

## Confusion

Confusion occurs when a consumer fails to correctly understand or interpret products and services. This, in turn, leads to them making imperfect purchasing decisions. This concept is important to marketeers because consumer confusion may result in reduced sales, reduced satisfaction with products and difficulty communicating effectively with the consumer. It is a widely studied and broad subject which is a part of consumer behaviour and decision making.

## Causes

### Choice Overload

Choice overload (sometimes called overchoice in the context of confusion) occurs when the set of purchasing options becomes overwhelmingly large for a consumer. A good example is wine in the UK where supermarkets may present over 1000 different products leaving the consumer with a difficult choice process. Whilst large assortments do have some positive aspects (principally novelty and stimulation and optimal solutions) any assortment greater than around 12-14 products leads to confusion and specifically transferring the ownership of quality assurance to the consumer. What this means in practice is reduced levels of satisfaction with purchases from large assortments as a consumer may be left with doubt that they have succeeded in finding the "best" product. Choice overload is growing with ever larger supermarkets and the internet being two of the main causes.

### Similarity

Similarity is where two or more products lack differentiating features which prevents the consumer easily distinguishing between them. Differentiating features could be any from the marketing mix or anything else associated with the product such as brand. Similarity of products has the negative effect on the consumer of increasing the cognitive effort required to make a decision. and reducing the perception of accuracy of decision. Both of these reduce the satisfaction with a decision and thereby satisfaction with the purchase.

## Lack of Information

A consumer may suffer from lack of information if the information doesn't exist, is unavailable to them at the required moment or is too complex for them to use in their decision making process.

## Information Overload

Too much information surrounding a product or service disturbs the consumer by forcing them to engage in a more complex and time-consuming purchasing process. This, and the fact that it is difficult to compare and value the information when it is superfluous, leaves the consumer unsatisfied, insecure regarding what choice to make, and more prone to delay the decision-making, and thereby the actual purchase.

## Lack of Consistency

When information provided on a product and/or service is not consistent with the consumer's previously held beliefs and convictions, ambiguity occurs in the understanding of the product.

## Law

Trademark infringement is measured by the multi-factor "likelihood of confusion" test. That is, a new mark will infringe on an existing trademark if the new mark is so similar to the original that consumers are likely to confuse the two marks, and mistakenly purchase from the wrong company.

The likelihood of confusion test turns on several factors, including:

- Strength of the plaintiff's trademark;

- Degree of similarity between the two marks at issue;

- Similarity of the goods and services at issue;

- Evidence of actual confusion;

- Purchaser sophistication;

- Quality of the defendant's goods or services;

- Defendant's intent in adopting the mark.

*Initial interest confusion* occurs when a mark is used to attract a consumer, but upon inspection there is no confusion. This type of confusion is well-recognized for Internet searches, where a consumer may be looking for the site of one company, and a second site mimics keywords and metadata to draw hits from the "real" site.

*Point of sale confusion* occurs when a consumer believes their product to be from a company which it is not.

*Post sale confusion* occurs after a product is purchased, and third parties mistakenly think that the product is produced by a different, generally more prestigious, brand.

## Consumer Complaint

A consumer complaint or customer complaint is "an expression of dissatisfaction on a consumer's behalf to a responsible party" (Landon, 1980). It can also be described in a positive sense as a report from a consumer providing documentation about a problem with a product or service. In fact, some modern business consultants urge businesses to view customer complaints as a gift.

Consumer complaints are usually informal complaints directly addressed to a company or public service provider, and most consumers manage to resolve problems with products and services in this way, but it sometimes requires persistence.

If the grievance is not addressed in a way that satisfies the consumer, the consumer sometimes registers the complaint with a third party such as the Better Business Bureau, a county government (if it has a "consumer protection" office) and Federal Trade Commission (in the United States). These and similar organizations in other countries accept for consumer complaints and assist people with customer service issues, as do government representatives like attorneys general. Consumers however rarely file complaints in the more formal legal sense, which consists of a formal legal process.

In some countries (for example Australia, the United Kingdom, and many countries of the European Community), the making of consumer complaints, particularly regarding the sale of financial services, is governed by statute (law). The statutory authority may require companies to reply to complaints within set time limits, publish written procedures for handling customer dissatisfaction, and provide information about arbitration schemes.

Internet forums and the advent of social media have provided consumers with a new way to submit complaints. Consumer news and advocacy websites often accept and publish complaints. Publishing complaints on highly visible websites increases the likelihood that the general public will become aware of the consumer's complaint. If, for example, a person with many "followers" or "friends" publishes a complaint on social media, it may go "viral". Internet forums in general and on complaint websites have made it possible for individual consumers to hold large corporations accountable in a public forum.

## Components of Culture

Culture is reflected through the various components that it comprises, viz., values, language, myths, customs, rituals and laws. These are briefly explained as follows:

- *Values*: Values are the beliefs and ideals shared by the people of a society, for which they have great respect and regard. They could assume both positive (do's) and negative (dont's) connotations, and are indicative of appropriate thoughts, feelings and acts of behavior.

- *Language*: Man is a social animal and needs to communicate with others. Language is used as a means to communicate with people in a social set up. It is the common language that binds together the people in a social structure.

- *Myths*: Myths are legendary folktales and stories that describe events and occurrences, and teach values to society. They are imaginary and fictitious, and comprise characters that are gods, heroes and common men, ultimately aimed at giving lessons to the people, with respect to the causes and effects, good and bad, right and wrong, etc. Myths describe the values that members of a social structure should share.

- *Customs*: Customs are habitual practices that formulate the established way of doing things and reflect culturally accepted patterns of behavior. They reflect practices that have permanent continuance and are so long established that they have the force of law; in other words they are conventions. People in a social system follow such practices collectively, and the habitual activity gets transmitted from one generation to another.

- *Rituals*: Rituals are prescribed processes and procedures for conduct of religious or social rites. They are established rites, ceremonies and proceedings that are symbolic in nature. Rituals are collective in nature, comprising many patterns of behavior that are interdependent to each other.

- *Laws*: Laws are principles, rules and regulations that are formulated/sanctioned by an authority (ruler, government, constitution etc.), and supported/protected by judicial authority. Their basis can actually be found in the society's values, customs, and rituals. Laws are universally applicable across people in a society/country. They are written collection of rules and regulations to be adhered to by the people, and non-adherence to which would lead to legal action from the judiciary.

## Measurement of Culture

Culture can be measured through use of many techniques, some of which are i) Projective Tests; ii) Attitude measurement tests and techniques; iii) Content analysis; iv) Consumer fieldwork; and v) Value measurement instruments. These techniques are used to study and assess cultural patterns, changes and trends.

   i) *Projective Tests*: Projective tests can be traced to the psychoanalytic psychology, which argue that human beings have conscious and unconscious attitudes, motivations and personalities that are hidden and unknown from conscious awareness. The projective tests attempt to measure underlying traits, fears, anxieties and attitudes, motivations and personalities. They help reveal people's orientations towards the cultural values, myths, customs, traditions and rituals.

The participants are shown pictures, images, cartoons and characters, inkblots and incomplete sentences/paragraphs to understand, interpret and comprehend them. The participants are asked to give as responses all that first comes into their minds. Gestures and body language, tone of voice and other reactions are also noted. The assumption behind use of such tests is that one tends to project and interpret to these ambiguous stimuli from ones' sub-consciousness. Such tests are used to study motivation and personality. The two commonly used tests are the Rorschach Inkblot Test and the Thematic Apperception Test (TAT).

ii) *Attitude measurement tests and techniques*: Attitude measurement tests and techniques are used to measure attitudes of people towards persons, objects, and situations. They reflect people's attitudes and orientations towards the cultural values, myths, customs, traditions and rituals.

iii) *Content analysis*: Content analysis focuses on the examination of verbal, written, non-verbal and pictorial compositions/communication. The content analysis helps reveal and explain the content of messages and the varying interpretations. Assessment about the society, and its culture as well as evolutionary socio-cultural changes can be gauged through the content of verbal, written, non-verbal and pictorial compositions/communication.

iv) *Consumer fieldwork*: Fieldwork may be conducted on consumers, so as to observe their behavior, and draw generalizations about the values, myths, beliefs, customs, traditions and rituals. Such generalizations are drawn on observable in store shopping behavior. Verbal and non-verbal body language are also observed and recorded. Sometimes, instead of being passive observers, the researchers may assume active roles and interact with the consumers (participants) as salespersons. Interviews and focus group sessions may also be used.

v) *Value measurement instruments*: Researchers today, are increasingly making use of value measurement instruments. These are scales that measure values by means of a questionnaire. Participants are asked to give their opinion on varied issues like peace, freedom and independence, comfort and convenience, ambition and success etc. Through interpretation of their responses and the observation of behavior, researchers can infer the dominant or underlying values of the society. Such values would influence general and specific consumption patterns and buying behavior. Commonly used value measurement instruments are the Rokeach Value Survey, the List of Values (LOV), and the Values and Lifestyles—VALS.

## Sub-culture

While culture is defined as the "personality of a society", (inclusive of language, customs and traditions, norms and laws, religion, art and music, etc), it is not entirely homogenous in nature. Not all people within a social system, share the same language, religion, customs and traditions. Every society is composed of smaller sub-units, homogenous within, and heterogeneous outside, all of which when put together make a complex society. Such sub-units or sub-groups are known as sub-cultures; people within sub-cultures possess distinctive sets of values, beliefs, customs and traditions etc. The members of a subculture possess such values and beliefs, as also customs and traditions that set them apart from people belonging to other sub-cultures.

For example, while we are all Indians, and our culture is Indian (with a common national language, Hindi, and common festivals like Diwali), North Indians are different from South Indians. While North Indians, celebrate Lohri, as a harvest festival in January, the South Indians celebrate

Pongal as their harvest festival at the same time. In other words, people within smaller units share the same language, religion, customs and traditions; and, this would be different in smaller or larger magnitude to people in other sub-units.

A single culture can be broken up into various consumer subcultures. A subculture can be defined as a culture that is not dominant in its society. As consumers from various sub-cultures, we are different to each other. We have varying values and beliefs, customs and traditions, etc. These get reflected in our perspectives and orientations that influence our purchase patterns and consumption behavior. That is why a study of sub-culture becomes important for a marketer.

## Types of Sub-culture

Based on the varying criteria, there can be different types of sub-cultures. The important sub-cultural categories are nationality, geographical location, religion, race and caste, gender and age. From a marketing perspective, these could also be discussed as market segments, which need to be studied and assessed carefully before deciding on a product/service offering and formulating a marketing mix for a particular segment(s).

- Nationality: Sub-cultures could be based on nationality. While we are all Asians, we are distinct with respect to culture, and are different in terms of language, customs and traditions etc. Thus, we are classified as Indians, Burmese, Nepalese, Pakistani etc.

- Geographical location: Within a country, we could be different across geography, climatic conditions, regions and terrains, and density of population. This is more so in cases where the country is large and borders spread across a huge population occupying a vast territory. People tend to develop regional affinity and identification, and this gets reflected in the food they eat, clothes they wear, interests they pursue, etc. They constitute as distinct sub-cultures and people across such sub-cultures are different to each other. For example, we can be classified as North Indians and South Indians. As consumers, our needs are different and would translate into various wants, for example, i) differences in food habits, and demand for poori-sabji, paratha, idli-vada etc.; or ii) differences in clothing, and demand for cottons, woolens and silk.

- Religion: People also exhibit differences when it comes to the religions that they belong to. Hindus, Muslims, Christians, Sikhs, Parsis etc. are all different from one another and have different values and beliefs, customs and traditions etc. As consumers, they make purchase choices and purchase decisions that are influenced by the dictates of their religious leaders, scriptures, and holy books. In fact, many products/services are symbolically and ritualistically associated with religion. For example, as per Islam, non-vegetarian food must be "Halal", and this itself comprises a huge segment that marketers across national boundaries are catering to. .

- Race and caste: Culture and its components also vary across race and caste. Jats, Jaats, Rajputs, Pathans and Yadavs are all different from one another. Such racial sub-cultures also impact buying behavior and consumption patterns.

- Gender: Because gender roles have an impact on acts of behavior, gender constitutes an important cultural sub-group. Males and females across all cultures are assigned different traits and characteristics that make them masculine and feminine. They also perform different roles in society and are two distinct sub-groups. It is true that gender roles have got blurred, and both men and women are performing such roles that they did not perform earlier. Product usage is common to both man and woman; for example, a man shown as using a LG washing machine or making Act II popcorn. Similarly products like shavers and razors exclusive to usage by men, are also being used by women (Gillette thus introduced a razor for women). All this has brought about a big socio-economic change and led to cultural transformation. The values espoused by the generation of today is much different to the one espoused by the previous generation. The pace of change has been further accelerated with households no longer being single income households, but turned to dual-income households. The role of women is no longer restricted to bearing children and managing the home. Women have started working outside, and are contributing to household income. This has impacted consumer needs and wants as also the priorities. The impact is evinced on consumption behavior, where the 'decider' role is no longer confined to a single person, i.e. the man of the family. Today buying decisions are jointly taken by husband and wife.

- Age: Infants, kids, teenagers and adolescents, adults and the aged, may all be looked up as distinct sub-groups. They have different values and beliefs, and all this impacts upon their priorities in life. Daily lifestyles, activities and interests, fashion and accessories, food and diet, etc. receive varying priorities across the various sub-groups. For example, an aged person would prioritize health and go in for nutritious home food as opposed to young man who would prioritize work and go in for fast food. Today we see a rising trend amongst kids, adolescents and the young towards junk food, and they constitute a lucrative segment for restaurants providing fast food.

## Exposure to other Cultures

As a result of rapid advancement and all-round development, we find ourselves exposed to people from various cultures. There has been a great deal of opening up, and the society has been impacted on all fronts, be it social, economic, cultural or technological. The cultural fabric has undergone a transformation and we see changes in our values and beliefs, customs and traditions, etc.

As consumers also, we have been exposed to other cultures. We have inculcated/adopted values and beliefs, perspectives and orientations that are much different to what existed earlier. The past decade particularly, has seen changes with respect to what we eat, what we wear and how we behave. All this has impacted our buying patterns and consumption behavior. There have been changes in demand with respect to our food and diet, clothing and lifestyles, etc.

It is important for a marketer to give consideration to three major issues; i) how do consumers in one culture get exposed to good/services being used by people of other cultures; ii) how should a marketer design/adapt his 4Ps so as to be accepted by people influenced by newer cultures (if he is serving in the home market only); iii) how should a marketer design/adapt his 4Ps so as to accepted by people of other cultures (in foreign markets).

Generally speaking, as consumers we are exposed to foreign cultures either i) through ones' own initiatives; or ii) through the marketers's efforts. Ultimately both these means of exposure lead to cultural transfer and amalgamation.

i) People get exposed and gradually influenced to newer cultures when they travel abroad for leisure; or live abroad while on foreign assignments; or work with people of foreign cultures while in their native country. They also get exposed through media, i.e. through books and magazines, movies and films, drama and theater, etc.

ii) Consumers also get influenced through marketer's efforts, who foresee potential and expand their markets by launching their products and services into newer geographical segments (often across national borders). They go in for promotional measures that lead to awareness and develop consumer interest for trial and adoption of newer products and services.

## Cross-cultural Consumer Analysis

The marketer needs to go in for a study of the socio-cultural fabric of the respective country where he intends to enter and serve. He needs to have an understanding of the consumption pattern and the consumption behavior across people from different cultures. He needs to assess the needs and wants as well as priorities and orientations of the people that he desires to serve.

Schiffman defines cross cultural consumer analysis as "the effort to determine to what extent the consumers of two or more nations are similar or different." The marketer must understand how consumers in targeted countries are similar and dissimilar from each other. It is important for a marketer to have this understanding as it helps him assess the social and cultural similarities and dissimilarities so that he can design appropriate marketing programs and strategies for such segment(s).

Application of Cross Culture Consumer Analysis: Relevance for Marketers

A cross-cultural consumer analysis helps the marketer assess the market potential and customer reaction for his product and service offering. People's values and beliefs, customs and traditions, as also perspectives and orientations have a bearing on customer's needs, wants and priorities, finally translating into their desire for product and service offerings. These would vary across nations and cultures, and marketers must thus go through an *acculturation process*. As has been defined earlier, acculturation is defined as the process of learning a new or a foreign culture.

It is essential that they learn about the culture of foreign countries, what their needs and wants are, how they prioritize them, how they form attitudes and opinions, etc. Thus, before taking decisions with respect to entering foreign cultures, and the manner in which they should be served, a marketer should conduct a cross-cultural consumer analysis. Such an analysis provides a marketer with inputs as to how he should be modifying his 4Ps so as to elicit quick adoption and diffusion of his product and service offering. Every component of culture should be carefully studied and a marketing program designed accordingly.

- Product names or brands should not have double meanings; they should not be insensitive in any manner, and they should not hurt the sentiments of people in the country where the marketer is planning to enter.

- They should be easy to remember, recall and pronounce. Else marketers should make sure that they help consumers remember and pronounce such names. For example, when Perfetti Van Melle India launched their candy Alpenliebe, they designed an advertisement that had a jingle that helped consumers pronounce the name.

- They should be distinct and not duplicate names already existing in the foreign country.

- The marketer must make sure that the product or service offering appeals to the needs and wants of people from foreign cultures.

- He must make sure that he keeps in mind local customs and traditions while formulating the strategy.

- While taking decisions on packaging and labeling as also design of advertisements, he must make sure of colors and symbols. Colors and symbols have varied meanings and connotations. The marketer should be careful that he should not be insensitive to people of foreign cultures.

- Marketers must make sure that they employ local (foreign) people for sales and marketing in foreign cultures. They should avoid sending their own people as the latter would take time to be acculturated. It would be better if local people are hired who would know the language, customs, tradition etc, and with whom the customers would be more comfortable. They would also be in a position to make localized decisions.

Through a cross-cultural analysis, a marketer would get inputs into how the foreign culture is different to his native culture. When customers across two or more countries are similar, the marketer can afford to have a similar marketing program; in case they are different, he would have to adapt his 4Ps and design a separate individualized marketing strategy for the foreign country.

The relevance of a cross cultural analysis for a marketer is summarized as follows:

- A cross-cultural consumer analysis helps predict customer reaction to a product and service offering; the marketer would get to assess the market potential and assess the viability of a segment(s).

- The marketer would get inputs into how the foreign culture is different to his native culture. This would help him decide whether to have a marketing program similar to the one that is present in the native country or to have a program that is 'individualized' to the foreign country.

- It would help him to position his product/service offering appropriately, keeping in mind the values and beliefs, customs and traditions, attitudes, opinions and lifestyles.

- It provides a marketer with inputs as to how he should be modifying his 4Ps so as to elicit quick adoption and diffusion of his product and service offering. This is particularly relevant for products that would be new to a foreign culture, and where the consumers would have to be taught about their importance and usage. The marketer would have to educate the consumers about such a product/service offering (cognition), create a favorable opinion and positive feelings (affect), and convince adoption and purchase (behavior).

## Strategies for Multinational Companies

The most important decision that multinational companies need to take is with respect to the international market segment(s) that they would be catering to, i.e. whether they would be making their product and service offerings available worldwide to all countries or they would be making it available only to certain select countries in the total international market. The decision would depend on the basis of the i) size of the market; ii) growth and attractiveness of the market; iii) stability in the market; iv) politico-legal environment and the accessibility of the countries involved.

Another major decision that the marketer needs to take is whether to pursue a standardized identical global strategy for all countries/cultures or to go in for a customized localized marketing strategy unique to a country/culture. The choice ranges across a continuum, where on one end, they market identical product and service offerings across cultures, and on the other end they market customized offerings unique to various cultures.

With advances in technology, the world is getting closer. Cultures are amalgamating and markets are getting similar. In this scenario, marketers believe that they can offer a standardized marketing mix, similar to the one that they offer in the native country. On the other hand, there are marketers who believe that there exist differences across culture and consumers across nations need to be served with product/service offerings that are adapted to the values, beliefs, customs and traditions. Thus, marketers need to take a decision as to whether they should go in for need benefit segmentation based on common needs and values (the former case) or go in for geographical segmentation based on national boundaries (the latter case).

In any case, an understanding of culture(s) becomes essential. This would help them formulate appropriate marketing strategies, particularly with respect to positioning and communication. Marketers need to have a proper understanding of the various components that constitute culture, be it values and beliefs, language, myths, customs and traditions, rituals and laws. Differences across cultures lead to variations in consumer behavior.

Thus, as companies decide to expand their markets to foreign territories, they need to follow one of the two strategies, viz:

i)  They could offer the product/service offerings with the same marketing mix (standardized and global), as in their native country. Such a strategy is known as an *undifferentiated* strategy, i.e., one marketing strategy for all countries. Such a global strategy maintains the same product name; the features, attributes and other ingredients also remain the same (maybe with slight modifications); so do the other Ps. A large number of companies prefer a "world brand", i.e. products and service offerings are positioned, designed, priced, promoted and sold all over the world in the manner that is similar to the country of origin. The approach leads to a worldwide brand name, company image, recognition and reputation. Examples of such brands are IBM, Sony, etc.

ii) They could adapt the product/service offerings in the foreign country. This would present a more "localized offering" where the and service offerings are positioned, designed, promoted and sold in a manner that is distinctive and specific to foreign countries and cultures. This strategy is referred to as adaptive global marketing or a "localized marketing strategy" where the objective is to meet the local needs in the most effective manner. The strategy has also been termed *concentrated* or *differentiated* marketing. The marketer offers differentiated marketing strategies for each country, with changes in product and /or brand name, as also product features, attributes and other ingredients as also the other Ps. The marketer would need to take into account differences in consumer behavior. McDonalds is a perfect example; when they entered India, they adapted their product offering by offering chicken burgers instead of the beef and pork (as consumption of beef and pork is a taboo with Hindus and Muslims). Further they introduced the McTikki Aloo Burger for vegetarians; they positioned themselves a "family" restaurant keeping in line with the Indian family concept. Companies that do not localize their offerings may find penetration into foreign cultures a difficult exercise. An example that can be quoted is Kellogg's Breakfast Cereal. They found it difficult to penetrate the Indian market as the very concept of cold milk at breakfast was against the traditional Indian belief (where hot milk was preferred especially at breakfast, and cold milk was regarded as unhealthy). It is thus concluded that a "world brand" may not always be favored. The marketer needs to adapt his product/service offerings.

Companies like Unilever, Nestle, Proctor and Gamble follow a mixed approach. They have standardized offerings in terms of their brands, but they blend and adapt their 4Ps to suit the needs of the local culture. Their offerings are generally standardized but the implementation strategy "local". Thus, they introduce under the same family brand name, soaps for different kinds of skin, shampoo for different kinds of hair (depending on the skin and hair types across countries and cultures), and detergents for different water types (hard water or soft water). This is where study of cross cultures becomes essential so as to identify differences and similarities across nations. A marketer has to go through the process of acculturation.

Marketers often face the challenge of dealing effectively with marketer in diverse cultures. This is more specific to decisions related to product and service offerings, and the communication strategy. Researchers have studied the issue and proposed changes in the product and service offering as also the communication programmes. Various frameworks have been proposed that determine the degree to which marketing and advertising efforts should be standardized (globalized) or localized. A few of such frameworks are discussed as follows:

I   A *product recognition continuum has been proposed by researchers, that explains produce awareness and recognition amongst consumers of foreign cultures.* The five-stage continuum explains product recognition from mere awareness of a foreign brand amongst consumers in a local market to a complete global identification of the brand.

Stage 1: In stage one, the local consumers are aware of a brand that is "foreign and alien." They have heard or read about this "foreign" brand, and may find the product/service offering as also the brand to be desirable. However, it is unavailable to them as it is not sold in their country. For example, Lamborghini and Porsche.

Stage 2: In stage two, the "foreign" brand is available in the local market. Local consumers are aware of the brand being "foreign" and made in a particular country. However, consumers have their own perceptions with respect to foreign brands which may be favorable or unfavorable. For example, BMW and Mercedes.

Stage 3: In stage three, the "foreign" or "imported" brand is widely accepted and accorded "national status". While it national origin is known, it does not affect their purchase choice. For example, Suzuki and Samsung.

Stage 4: In stage four, the foreign brand is converted partly or wholly into a domestic brand. The local consumers no longer consider it to be a foreign brand and perceive it as a local brand. While its foreign origin may be remembered, the brand has been adopted so very well that is "naturalized." For example, Colgate and Cadburys.

Stage 5: In this last stage, the foreign brand has so very well adopted and assimilated that the people no longer regard it as "foreign". In fact, many are not even aware of the country of origin, and never even bother to ask so. It is regarded as purely global or "borderless." For example, Unilever (Hindustan Unilever), Xerox and Dettol.

II  Another framework presents four alternative marketing strategies that could be made available to a marketer who wants to expand beyond national territories. A company could opt for *standardizing or localizing either or both of the i) product; ii) communication program.* This can be better explained through a grid or through a two-by-two matrix which is presented below. Based on a combination of both, the various alternative strategies are as follows:

a)  Standardized product and standardized communication strategy: The marketer should use the same marketing strategy that he uses in his home country.

b)  Standardized product and localized communication strategy: The marketer would offer the same product in another country but adapt the promotion message.

c)  Localized product and standardized communication strategy: He would adapt the product offering and use the current communication strategy that he is using in his native culture.

d)  Localized product and localized communication strategy: This would mean a total adaptation, a new product and a new communication strategy.

| PRODUCT STRATEGY | COMMUNICATION STRATEGY | |
| --- | --- | --- |
| | Standardized Communications | Localized Communications |
| Standardized Product | Global Strategy: Uniform Product/ Uniform Message | Mixed Strategy: Uniform Product/ Customized Message |
| Localized Product | Mixed Strategy: Customized Product/ Uniform Message | Local Strategy: Customized Product/ Customized Message |

Framework for Alternative Global Marketing Strategies

The grid thus, represents alternative growth opportunities for a marketer, ranging from merely "exporting" a standardized product and service offering with the same mix to developing a completely new product and service offering with a new mix particularly with respect to communication. Which of the strategies would work best for a marketer would depend on a cross cultural analysis.

III Another framework has been proposed that evaluates *the degree of global standardization that would be feasible for a product or service offering when it is offered in another country*. It helps a marketer make a decision whether he should go in for a standardized approach a global product or service offering and global marketing mix, or opt for a localized approach with a customized marketing mix, typical for that foreign country. The marketer has to make a trade off; while the former is economical, with technological, economic and marketing synergies, the latter is more appealing and welcoming to people of foreign cultures.

According to the framework, before deciding on a viable marketing strategy, a marketer should keep certain factors in mind. These factors are i) characteristics of the target segment(s); ii) assessment of the firm's market position with respect to growth rate and market share; iii) nature and attributes of the product and service offering; iv) the environment; and v) organizational factors.

i)   Characteristics of the target segment(s): this would include a study of the geographic area and also the economic factors.

ii)  Assessment of the firm's market position: the marketer needs to assess the extent of market development, market conditions and competition.

iii) Nature and attributes of the product and service offering: this implies a study of the type of product as well a product positioning.

iv)  The environment: this would include a study of the politico-legal as well as the economic environment, and also the marketing infra-structure.

v)   Organizational factors: this would include factors like corporate orientation, authority relationships etc.

According to the framework, *performance in program markets* affects the *degree of program standardization. The degree of standardization is affected by the five factors mentioned above.*

IV There is another framework that helps a marketer assess whether to use a *global or a local marketing strategy*. The framework lays emphasis on a *high-tech to high-touch* continuum. According to the framework, for high-involvement products that approach either end of the high-tech/high-touch continuum, product standardization is more successful. It would be suitable for a marketer to position such products as global brands. On the other hand, for low-involvement products that lie on the mid-range of the high-tech/high-touch continuum, the marketer should follow a localized approach and go in for a market-by-market execution. The marketer should position such products as local brands.

Thus it can be observed that both marketers and consumers use a common vocabulary for high-tech products, like, kilo bytes, mega bytes for RAM storage capacity in computers or Bluetooth for data transfer in mobiles etc. In case of internet connections, the speed is marketed in MBPS (Mega bits per second); or In the case of hand held electronic devices, the marketer communicates in terms of GPS (Global Positioning System), Bluetooth, Camera with certain Mega-Pixel, MP3 etc. They use rational appeals for products like computers, laptops, cameras, DVD players etc. High-tech positioning is used for such products. On the other hand, marketers use social and emotional appeals or even status/image for high-touch products, be it perfumes, mobile phones, apparel wear etc. High-touch positioning is used for such image related products.

## Culture Relevance for a Marketer

A study of culture, sub-culture and cross culture holds great relevance for a marketer. A study of culture is inclusive of language, customs and traditions, norms and laws, religion, art and music, etc. It also includes the interests of people, their lifestyles and orientations, and their attitudes towards general and specific issues. An understanding of culture helps the marketer in designing a strategy that would address and appeal to people of a particular culture. It would help him to design his 4Ps in an efficient and effective manner. The relevance of a study of culture and cross culture is discussed as follows:

-   The culture of a society has a bearing on buying patterns and consumption behavior. The kinds of products and services and/or brands that consumers' buy and use, are all based on their cultures and sub-cultures. Through a study of culture, the marketer would get to know about the viability of target segment(s), and also about how quickly the product/service offering would be diffused and adopted by people.

-   Marketers must also be conscious of newly developed and embraced values, customs and traditions, so as to be able to take advantage of the situation.

-   Subcultures are relevant units of analysis for market research. A sub-cultural analysis helps a marketer identify distinct segments that are "natural", sizable and easy to cater to.

-   Every component of culture should be carefully studied and a marketing program designed accordingly; Product names or brands should not have double meanings; they should not be insensitive in any manner; they should be distinct, easy to remember, recall and pronounce.

-   While deciding on positioning and communication, marketer must be sensitive to culture, and particularly, cross-culture; the colors, language and symbols, should all be kept in mind.

-   The analysis of the culture, sub-culture and cross-culture helps profile consumers into segments that a marketer could take advantage off through formulation of an appropriate marketing strategy. The marketer could choose from two options, viz., either decide on a standardized global strategy or go in for a localized customized strategy.

-   MNC's who desire to enter foreign markets should carefully study and understand the cultures of such countries; They need to go through an elaborate process of acculturation so that they can understand the inhabitants of such cultures and their needs.

-   It is crucial that a marketer has a proper understanding of the social and cultural similarities and dissimilarities across cultures so that he can design appropriate marketing programs and strategies for such segment(s).

- The marketer must make sure that the product or service offering appeals to the needs and wants of people from foreign cultures. He must make sure that he keeps in mind local customs and traditions while formulating the strategy.

- Marketers must make sure that they employ local (foreign) people for sales and marketing in foreign cultures. They should avoid sending their own people as the latter would take time to be acculturated.

- Especially with reference to international marketing, marketers must make sure that they i) modify their product and service offerings so as to meet local cultures, and gain easy and quick acceptance in the foreign country; ii) design a communication /promotion programme where the message content, language etc. is consistent with those of the segment; iii) adjust the prices and payment terms and conditions to meet local expense and consumption patterns; iv) adapt their distribution policies, including retailing to adjust with what the target segment in foreign cultures is used to.

- Marketers must give due consideration to three major issues; i) how do consumers in one culture get exposed to good/services being used by people of other cultures; ii) how should a marketer design/adapt his 4Ps so as to be accepted by people influenced by newer cultures (if he is serving in the home market only); iii) how should a marketer design/adapt his 4Ps so as to accepted by people of other cultures (in foreign markets).

- When customers across two or more countries are similar, the marketer can afford to have a similar marketing program; in case they are different, he would have to adapt his 4Ps and design a separate individualized marketing strategy for the foreign country.

## References

- Arnould, E. J.; Thompson, C. J. (2005). "Consumer culture theory (CCT): Twenty Years of Research". Journal of Consumer Research. 31 (4): 868–882. doi:10.1086/426626

- Berger, Arthur (2004). Ads, Fads, and Consumer Culture. Lanham, MD: Rowman and Littlefield. pp. 25–43. ISBN 0-7425-2724-7 – via Hard Text

- Firat, A. F.; Venkatesh, A. (1995). "Liberatory Postmodernism and the Reenchantment of Consumption". Journal of Consumer Research. 22 (3): 239–267. doi:10.1086/209448. JSTOR 2489612

- Espejo, Roman (2010). Consumerism. Farmington Hills, MI: Greenhaven Press and Gale Cengage Learning. pp. 65–74. ISBN 978-0-7377-4507-8 – via Hard Text

- Arnould, E. J. (2006). "Consumer culture theory: retrospect and prospect" (PDF). European Advances in Consumer Research. 7 (1): 605–607. Retrieved 14 August 2010

- Kozinets, R. V. (2001). "Utopian Enterprise: Articulating the Meanings of Star Trek's Culture of Consumption". Journal of Consumer Research. 28 (3): 67–88. doi:10.1086/321948. JSTOR 254324

- Husband, Julie; O'Loughlin, Jim (2004). Daily Life In The Industrial United States, 1870-1900. Westport, CT: Greenwood Press. pp. 151–177. ISBN 0-313-32302-X – via Hard Text

- Schouten, J.; McAlexander, J. H. (1995). "Subcultures of Consumption: An Ethnography of the New Bikers" (PDF). Journal of Consumer Research. 22 (3): 43–61. doi:10.1086/209434

- Keene, Jennifer; Cornell, Saul; O'Donnell, Edward (2015). Visions of America:A History of the United States. Boston: Person. ISBN 978-0-13-376776-6 – via Hard Text

- Schau, H. J.; Gilly, M. C. (2003). "We Are What We Post? Self-Presentation in Personal Web Space". Journal of Consumer Research. 30 (4): 384–404. doi:10.1086/378616. JSTOR 3132017

- "Learning to be tribal: facilitating the formation of consumer tribes". European Journal of Marketing. 47 (5/6): 813–832. May 24, 2013. doi:10.1108/03090561311306886. ISSN 0309-0566

- Maffesoli, Michel (1995-12-05). The Time of the Tribes: The Decline of Individualism in Mass Society. SAGE. ISBN 9781848609532

- Holt, D. B. (1998). "Does Cultural Capital Structure American Consumption". Journal of Consumer Research. 23 (3): 1–25. doi:10.1086/209523

# Opinion Leadership and its Role in Consumer Behavior

Opinion leadership is the higher form of media that interprets and advocates the media content. This can greatly influence ideas and perceptions of individuals or groups who hold the opinion leader in high esteem. These leaders play the role of authoritative figure, trend setter and of a local opinion leader. Consumer behavior in consumer behavior is best understood in confluence with the major topics listed in the following chapter.

## Opinion Leadership

Opinion leadership is leadership by an active media user who interprets the meaning of media messages or content for lower-end media users. Typically the opinion leader is held in high esteem by those who accept his or her opinions. Opinion leadership comes from the theory of two-step flow of communication propounded by Paul Lazarsfeld and Elihu Katz. Significant developers of the theory have been Robert K. Merton, C. Wright Mills and Bernard Berelson. This theory is one of several models that try to explain the diffusion of innovations, ideas, or commercial products.

### Types

Merton distinguishes two types of opinion leadership: monomorphic and polymorphic. Typically, opinion leadership is viewed as a monomorphic, domain-specific measure of individual differences, that is, a person that is an opinion leader in one field may be a follower in another field. An example of a monomorphic opinion leader in the field of computer technology, might be a neighborhood computer service technician. The technician has access to far more information on this topic than the average consumer and has the requisite background to understand the information, though the same person might be a follower at another field (for example sports) and ask others for advice. In contrast, polymorphic opinion leaders are able to influence others in a broad range of domains. Variants of polymorphic opinion leadership include market mavenism, personality strength and generalized opinion leadership. So far, there is little consensus as to the degree these concept operationalize the same or simply related constructs.

### Characteristics

In his article "The Two Step Flow of Communication" by Elihu Katz, he found opinion leaders to have more influence on people's opinions, actions, and behaviors than the media. Opinion leaders are seen to have more influence than the media for a number of reasons. Opinion leaders are seen as trustworthy and non-purposive. People do not feel they are being tricked into thinking a certain way about something from someone they know. However, the media can be seen as forcing a concept on the public and therefore less influential. While the media can act as a reinforcing agent, opinion leaders have a more changing or determining role in an individual's opinion or action.

## Factors for Leadership

In his article, Elihu Katz answers the question, "Who is an opinion leader?" One or more of these factors make noteworthy opinion leaders:

1. expression of values

2. professional competence

3. nature of their social network.

Opinion leaders are individuals who obtain more media coverage than others and are especially educated on a certain issue. They seek the acceptance of others and are especially motivated to enhance their social status. In the jargon of public relations, they are called thought leaders.

## Example

In a strategic attempt to engage the public in environmental issues and his nonprofit, The Climate Project, Al Gore used the concept of opinion leaders. Gore found opinion leaders by recruiting individuals who were educated on environmental issues and saw themselves as influential in their community and amongst their friends and family. From there, he trained the opinion leaders on the information he wanted them to spread and enabled them to influence their communities. By using opinion leaders, Gore was able to educate and influence many Americans to take notice of climate change and change their actions.

## Word-of-mouth Communication and Opinion Leadership

The informal interpersonal communication that occurs between two people is referred to as *Word-of-Mouth (WOM) communication*. In terms of marketing, such a conversation relates to purchase activity and consumption behavior, and thus pertains to anything and/or everything about product and service offerings. The major characteristic features of WOM communication are:

i) WOM is informal in nature.

ii) It is interpersonal and takes place between two or more people. The people could be actual consumers or prospects; and are in no way representative of the marketer.

iii) Unlike commercial sources, the people involved in WOM communication do not have ulterior or hidden motives of making a sale and earning profit.

Word-of-mouth communication generally relates to face-to-face informal communication. However, it could also occur through a telephonic conversation or chatting and blogging on the Internet. It could assume verbal and non-verbal forms (in the form of behavior).

As people communicate with each other in a purchase decision making situation, one of those involved in the informal communication process is able to influence the attitude and purchase decision of others. He is an Opinion Leader and the process is known as *Opinion Leadership*. Schiffman defines Opinion Leadership as "the process by which one person (the opinion leader) informally influences the actions or attitudes of others, who may be opinion seekers or merely opinion recipients".

An identification of Opinion Leaders, their behavior and the very dynamics of the Opinion Leadership process is helpful to the marketer. Once the marketers have identified the Opinion Leaders, marketers can target their marketing efforts to them. They can provide product information and advice to them and Opinion Leaders through WOM can make the task easier for marketers.

## Opinion Leaders

One of those people who indulge in informal product related communication, usually provides information about a product or product category, whether it would useful to buy, how it would be used etc. He would also offer advice as to which of several brands is the best and from where it should be bought. This person is known as the Opinion Leader and the process is known as *Opinion Leadership*.

In some cases, the Opinion Leader just likes to talk and discuss about a product or service category. He voluntarily provides information about the product and product category and/or about brands. The people who form the audience and listen to him are called Opinion Receivers.

In other cases, prior to a purchase, people could approach an Opinion Leader and request him for information and advice about the product category and/or about brands. That is, the Opinion Leader would provide information only when asked for. In such cases, the persons (audience/or the receiver of information) are known as Opinion Seekers. Individuals who on their own seek information and advice about products and brands are called Opinion Seekers.

There is a two-way exchange of information, and both opinion leaders and opinion receivers/seekers interact with each other. Opinion leaders provide the receivers/seekers with product information, advice, and relate to them their experiences. In return for this, they gather more information, personal opinion and personal experiences from the receivers/seekers.

Opinion Leaders are not generic in nature; they are specific to a product category and the Opinion Leader for a product category would become an Opinion Receiver/Seeker for another product category.

### Role Played by Opinion Leaders

Opinion leaders play a key role and act as a vital role between the marketer and the consumer. He communicates informally about product and service offerings and/or brands; he gives product news and advice to consumers (current and potential) and also narrates his personal experience to others. The major roles played by opinion leaders are, i) authority figure; ii) trend setter; and iii) local opinion leader. These roles are discussed as follows:

i)   *Authority figure*: The role that is played by an Opinion Leader when he gives product news and advice, and also narrates his personal experiences to consumers, is known as the *authority figure role*. By providing product news and advice, as also narrating his personal experiences, he helps current and potential consumers satisfy their needs and wants.

Opinion leaders are highly involved with a product category. They gather information about new, technically complex and risky products by reading about them in newspapers, journals and magazines (also special interest magazines). They attend product launch parties, trade fairs and trade shows, conferences and symposiums etc. They also enter into conversations and discussions with subject experts, researchers, scientists, and even innovators. Innovators provide them with accounts of their first hand experience. It is noteworthy that sometimes even Opinion Leaders act as innovators and are the first to try out a new product offering in the product category of their interest.

Opinion Leaders are said to be performing the *authority figure role* as they act as experts and authorities for a particular product category. They have knowledge, expertise and experience with the product category. They are aware of the various evaluative criteria on which the product and service offerings should be assessed and they are also aware of the decision rules that need to be applied to make a final purchase decision. Opinion Leaders are also aware of the various brands that are available, and the value associated with each. So they are in the best position to provide information and advice to consumer as to i) whether to make a purchase? ii) If yes, which brand to buy? Because of this role that they perform as experts, consumers prefer approaching them for information and advice. This helps the consumers i) reduce the level of physical and cognitive effort associated with a purchase; ii) reduce the level of risk associated with the purchase.

Opinion Leaders enjoy playing this role because of the prestige and pride associated with it. As mentioned above, they may voluntarily play this role and enjoy talking about a product category, or they may be approached and requested for it by the consumers. In any case, they derive pleasure and pride in acting out the expert's role.

Opinion Leaders are specific to a product or service category. It is very rare that an Opinion Leader is an expert or authority for more than one product category. This is because of the fact that it would involve a lot of effort and would difficult for a person to be well informed and educated about any and every product category. Further, the expertise would be maintained only if it is an ongoing effort of information gathering, storage and retention. It would involve a huge amount of effort to develop and maintain expertise in more than one or few areas. Thus, as an expert, Opinion Leaders specialize in one product category. However, Opinion Leadership could tend to overlap across certain combinations of interest areas, i.e., Opinion leaders in one product category can often be Opinion Leaders in related areas, like kitchen ware and household goods, fashion apparel and cosmetics, computers and mobiles, tourism and travel.

    ii) *Trend setter*: Opinion Leaders act as trend setters. They are inner oriented and do not bother about what others in the society say or do. They are also innovative and often go in for purchase of new product and service offerings (of their interest category) and through the purchase and usage, they set the trend.

Opinion Leaders play the *trend setter role* when they narrate accounts of their personal experiences to others to copy and emulate. In other words, if they purchase a new innovative product of their interest, they speak of their experience as acts of behavior that the audience (opinion receivers/ opinion seekers) should emulate.

Unlike the authority role (of providing news and advice), they emphasize more on narrating their personal experiences. Rather than knowledge and expertise being the source of credibility, it is the personal experience that provides credibility.

Once a trend is set by trend setters, people begin to copy them. In fact they act as a reference group for others who want to use the same product and service offerings that are used by former. As trend setters, Opinion Leaders could belong to membership or non-membership reference groups.

     iii) *Local Opinion Leader*: People like to behave like others in their reference groups. They desire social approval from contactual (membership) and aspirational (non-membership) groups. People from such groups directly or indirectly provide information and advice that helps consumers to make purchase decisions, and buy such goods and services and/or brands that the contactual and aspirational groups approve off.

Opinion Leaders are said to act a *local opinion leaders* when a) they constitute a person's positive reference group; and b) they provide information about such product and service offerings and/or brands that help satisfy their needs and wants of the consumer group in a manner that is consistent with group values and norms. As *local opinion leaders,* theyprovide knowledge and advice, and narrate personal experiences about product and service offerings. Their credibility lies in the fact that as they belong to the same group as others who approach them, they are able to advise on the "good" or "bad", and thereby guarantee social approval and appreciation.

## Motives Behind Opinion Leadership

Both Opinion Leaders and Opinion Receivers/seekers have their own reasons for providing information and receiving/seeking product information and advice. Opinion Leaders give product related information and advice sometimes voluntarily on their own and sometimes when are approached and asked for. Similarly Opinion Receivers/Seekers request for information or listen with listen with patience to all that the Opinion Leader has to say. There are various reasons as to why such communication exchange takes place between Opinion Leaders and Opinion Receivers/ Seekers, be they relatives, friends, acquaintances or even strangers. Some of the reasons why Opinion Leaders provide information and why Opinion Receivers/Seekers receive or seek information and advice are discussed below. These explain the motives behind the Opinion Leadership process.

*i) Why do Opinion Leaders provide information?*

    -   Opinion Leaders like to give product news, provide expert advice and also love to share their experiences with others. This is because they are involved and interested in a product or service category, and love to talk about it (*product involvement*).

    -   WOM communication gives them an opportunity to talk about their interests to others. Further they may feel so positively and favorably or negatively and unfavorably about a product and/or brand that they feel like telling about it to others (*product involvement, self involvement and social involvement*)

- As they possess knowledge, expertise and experience with a product category, they feel important and powerful when people approach them for information and advice. It confers upon them a sense of superiority or special status over others. They take pride in providing information and advice (*self gratification, power and pride*). They also feel that others to whom they have given information and advice on new products or services have bought them because of them.

- They may be genuinely be benevolent and generous, and out of altruistic concerns may like to help others, especially family, friends, relatives and neighbours (*selfless motive: social involvement*).

- Opinion Leaders may be also trying to reduce their own level of post-purcahse cognitive dissonance (*self-interest*).

- Interestingly true, many provide information as a) they may be wanting to try out a new product or service offering after someone else buys and uses it first; or b); or

c)  they may themselves be trying to reassure themselves of their own purchase decision by recommending it to others; and d) they may be dissatisfied with a purchase and like to complain about the purchase of the product and service and/or brand and/or company and/store from where it has been purchased.

*ii) Why do Opinion Receiver/Seekers request for information?*

- Opinion Receivers/Seekers gather information so that they can make the right purchase decision, with respect to the right product and service offering, the right brand, at the right price, from the right store and at the right time. Especially in cases of high involvement products, a person may be less knowledgeable and less involved and can take advice from someone who is more experienced and knowledgeable for that product category.

- They obtain information about new-product or new-usage.

- It reduces the physical and cognitive effort that the Opinion Receivers/Seekers has to take to gather information, evaluate alternatives and take the right decision. They also save on time required to gain information about product and the varying brands.

- Product knowledge and advice reduces the level of uncertainty associated with a purchase. It helps them reduce the perceived risk as they are able to gain product and/or brand knowledge from experts, who are also many a times innovators and first-time users of the product.

- They prefer word-of-mouth communication over other marketing communication as they believe that while the latter have an ulterior interest in making sales, the former is more credible with no ulterior motives.

- People also turn to Opinion Leaders so as to confirm their purchase decisions. This is particularly true for high involvement products, as also for products that need social approval and/or match social class and social status

## Dynamics of Opinion Leadership Process

The Opinion Leadership process is highly dynamic in nature. Opinion Leaders communicate informally about product and service offerings and/or brands. They offer product information and advice, and narrate experiences. They are not generic in nature; they are specific to a product category, and an expert in one product category would not be an expert for another product category. Thus, a person may be an Opinion Leader for a product category and an Opinion Receiver for another. The dynamic nature of Opinion Leadership is discussed as follows:

*Opinion Leaders provide product information, advice and narrate experiences:* Opinion Leaders communicate informally about product and service offerings and/or brands; they give product news and advice to consumers (current and potential) and also narrate their personal experience to others. As such they act as authority figures, trend setters and local opinion leaders.

*Opinion Leaders provide both positive and negative information:* Opinion Leaders provide both favorable and unfavorable information about product and service offerings and/or brands, and this adds to their credibility. Compared to positive and neutral information and/or evaluation, the impact of negative information and/or evaluation is much greater and has a bigger impact on Opinion Receivers/Seekers. Thus, they would avoid such product and service offerings and/or brands that are spoken negatively by Opinion Leaders.

*Opinion Leaders are influential and persuasive:*Opinion Leaders are highly influential and very effective at persuading people around them. They are credible informal sources of product knowledge, information and advice. People look up to them for advice and they are good at influencing the former because of the following:

- they are regarded as subject experts, i.e. it is believed that opinion leaders are knowledgeable and experienced about a product or service category.

- since they receive no monetary compensation, their information, advice, opinion and experiences about a product or service category, are perceived as genuine, objective and unbiased.

- they are thought to have no selfish, ulterior or hidden motives, and this adds to their credibility (unlike a marketer who wants to make a sale).

- because they have no self-interest, their advice is regarded as being in the best interests of others (potential and actual consumers).

*Opinion Leaders are not generic in nature*: They are specific to a product or service category, and possess expertise and specialization in it. Because of the in depth knowledge they have about the product category, people approach them for information and advice for that product or service category.

It is important to distinguish between Opinion Leaders and Market Mavens. There are some people who seem to know about everything and offer their advice about anything and everything. Such people are called market mavens. They are different from Opinion Leaders in the sense that actually they do not provide information about a product or service category. They provide information, advice and narrate experiences of general buying and consumption behavior. They also seem to know less intensive about a product or service category, and more extensively about many products and services. They know more about what should be bought, how should it be used, when it should be bought, where it would be available (retail outlets) etc. In a nutshell, they possess more of general knowledge or market expertise.

*Opinion Leaders could also become Opinion Receivers/Seekers:* As explained above, Opinion Leaders are category specific. They are experts in one product/service category, and act as Opinion Leaders. However, when it comes to another product/service category, they may become Opinion Receivers/Seekers. They may even seek information from people to whom they had given information earlier about another product category. Thus, the roles may get reversed from Opinion Leaders to Opinion Receivers/Seekers in the context of other product/service categories.

Sometimes a person may become an Opinion Receiver/Seeker for the same product also. This is when he is in a product-related conversation/discussion with a Opinion Receiver/Seeker who is more informed, enlightened and updated with information product knowledge. This information then adds to the Opinion Leaders' knowledge database in his memory (adds to his *associated network*).

## Measurement of Opinion Leadership

As Opinion Leaders act as a vital link between marketers and consumers, the marketers are always concerned with i) the identification of such people in a social structure who are Opinion Leaders; ii) the identification of people who have the potential to become Opinion Leaders; and iii) the measurement of Opinion Leadership.

In order to measure Opinion Leadership, it is essential that Opinion Leaders with respect to the product/service category are identified. It is also important that people who have the potential to become Opinion Leaders are also identified. There are three ways in which Opinion Leaders can be identified; these are listed as follows:

a)  marketers directly ask the consumers whether they are Opinion Leaders.

b)  they ask a subject expert to identify who the Opinion Leaders are.

c)  they study the communication patterns and flows among consumers, interpret the dynamics and identify the leaders

These methods, in particular the third one help marketers to identify the traits and characteristics that make up an Opinion Leader for a type of product or service category. It also helps the marketer understand the behavior of Opinion Leaders and the dynamics underlying the Opinion Leadership process. Marketers are interested in identifying, measuring and analyzing the impact of the opinion leadership process on consumption patterns and consumption behavior.

An understanding of the traits and characteristics of Opinion Leaders, their behavior and the very dynamics of the Opinion Leadership process is helpful to the marketer. Once the marketers have identified the general traits and characteristics of Opinion Leaders, they can target their marketing efforts, particularly the communication programme at all such consumers who possess such traits and characteristics. Marketers would provide them with information about the product and product category, about the brand, about the usage, its benefit and utility etc. They would also tell them about the various attributes and features, the price and the availability. Once such people (Opinion Leaders or those who have the potential to become Opinion Leaders) are exposed with such a message, they would in turn talk about it to others in their social group. This would make the job easier for a marketer.

All this would ultimately lead to an informal spread of product news, advice and experiences. As has been discussed earlier, WOM communication has a greater impact on consumption behavior as it is regarded as being credible, without any hidden/ulterior motives.

As far as measurement of Opinion Leadership is concerned, researchers make use of various methods. According to Rogers, there are four basic techniques for measuring Opinion Leadership, viz., i) the self-designating method; ii) the sociometric method; iii) the key informant method; and iv) the objective method. Each of these is explained and critically assessed as follows:

i) *The self-designating method*: A marketing survey is conducted and people are asked a series of questions to determine the degree to which they behave as Opinion Leaders. Questions pertain to:

a) the extent to which they have given information and advice about a product/service category and/or brands to others in the social system

b) how often they have been able to influence the purchase decisions about others.

c) how often they have been approached by others for information and advice about that particular product/service category

*Advantages*: It is easy to include and apply in market research questionnaires. It helps measure an individual's perception and assessment about his/her actual Opinion Leadership and related capacities.

*Disadvantages*: As the technique is based on self assessment and evaluation, it could be to lead to over-estimation of self and thus, suffer from bias. People could portray themselves as being "knowledgeable and important advisors" to others when it comes to making purchase decisions. It is also difficult to assess the outcome of the informal communication in terms of knowledge and advice. While a person may report that he provides information and advice, and helps people make purchase decisions, it may not be essential that the receivers may be actually using this information and advice. Thus, success of the technique would depend on the objectivity with which a respondent can identify, assess and report his personal influence.

The final assessment needs to be made by the marketer. The marketer must understand the degree of relevance the Opinion Receivers/Seekers attach to the information and advice that they receive from the various so called Opinion Leaders. This assessment would help the marketer identify who among the many are Opinion Leaders and who are not.

ii) *The sociometric method*: The sociometric method of measuring Opinion Leadership basis itself on the study of the social system, and particularly the communication patterns and flows to identify those to give information and advice as act as Opinion Leaders. Researchers examine complete patterns of informal information flows among consumers of a particular product/service category, and identify those who provide information to others as Opinion Leaders.

While the technique makes use of the analysis of the communication flow, it also uses questionnaires that are administered to people in a social system. People in a social system are asked to identify:

a) those people to whom they have given information and advice about a product/service category. In case the respondent identifies one or many people to whom he has provided information and advice, he is regarded as an Opinion Leader. Researchers could cross-examine by contacting and questioning the Receiver/Seekers of information and confirming from them.

b) those people to whom they have gone for information and advice about a product or service category and/or brand. Her again, researchers could cross-examine by contacting and questioning the Opinion Leaders and confirming from them.

*Advantages*: The technique can meet tests of validity and reliability. Chances of misconception and bias are less.

*Disadvantages*: It is a costly in terms of both money and time. In order to obtain results that are valid and reliable, it requires intensive and extensive data, i.e. a large amount of information from a large sample of respondents. This could be expensive and time consuming. The analysis could also be complex and would require experts in the area.

iii) *The key informant method*: Based on careful observation and analysis of social communication, key informants in a social system are identified. These key informants are asked to identify and/or designate individuals in the social group who are Opinion Leaders or who are most likely to be Opinion Leaders. The key informants are those who are aware about the communication patterns in a social environment and able to provide a fair and impartial assessment of these patterns. They may or may not be a member of such group(s); they may be active participants or passive observers. In this way (where an expert is asked to identify Opinion Leaders), the technique is better than the self-designating method (where a person is asked to assess himself as an Opinion Leader).

*Advantages*: This is relatively less expensive and time consuming, as compared to the sociometric method. The study is based on a chosen few rather than large samples in the self-designating and sociometric methods.

*Disadvantages*: If informants are not carefully chosen, they may provide wrong information.

iv) *The objective method*: The objective method is based on simulation. It identifies and measures Opinion Leadership by placing people in controlled environments (just as controlled experiments). People are chosen, given information about new products and service categories, and the asked to act out as Opinion Leaders. The resulting "web" and "patterns" of informal interpersonal communication regarding the relevant product or service category are traced and analyzed. The technique thus measures the results of their efforts and assesses how successful their impact is on consumption behavior.

*Advantages*: It measures people's abilities to provide news and advice and influence purchase decisions in controlled environments.

*Disadvantages*: It is time consuming as it requires setting up of experimental designs. It is a complex process and requires subject experts and trained psychologists.

## Traits and Characteristics of Opinion Leaders

As discussed above, an understanding of the traits and characteristics of Opinion Leaders is helpful to marketers so that they can target their marketing efforts, particularly their promotional efforts and their communication programme at all such consumers. Marketers assume that given their characteristics, the Opinion Leaders would indulge in WOM communication and spread product news, advice and experiences. They would successfully be able to influence consumption patterns and consumption behavior of others.

Consumer researchers and market practitioners have successfully identified traits and characteristics of Opinion Leaders, and developed their profile. Such traits and characteristics are discussed as follows:

i) Opinion leaders possess high levels of *involvement and interest* in a specific product or service category. They gather information from various sources (print, electronic and audio visual, internet and websites etc.) about product development, and are updated about information. They have greater interest for exposure to media and news specifically relevant to their subject areas of interest and specialization. They like to read and hear more about what interests them. The information search is ongoing because of the level of interest that they possess.

ii) They are *subject experts and have tremendous knowledge* about the specific product or service category. They are well-informed about product attributes and features, benefits and utility, knowledge about brands, price and availability. Because of their knowledge and expertise, people turn to tem for advice. They are authority figures and provide information, advice and narrate experiences to Opinion Receiver/Seekers.

iii) They are product or service *category specific*; a person who is an opinion leader in a particular product/service category would be an Opinion Receiver/Seeker for another. However, Opinion Leadership could tend to overlap across certain combinations of interest areas, i.e., Opinion leaders in one product category can often be Opinion Leaders in related areas, like kitchen ware and household goods, fashion apparel and cosmetics, computers and mobiles, tourism and travel.

iv) In most cases, Opinion Leaders are also *consumer innovators*. Because of their interest in a product or service category, they have a tendency to purchase a new product offering as soon as it is launched in the market. Also, because with their fist hand experience with the product, they speak with authority and experience. They act as trend setters and are in a better position to give advice and convince others to make a purchase.

v) Opinion Leaders also possess certain *personal characteristics*; by nature, they are *self-confident and gregarious*. Because of the knowledge and experience that they possess, they are self-confident. They are extroverts and sociable by nature, who enjoy being in company of others, love talking to others and provide them with product news and advice and share their experiences.

vi) As far as characteristics related to *social class* and social standing are concerned, Opinion leaders generally belong to the *same socioeconomic group* as Opinion Receivers/Seekers. The reasons for this are quite logical. First, Opinion Leaders indulge in informal communication, and the Receivers/Seekers would in most cases be their own friends, neighbours, peers and colleagues. It is with them and other members of their social class that a regular exchange of information takes place, and it is to them that they would give information and advice and share their experiences. Secondly, it is only when there is a match of economic class, that Opinion Receivers/Seekers would approach an Opinion Leader. This is because there would be a better level of comfort and understanding between the two. Opinion Leaders would recommend a product and/or brand that he has been able to monetarily afford and use and it would also be something that the Receivers/ Seekers can also afford. Thirdly, the Receivers/Seekers desire social approval and social approval and acceptance, and thus all the more reason that he approaches someone from his socio-economic class.

## Relevance of Opinion Leadership for a Marketer

The study of informal interpersonal communication, particularly through Opinion Leadership holds relevance for a marketer. The Opinion Leader provides product news, advice and experience to Opinion Receivers/Seekers (potential consumers). This reduces the latter's physical and cognitive effort associated with the purchase decision making process. It also reduces their level of perceived risk. Marketer realize that Opinion Leaders are regarded as credible sources of WOM communication. They also successfully exert tremendous amount of influence on consumers' choice and preferences as also the actual purchase activity. Thus, the study of Opinion Leadership holds relevance for a marketer.

As Opinion Leaders act as a vital link between marketers and consumers, the marketers should concern themselves with the identification of Opinion Leaders, as also the identification of those who have the potential to become Opinion Leaders. For this they need to have an understanding of the traits and characteristics that make up an Opinion Leader for a type of product or service category. Once they have identified the general traits and characteristics of Opinion Leaders, they can target their marketing efforts, particularly the communication programme at all such consumers. Marketers would provide them with information about the product and product category, about the brand, about the usage, its benefit and utility etc. They would also tell them about the various attributes and features, the price and the availability. Once such people (Opinion Leaders or those who have the potential to become Opinion Leaders) are exposed with such a message, they would "carry around the word" to the masses, by talking about it to others in their social group. This would make the job easier for a marketer.

Marketers often attempt to encourage Opinion Leadership through their marketing strategies:

- through schemes like "share you experiences", "tell others that you like our brand", etc., marketers encourage consumers to discuss their experiences with others (eg. Electronic goods etc).

- through showing advertisements that portray product/service informal discussions about products/services amongst people (eg. health drinks, skin and hair care products etc.).

It needs to be mentioned here that WOM communication is difficult to manage and control. When a person is satisfied with the purchase of a product and/or brand, he would speak in favor of it. On the other hand, when he is dissatisfied with the purchase and the usage, he would speak unfavorably about it to others. Similarly, Opinion Leaders provide information that could be both favorable and unfavorable to a product or service category and/or brand. Negative remarks could also arise in the form of rumors, especially with new product categories. Needless to say, quite logical that the unfavorable or negative information has a deeper and profound effect. To counter this, marketers are desirous of handling customer relations in a better manner, and have introduced help lines and toll free numbers.

Marketers should also measuring and analyze the impact of the Opinion Leadership process on consumption patterns and consumption behavior. This would help him understand those amongst Opinion Leaders who are genuine and powerful and those who are fake and superficial. This is because they can then focus more on the former than on the latter.

All this would ultimately lead to an informal spread of product news, advice and experiences. As has been discussed earlier, WOM communication has a greater impact on consumption behavior as it is regarded as being credible, without any hidden/ulterior motives.

## References

- Childers, T. L. (1986). "Assessment of the psychometric properties of an opinion leadership scale". Journal of Marketing Research. 23: 184–188. doi:10.2307/3172527

- Feick, L. F.; Price, L. L. (1987). "The market maven: A diffuser of marketplace information". Journal of Marketing. 51: 83–97. doi:10.2307/1251146

- Flynn, L. R.; Goldsmith, R. E.; Eastman, J. K. (1996). "Opinion leadership and opinion seekers: Two new measurement scales". Journal of the Academy of Marketing Science. 24: 147–147. doi:10.1177/0092070396242004

- Gnambs, T.; Batinic, B. (2011). "Convergent and discriminant validity of opinion leadership: Multitrait-multimethod analysis across measurement occasion and informant type". Journal of Individual Differences. 39: 94–102. doi:10.1027/1614-0001/a000040

- Weimann, G. (1991). "The influentials: Back to the concept of opinion leaders?". Public Opinion Quarterly. 55 (2): 267–279. doi:10.1086/269257

- Katz, Elihu (1957). "The two-step flow of communication: An up-to-date report on an hypothesis". Public Opinion Quarterly. 21: 61–78. doi:10.1086/266687

- Rose, P.; Kim, J. (2011). "Self-Monitoring, Opinion Leadership and Opinion Seeking: a Sociomotivational Approach". Current Psychology. 30: 203–214. doi:10.1007/s12144-011-9114-1

# Permissions

All chapters in this book are published with permission under the Creative Commons Attribution Share Alike License or equivalent. Every chapter published in this book has been scrutinized by our experts. Their significance has been extensively debated. The topics covered herein carry significant information for a comprehensive understanding. They may even be implemented as practical applications or may be referred to as a beginning point for further studies.

We would like to thank the editorial team for lending their expertise to make the book truly unique. They have played a crucial role in the development of this book. Without their invaluable contributions this book wouldn't have been possible. They have made vital efforts to compile up to date information on the varied aspects of this subject to make this book a valuable addition to the collection of many professionals and students.

This book was conceptualized with the vision of imparting up-to-date and integrated information in this field. To ensure the same, a matchless editorial board was set up. Every individual on the board went through rigorous rounds of assessment to prove their worth. After which they invested a large part of their time researching and compiling the most relevant data for our readers.

The editorial board has been involved in producing this book since its inception. They have spent rigorous hours researching and exploring the diverse topics which have resulted in the successful publishing of this book. They have passed on their knowledge of decades through this book. To expedite this challenging task, the publisher supported the team at every step. A small team of assistant editors was also appointed to further simplify the editing procedure and attain best results for the readers.

Apart from the editorial board, the designing team has also invested a significant amount of their time in understanding the subject and creating the most relevant covers. They scrutinized every image to scout for the most suitable representation of the subject and create an appropriate cover for the book.

The publishing team has been an ardent support to the editorial, designing and production team. Their endless efforts to recruit the best for this project, has resulted in the accomplishment of this book. They are a veteran in the field of academics and their pool of knowledge is as vast as their experience in printing. Their expertise and guidance has proved useful at every step. Their uncompromising quality standards have made this book an exceptional effort. Their encouragement from time to time has been an inspiration for everyone.

The publisher and the editorial board hope that this book will prove to be a valuable piece of knowledge for students, practitioners and scholars across the globe.

# Index

**A**

Adoption Rates, 23-24
Advertising Management, 108-109, 140, 171
Advertising Planning, 120
Affect, 2-3, 11, 27-28, 36, 39-40, 47, 49, 51, 58, 83, 85, 87, 93, 114-116, 120, 163, 170, 173, 182, 208, 210
Airline Accident, 19
Analysis Paralysis, 45
Analytical, 40, 52, 101
Anthropology, 3, 31, 39-40
Aspirational Groups, 17, 163, 181, 219
Associative Reference, 17
Attitudinal Segments, 68
Audience Share, 131
Average Audience, 131

**B**

Behavior, 1-3, 34, 39-42, 78-79, 83, 93-94, 97, 144-145, 172, 179-182, 208-209, 212 215-217, 219, 227
Benefit-sought, 67-68
Brand Advocacy, 3, 19
Brand Loyalty, 19, 81, 83, 92-93, 95, 119, 143, 145, 147, 151, 157, 159
Brand-switching, 24-25
Buyer, 6, 34, 40-41, 61, 67, 79 81-87, 102, 106, 112, 135, 143 158, 160-162, 164-165 167-169, 190

**C**

Channel-switching, 25
Cognition, 2-3, 39, 85, 93, 115-116, 120, 167, 208
Common Terms, 106
Communications Objectives, 120-123, 135, 139
Compatibility, 23-24
Consideration Set, 9, 15, 94-95
Consumer Confusion, 83, 199
Consumer Culture, 188-190, 198, 213
Contactual Group, 181
Corporate Hierarchy, 107
Creative Strategy, 125-126
Cultural Segmentation, 70
Culture Theory, 198, 213
Customer Citizenship, 4, 19, 31

**D**

Decider, 5, 41, 85-87, 205
Decision Making, 2, 39-40 42-43, 78, 80, 85, 87 93-94, 96, 102, 105, 157 159-161, 180, 196, 199-200, 216, 226
Demographic Segmentation, 56-57, 62-65, 75, 146
Differentiated Approach, 57
Disassociative Reference, 17
Dissatisfaction, 8, 11, 123, 164, 201
Drawbacks, 190

**E**

Economics, 1, 3, 31, 36, 39-40, 42, 49, 96, 195-196
Emotions, 3, 11-13, 27-29, 53, 90, 126, 158
Esteem, 12, 20, 30, 144, 147, 161, 163, 182, 215

**F**

Financial Risk, 19-20

**G**

Generational Segments, 69
Geographic Segmentation, 61-63, 96, 142, 144, 146

**H**

Hierarchy-free Models, 114, 120
High-involvement, 84, 118-119, 211

**I**

Impulse Purchases, 26-27, 119
Income Effects, 194
Information Overload, 19, 45, 200
Information Search, 5-8, 12, 15 20, 27, 34, 40, 78, 80-84, 87 89, 94, 159, 164, 225
Initiator, 5, 41, 85-86
Inkblots, 202
Integrative Models, 114, 117
International Plan, 106
Interpretive, 40, 199

**L**

Labor-leisure Tradeoff, 197-198

**M**

Market Segmentation, 4, 19, 55-58, 62, 96, 98, 141-143, 145-147

Marketing, 1, 3-4, 6, 17, 20-22, 24, 26-28, 90, 94 96-107, 120-124, 126, 140-143 165 169-171, 189, 199, 225-227

Marketing Plan, 120, 122, 146, 150

Media Buying, 109, 133

Media Channel Strategy, 126, 128-129

Media Planning, 109, 126-127, 131, 152, 154, 156-157

Methodology, 37, 106, 131

Motivations, 1, 12-13, 55, 57, 63, 66, 76, 99, 123, 137, 146, 190, 202

Myers-briggs Type, 52

**N**

Natural Depletion, 8

Neuroscience, 4, 31-33, 53, 85, 96, 102, 120, 138

**O**

Opinion Leaders, 4, 17, 22, 42, 90, 94, 163, 215-227

Organisational Responsibilities, 110

Out-of-stock, 8

**P**

Perception, 9, 14, 19-20, 39, 48-49, 51-52, 84, 159, 162, 170, 187, 199, 223

Personal Biases, 49, 84

Personality, 3, 11, 39, 61, 63, 88-89, 91, 117-118, 126, 142 144-147, 159, 162-163, 167 171, 183, 185, 202, 215

Physiological, 12, 136-137, 143

Price Change, 105, 192, 194-195

Prior Experience, 9, 11, 14-15, 72

Problem Recognition, 6-8, 80, 87-88, 94, 163

Product Specification, 167

Promotional Mix, 109, 111-113, 124

Proposal Solicitation, 167

Psychographic Segmentation, 66, 142, 144

Psychology, 3, 36, 39-40, 42-43, 96, 107, 120, 151, 202, 227

Pull Strategy, 122

Purchase Decision, 5-12, 14-15, 19, 23, 41, 81-84, 87, 89 92-96, 115, 135, 164, 180, 216, 218, 220, 226

**R**

Rational Purchase, 118-119

Readership Profiles, 131

Regular Purchase, 8

Relative Advantage, 23

**S**

Safety, 12, 172-173

Segment Size, 71

Self-concept, 91, 162, 181

Site Traffic, 132

Social Class, 15-16, 39, 144, 163, 220, 225-226

Social Risk, 6, 19-20

Social System, 22, 185-187, 202-203, 223-224

Sociology, 3, 39-40, 97

Structural Attractiveness, 71

Substitution, 191, 194-195, 197-198

**T**

Target Audience, 99, 109, 117, 121-122, 135, 153, 155, 171

Target Market, 55, 71-72, 75, 97-98, 103, 108-110, 120-121 127-129, 140-143, 147 149-151, 153-154, 157, 171

Task Method, 124

Trialability, 23

**U**

Up-market, 6, 17, 19, 119

Usage Occasion, 3, 67, 74

Usefulness, 32, 184

User, 5, 25, 41, 65, 67, 70, 74 76, 85-87, 126, 145, 152, 161 169, 215

**W**

Wage Work, 189